Social Care
Learning from Practice

Social Care
Learning from Practice

Edited by Noel Howard and Denise Lyons

Gill & Macmillan

Gill & Macmillan
Hume Avenue
Park West
Dublin 12
www.gillmacmillan.ie

978 07171 5969 7

Print origination by Síofra Murphy
Printed by GraphyCems, Spain
Index by Cliff Murphy

The paper used in this book comes from the wood pulp of managed forests. For every tree felled, at least one tree is planted, thereby renewing natural resources.

A CIP catalogue record is available for this book from the British Library

Acknowledgements

As the first book on social care in Ireland to be written from the heart as well as the head, the task was a daunting one from the beginning.

Without the patience, diligence and, in many cases, the courage of the contributors, this book could not have been written. To them goes a big thank you.

Marion O'Brien and Catherine Gough of Gill & Macmillan provided us with the necessary professional guidance and encouragement from the beginning. This was hugely important.

A special thanks to Una O'Grady, Laura Kane and Jim Donnelly for their continued interest in the project and for their attention to detail.

For the continued support and tolerance of our family members and friends, we express our absolute appreciation.

Contributors' Profiles

Laura Behan has been a practising social care worker since 2005. While undertaking her degree she volunteered in the area of youth and community work, where she discovered her passion for working with young people. Since qualifying, Laura has worked in various residential centres with children and adolescents. Laura currently works in the Child and Adolescent Mental Health Services (CAMHS). As part of a multidisciplinary team, she is involved in the assessment and treatment of children and their families who present with a wide range of mental health difficulties. Her particular interests include the use of process-oriented therapeutic work to address the impact of childhood trauma on young people and the application of family-based models of intervention. Laura is a committee member of the Special Interest Group for Social Care in CAMHS.

Helen Buggle worked in community development in Latin America for a number of years before coming to social care. She has worked in residential social care for over twenty-seven years and manages a mixed therapeutic community unit in Dublin. She holds an MA in Therapeutic Child Care and facilitates training for workers on attachment and relationship skills in care work on behalf of the HSE Dublin Mid-Leinster. A psychodynamic perspective on difficult behaviours is another area of interest for her and she recently helped set up a 'care and treatment' meeting space for social care workers to come together for mutual support and learning.

Lillian Byrne-Lancaster is President of the Irish Association of Social Care Educators (2012–2015) and a lecturer in Social Care and Early Childhood Education Theory and Practice at the Wexford Campus of IT Carlow. Lillian has worked as a social care worker in a variety of community and residential settings. Her MA dissertation (Cork Institute of Technology) explored placement in social care education and she is currently exploring placement-based learning for her PhD with IT Sligo.

Caroline Coyle began a foundation course in Athlone Institute of Technology as a mature student in 2001. One module was in social care and this led her to undertake a BA in Applied Social Studies in 2007. In 2009 she achieved a master's in Child and Youth Care. Caroline has worked in various residential units and currently lectures in the Humanities Department of Athlone IT.

Kathy D'Arcy is a social care leader who has worked in emergency care in the HSE South for the past ten years. She is also a published poet, and holds the post of Poet in Residence with Tigh Filí Cultural Centre, Cork. She is a youth arts facilitator, and runs creative writing workshops for children and young people all around the country, both as part of Tigh Filí's Eurochild and Youthlife poetry programmes (which she designs) and as a freelancer. In 2013 Kathy and the four young people who edited the collection under her guidance presented the first *Youthlife* anthology to President Higgins at Áras an Uachtaráin. Kathy originally qualified and worked as a doctor.

Dr John Digney has worked with troubled children and families for over twenty years. He holds qualifications in psychology, psychotherapy and project management. Other areas of expertise include being a certified senior trainer in programmes such as RAP, outcomes that matter, therapeutic use of daily events (DLE) and deep brain learning. His PhD focused on the therapeutic potential and uses of humour in child and youth care.

Fiona Doyle has been involved in social care practice for almost sixteen years. A social care worker since 1999, she graduated in social care in 2010. Since 2011, Fiona has been working as a social care leader and has completed courses in neuro-linguistic practice. She has also qualified as an NCI instructor and is currently completing a course in human resource management. During her time as a social care worker Fiona was involved with adults and children with a broad range of disabilities, predominantly in residential care.

Angela Feeney holds a BA in Applied Social Studies in Social Care from Athlone IT and an MA in Child, Family and Community Studies from Dublin Institute of Technology. Angela has been involved in social care practice and management since 2000 and has worked in the areas of intellectual disability, residential childcare and family services. In 2006 Angela was involved in the establishment of a Family Assessment and Intervention Service, which specialises in systemic/ecological home-based assessments, where she continues to work.

Maurice Fenton entered social care as a volunteer in 1992. Over the intervening years he has worked at all levels in residential care, from trainee to director, in the statutory, voluntary and private sectors. He returned to education at the age of forty and has remained there ever since. He founded Empower Ireland in 2009 to support care leavers in Ireland and in March 2013 left his post as director of services to focus on developing Empower Ireland and to concentrate on his doctoral studies at Queen's University.

Noel Howard is a former president and current publications editor of the Irish Association of Social Care Workers (IASCW) and has been a member of the Social Care Ireland executive since its inception. He has worked as a teacher in the United States, Pakistan and Ireland. At various times he was a bus conductor, postman and bible salesman. In 1973 he moved from teaching to work in a remand and assessment unit for boys in Finglas, Dublin. In 1996 he took up the position of Deputy Director at Ferryhouse, Clonmel and retired from there in 2008.

Aoife Killeen is a social care worker and researcher who is currently completing her PhD in Social Care at Cork Institute of Technology. Her chapter is based on her experience in working in a large supported living unit, and she also has experience of working in the community and in larger residential care settings. She has gained valuable experience on the ground and hopes to lecture and pursue an academic career full time with an emphasis on linking theory to practice, and emphasising the importance of the person in the provision of care. Aoife believes that before we can achieve the rights of people with disabilities to choose, to be respected and to be included in the community, we must link government policy to the reality of service provision on the ground.

Keith King, a name chosen for his contribution to this book, is a social care worker currently studying for a master's in Social Work. Keith very kindly shared a story from his experience of being on the other side of residential care.

Claire Leonard has worked in social care since 1994, and in 2003 received her MA in Social Studies from NUI Maynooth. Claire is currently managing a service for adults with an intellectual disability (including people who have a dual diagnosis and ageing-related support needs). She also has extensive experience in providing independent living supports for adults with physical disabilities.

Denise Lyons is President of Social Care Ireland (2012–2014) and a lecturer in the Personal and Professional Development and Creative Studies modules at the Institute of Technology Blanchardstown. Prior to becoming a lecturer in 2000, Denise worked as a social care worker in several residential care settings. She is an art therapist, and editor of *Creative Studies for the Caring Professions* (Gill & Macmillan 2010). She is a PhD candidate at the School of Education, University College Cork, researching what social care workers do in various settings.

Derek McDonnell has worked in various settings as a social care worker for the last twenty-two years, fourteen of which were spent working in Lucena Clinic in Orwell Road, Dublin, in the Child and Adolescent Mental Health Services. He is currently working as a community social care leader in the Laois/Offaly Social Work Department, providing therapeutic intervention to children. He is trained in a process called 'focusing', which he has incorporated into his therapeutic intervention, and is currently running training programmes in this process for foster carers, staff and a group focusing programme for pupils in primary school.

John Molloy has over thirty years' experience as a social care manager. In the 1970s he joined the staff of Scoil Ard Mhuire Detention School in Dublin, having been a youth worker and teacher prior to that. He then worked in Trudder House in Wicklow, a unit for Traveller children, and began his management career there. He qualified in social care from Cathal Brugha Street, Dublin (now DIT). John has a master's in Child Protection and Welfare from Trinity College.

Des Mooney is a social care worker currently practising in a residential care centre in the southeast. He also tutors adult students in the areas of child development and early carer and education practice. His research interests include the provision of a healing environment for young people in care, the links between continuing professional development and the practice of social care, and adult and lifelong learning. Des holds a BA in Social Care and an MA in Higher Education. His research thesis focused on the experience of adult child care workers returning to education.

Frank Mulville has worked in social/child care, social work and youth services for over thirty years, both in Ireland and in England. He trained in child care in Kilkenny and in social work in Croydon, England. Since 1995 he has been working as a facilitator, trainer, lecturer and external supervisor in the areas of social care, youth and community work, social work and addiction services. Frank works as a staff consultant in a number of residential centres. He has a continuing interest in the way in which social care workers engage with children and young people and with each other. He stresses the importance of effective management, clearly developed approaches and reflective practice that acknowledges the importance of understanding the transferences and projections that are at play in the relationships between children/young people and staff, and how these can be used to gain insight into their needs and potential.

Pauline Clarke Orohoe entered the social care field in 1997 and completed the Diploma in Social Care, later returning to college to complete her BA. Her work has ranged from mainstream residential care to community childcare and project work. She currently works as a social care manager.

Maria O'Sullivan has over twenty years' experience as a social care worker and manager in High Support and Special Care. She has brought her expertise to academia and now lectures part time in the Institute of Technology Tralee.

Iseult Paul graduated in 2007 with a first-class honours degree from the Institute of Technology Blanchardstown. She has a diverse range of experience in social care on a personal and professional level. Iseult has a particular passion for the continuing professional development (CPD) of social care workers and recognises the importance of CPD in the provision of best practice. Since 2005 Iseult has worked in the area of intellectual disability; her varied role includes formal and informal training and support to staff and individuals with an intellectual disability. She is also a qualified holistic therapist and takes a holistic approach to practice.

Paddy Ormond studied in Trinity College, where he achieved an Advanced Diploma in Child Protection and Welfare. He began his involvement with residential care in the late 1970s as a volunteer and quickly became absorbed by the nature of the work. He took up the offer of a full-time position in 1979 and in 1984 commenced working in a very specialised children's community-based residential centre in Dublin's north inner city, where he worked very closely with families from the local community. He took up the position of project leader there in 1990 and continued to manage this unit until 2012. He is currently project leader in the Neighbourhood Youth Project 1 in the north inner city – this is a child and family support service provided under the HSE Community Development and Family Support Team.

Niall Reynolds graduated from Dublin Institute of Technology with a first class degree in Social Care in 2010. He has experience of many different settings, from special care to high support to community-based interventions. He is currently completing a master's in Systemic Psychotherapy and his areas of interest include family systems of children in care, management of sexually harmful behaviour in residential care settings and collaborative practice in social care. He is part of the Southside Inter-Agency Treatment Team (SIATT) that deals with adolescent boys who have sexually offended.

Maxwell Smart took up a position in 1995 at Lothian Villa, a residential child care centre in Scotland, having worked in child protection and family practice following his social work qualification in 1986. He gained an MSc in Advanced Residential Child Care from the University of Strathclyde in 2010 and is involved in training residential staff groups and foster carers in the reclaiming needs of the RAP programme.

Marguerita Walsh began her social care career working with children with intellectual disabilities, including in residential and respite services. In 2007 she began working in children's respite services. She qualified with a BA (honours) from Cork Institute of Technology in 2009 and in 2013 qualified with an MA (research) in Social Care. She also has qualifications in training and professional practice and development. Currently, she works in an assisted living service for people with acquired brain injuries.

David Williams has been involved in social care practice, management and education for almost twenty years. He has worked in the areas of youth work, elder care, and residential child care and intellectual disabilities. He lectures on the social care programmes at Dublin Institute of Technology and his research interests include approaches to managing difficult behaviours, the professionalisation of social care work and foster care. He is currently completing his doctoral research thesis on the experiences of the birth children of foster carers.

Contents

Contents

My Daddy Didn't Hold Me Down

My daddy didn't hold me down, no, he never got me.
All the girls were got but no, not me.
I hear them whisper under dark circles of watery arches
And in the sleeve of leaves along the quay.
My daddy wasn't fast enough to catch me
My daddy stumbled over quite a lot
He didn't haw his breath upon my cheekbone
His snorting nostrils didn't spit and snot.
I didn't smell the sweetness of the cider
Or look into his glaucomatous eyes
I didn't scream and kick to get him off me
I didn't drown the Shannon with my cries.
Street people think that they can see right through me,
Narrow eyes from girls and sneers from boys
They rail against the inside of my insides
But everything they heard is all just lies.

Caroline Coyle

Overview of Social Care Practice

Chapter 1
Learning from Stories of Practice

Denise Lyons and Noel Howard

INTRODUCTION

'We need a book about the practice of social care, written by people on the front line, workers and managers.' I (Denise) had this thought several times over the years, sparked mostly by a need for realistic case studies to share with students. Becoming a member of the executive of Social Care Ireland (SCI) in 2010, the umbrella group for the three representative bodies of social care, enabled me to meet social care workers who were also interested in the idea of a book about practice. As well as needing a selection of stories from experienced workers, this book required a veteran social care worker to guide the process. I was privileged to work with Noel Howard on the committee of SCI and fortunately he required no persuasion or bribing to take up the challenge.

This book is the collaborative effort of a number of social care workers who were brave enough to share insightful stories of practice with us. Each worker has valuable experience worth sharing about his or her own area of work, with enlightenment gained from years working with vulnerable people. The stories you will read in this book are based on real practice experiences. In some you will see the personality of the author coming through and this is refreshing at a time when personality in social care is being slowly eroded. This factor alone distinguishes the book from worthy studies that deal with theory alone.

Nothing in this book is specifically presented as a panacea or recipe for best practice in social care. Neither should it be taken that the editors are necessarily endorsing any of the methods, approaches or interventions outlined in any of the chapters. We would advise that methods of intervention and therapeutic techniques outlined in some of these chapters are the advanced practice of social care workers with expertise, training, experience and supervision. The social care workers using therapy in their practice have advanced training. Such practice is therapy rather than the general therapeutic benefits that flow from effective social care practice. Many of the interventions and approaches may apply in a general sense, but social care workers do not need to be reminded that what worked yesterday may not work today because of the ever-changing dynamic that is so much part and parcel of what they do. The stories are offered as a lens through which we can bear witness to the emergence and continued professional development of each worker that go beyond the challenges that working with vulnerable people inevitably brings.

WHERE DO WE WORK AND WHAT DO WE DO?

Each individual author was given the challenge to write about their practice through the guise of a case study, or by using real examples to demonstrate the issues they deemed pertinent to their specific area. As you will discover from reading this book, the emphasis here is on practice rather than the theoretical approaches that have influenced or that underpin the approach. As a lecturer I continuously drill home to students that they should support all their opinions and discussion with relevant theory. In this case we invited social care workers to focus on practice, with an acknowledgment that all the contributors to this book are either qualified social care workers or are eligible for statutory registration. Several of the contributors have engaged in further education to support the practice they are involved in and consider the degree as the foundation of their education. Many explain why they were attracted to social care, and how the chosen issue impacted upon them as a worker. We hope this book will spark discussions in lecture theatres and staffrooms about what theories may be relevant to the case studies presented.

We also aimed to provide a broad picture of social care from a variety of different practice areas, which led us to the question, 'Where do social care workers in Ireland work?' In 2011 social care workers, managers and educators collaboratively described the range of social care settings as 'children and adolescents in residential care; young people in detention schools; people with intellectual or physical disabilities; people who are homeless; people with alcohol/drug dependency; families in the community; or older people' (Lalor & Share 2013:5). This may not represent the full spectrum of practice, as there is currently no empirical data available on where social care workers actually work or how many are employed in the different areas. According to the 2009 report of the Skills and Labour Market Research Unit (SLMRU), there were 7,900 social care workers employed in Ireland (SLMRU 2009:92), which may include workers in the Health Service Executive (HSE), the voluntary sector, agencies and the private sector. The statutory registration of social care workers will enable us to know the exact number of people in Ireland eligible to legally use the title Social Care Worker and to determine where those who are employed are working.

This book does not include every area of practice. Of that we are sure. However, we are confident that the themes and issues identified within the chapters are relevant to a wide audience of workers struggling to form and maintain relationships; trying to engage with people in various types of care provision; or dealing with a variety of challenges every day. Many of the scenarios are mirrored across numerous areas of social care work. We also hope that this book will encourage other social care workers to write about practice and increase our knowledge base on the broad profession that is social care. You will notice that some chapters are heavily referenced; others less so. The editors believe this is a healthy reflection on the practice issues as well as theory supporting that practice.

SOCIAL CARE STORIES

At the 2012 annual planning meeting of the Health and Social Care Professions (H&SCP) Advisory Group, Dr Michael Byrne presented some of the findings from the 2011 *Survey of the Research Activity, Skills and Training Needs of Health and Social Care Professionals in Ireland*, specifically the twelve professions covered by the 2005 Health and Social Care Professionals Act (McHugh & Byrne 2011). According to the report there were 3,367 social care workers employed by the HSE in Ireland. This figure is much lower than that quoted in the SLMRU report (7,900), but this may reflect the large number of social care workers estimated to work for agencies and the private sector. In his presentation, Dr Byrne took social care workers as an example, stating that for the largest professional group covered under the H&SCP Act, we had the smallest number (n=3) of workers engaged in evidence-based research. The reasons presented in the report for the low engagement of our profession in research included: the heavy workload, leaving no time for research; workers feeling insecure about academic writing skills; that research was not valued in the service by management; and that there was no culture of undertaking research (McHugh & Byrne 2011).

After attending the planning meeting I felt disheartened about the statistics presented and wondered if there was something we could do to encourage people to write about their practice. The education sub-group of the H&SCP Advisory Body is interested in 'mentoring' as a possible way to encourage workers to engage in research. Here the worker becomes a research partner with an academic or student on placement. The worker is the link to practice, using his or her experience as evidence. Each contributor to this book has demonstrated that the insights social care workers have acquired through experience in specific social care settings are worth sharing for the development of our profession.

The 2011 report was funded by the HSE because of a recognition that each of the twelve professions due for statutory registration will need current information about the profession. Social care is no exception. So we need to encourage workers to write about practice and we need to do it soon in preparation for statutory registration. The 2011 survey was distributed to HSE staff only and the results do not include any social care workers engaged in research from any other sector, or those who are employed in education. This is interesting because social care educators are the main contributors to the knowledge base for social care, evident from the *Irish Journal of Applied Social Studies* (*IJASS*), the various Irish texts on social care and the role of educators in the development of the educational guide for social care education, *Awards Standards – Social Care Work* (HETAC 2010).

The Higher Education and Training Awards Council (HETAC) devised standards that may help guide the future Social Care Registration Board on the 'Draft Criteria and Standards of Proficiency for Education and Training' for social care education. The board members included Lorraine Ryan, who was nominated by the Irish Association of Social Care Workers (IASCW) and the Resident Managers' Association (RMA), now the Irish Association of Social Care Management (IASCM); John Fox, who was released by the HSE; and David Power (IASCW Vice President at the time), who represented the Health and Social Care Professional Council (CORU). The following were also included in the group, which was chaired by Pat McGarty (IT Tralee and IASCE): Kevin Lalor (DIT and IASCE); Karen Finnerty (Open Training College); Judy Doyle (DIT); Margaret Gilmore (IT Sligo); Mark Smith (Edinburgh University) and Reidar Osterhaug (Stavanger University, Norway) (HETAC 2010:2).

The standards were presented as a guide for programme development and accreditation and thus applied to the majority of social care institutes of education. The document frames the knowledge, skills and competencies of social care under the standards expected at each National Framework of Qualifications award level (levels 6 to 9). The members of the board were invited because of their involvement in social care education and practice, and several members had experience of social care work. Williams and Lalor (2001:82) state that the 'training of social care personnel must be appropriate and informed by the needs of the profession', which should include all services. However, as social care is such a broad profession it is practically impossible to have all sections of practice represented on this board. By writing about practice, social care workers from diverse services can ensure that educators include the core competencies of practice specific to their area in social care programmes.

ARE THESE STORIES RESEARCH?

When you ask questions about your practice or reflect on how you could have done something differently, you are engaging in research (Farrelly 2013). Pawson *et al.* (2003) devised a table depicting the types and sources of social care knowledge. 'Practitioner knowledge' was listed as one of the four types, and surmised by Farrelly (2013:126) as knowledge 'gained from doing social care, which tends to be tacit, personal and context specific'. In their article on sharing knowledge between health workers and academics, Bartunek *et al.* (2003) stated that both tacit and explicit knowledge are required for an in-depth understanding of practice. Tacit knowledge is described as individual, subjective and based within a setting, whereas explicit knowledge is articulated through deduction and theorising, and can be coded and generalised. Practitioner knowledge is tacit knowledge, and according to Bartunek *et al.* (2003) it is essential to have both: 'Practitioner knowledge is acquired directly through the practice of social caring and the distillation of collective wisdom at many points through media such as education and training, requesting and receiving advice, attending team meetings and case conferences, and comparing notes' (Pawson *et al.* 2003:17). The chapters are evidence of both a tacit and an explicit approach to understanding social care practice.

In this book social care workers explore and question practice, describe new and interesting ways of working and reflect on the merits or otherwise of the different approaches used. These stories are our contribution to the knowledge base for social care into the future.

USING POETRY TO TELL A STORY

We are very fortunate to have two original poems by Caroline Coyle featured in this book. Caroline was a social care worker caring for young people through traumatic experiences, which she has narrated in her poems. The first poem, 'My Daddy Didn't Hold Me Down' (page xvi), was inspired by the intimate and trusting relationship between the carer and the young person, who feels safe enough to disclose, or safe enough to deny disclosure. Through the shared experience of receiving a young person's story, the social care worker can help on many different levels. The actual verbalisation of the stories can act as an avenue for those experiences to escape, thus helping to alleviate the young person's stress and their internalisation of the experience.

This book concludes with a second poem, 'No Womb at the Inn' (page 275), which explores the story of a Traveller girl in care becoming pregnant and being moved, looking at religion in the Travelling community, its importance and the connected symbolism. Themes such as generational experiences of being in care, knowing about the care systems and trying to prevent your own child from going into care, feelings of powerlessness, pleading for help and the perception that nobody cares emerge from this poem. The poem highlights the intergenerational culture of being in care for some groups in Irish society.

Chapters 2 and 3 illustrate where both editors have spent most of their working lives: Noel in practice and working with the IASCW (Chapter 2); and Denise in social care education and the Irish Association of Social Care Educators (IASCE) (Chapter 3).

Chapter 2 gives an overview of the origin and development of what is today the IASCW. The road travelled over forty years is one of hope and despair; relative success overshadowed by broken trust; enormous generosity of spirit, but also its very antithesis. It is a road strewn, literally, with blood, sweat and tears. The chapter sketches the ebb and flow of major social and political influences on the lives of social care workers and those for whom they care over years marked by huge social change, upheavals and scandals as well as legislative and regulatory change. What has not changed is the simple, yet enormously complicated, task that social care workers face daily – how can I make a difference?

Social care education is the focus of Chapter 3, which looks at how it has evolved since the first training programme began in 1971. The change from the single focus of child care to the multi-faceted profession of social care has implications on the ability of programmes to be fit for purpose and to educate workers for diverse fields of practice. On the front line, educators have themselves collaborated in order to improve the education provided across the country. In particular, the role the IASCE plays in this process is worth noting.

In Chapter 4, 'Keith' graphically describes the journey from dysfunctional yet loving family through the residential and aftercare system. As with many of the chapters in the book, this one throws the importance of the key worker, the 'I', into sharp focus. It proves that one person in a vulnerable individual's life, in this case the right person at the right time, can make all the difference. The editors believe that this account, from someone who has seen the best and worst of the care system and its aftermath, is well placed at the book's beginning. In the chapters that follow, other 'Keiths' emerge in many different guises.

We are fortunate to have Keith's story reflected from the other side, as it were, by Maurice Fenton in Chapter 5. Maurice has allowed himself to be identified in order to contextualise the lessons learned and the implications of wider issues – as relevant today as then – that were at play when he worked with Keith. 'The Impossible Task: Which Wolf will Win?' is an intriguing title and the chapter, inter alia, challenges some of the conventional wisdom around what works and what doesn't.

In a similar vein, Chapter 6 is the story, by Dr John Digney and Max Smart, of doing small things with great kindness. Both John and Max have worked on the floor, in management and clinical roles, for fifty-plus years between them. Here the authors challenge us to learn a new dance where change is 'inside-out', to use the concepts of love and kindness, through the relationship as a vehicle for this. They present a model for practice illustrated as the therapeutic use of daily events, where the main characteristics of practice are explained in depth, supported throughout with real-life stories. Central to working inside-out is taking the risk to show genuine love and kindness in an attempt to create positive change.

Pauline Clarke Orohoe's chapter (Chapter 7) raises some pertinent question about social care work, flooded – as are other disciplines – with jargon posing as clarity. Much of the language we automatically use as professionals can confuse and, at times, intimidate vulnerable people. Terms that to us are routine and don't cost us a second thought can leave those we care for, who are sometimes educationally disadvantaged, even more disadvantaged: we must be clear, deliberate and definite in the language we use and in how we explain what professional terms actually mean.

As social care expands into different areas of practice, workers are now involved in family assessment and all the challenges that the worker experiences in trying to encourage families to engage in the service. In Chapter 8 Angela Feeney explains the benefits of the 'home-based ecological assessment' tool in her practice, and brings us on a journey from our usual habitat in a service setting into the home.

The home is also featured in Chapter 9, in which Aoife Killeen talks about the benefits of living semi-independently in a congregated setting. Aoife provides instruction on the relevant policies and legislation for social care workers in the disability sector, using examples from her practice and the voice of her colleagues to critically explore this as an approach to semi-independent living. Frontline staff are faced with a virtual reversal in policy, where due to budget constraints service users are returning to almost institutional living; and Aoife offers a practical, cost-saving alternative.

In Chapter 10 we stay with the disability sector, but this time the setting is a day care centre for people with an intellectual disability, and Iseult Paul explores the challenges her team faces with an ageing population. Central to her practice is the notion that the worker integrates personal and professional past experiences into their practice, and that our placements, part-time jobs and life experience influence the worker we become.

In a similar vein, in Chapter 11 Frank Mulville draws on many years of experience to concentrate on the 'I' and self-understanding in social care. He is forthright and honest in looking at himself in the context of examples where one is not only powerless physically but also, at times, emotionally. Times, indeed, when we feel silly, worthless and at the bottom of the pile. He looks at areas where social care workers need downtime as a team, something rare in today's bureaucratic world of social care, and stresses the need for self care and the necessity of a life outside work, without which we benefit nobody, least of all those who need our care so much.

Focusing, developed by Eugene Gendelin, is a topic taken by Derek McDonnell in Chapter 12, 'Precious Cargo'. It details the development of an 'inner dialogue' that can be used to great advantage in relation to any aspect of one's life. The examples from Derek's practice outline in a step-by-step process the key elements that focusing requires in order to be effective in addressing specific areas of difficulty, past or present, in one's life.

Des Mooney begins Chapter 13 by also stressing the influence past life experiences had on his practice; and his understanding of resisting the urge to rush in, and what can happen when we adopt the approach of 'waiting'. He is not telling us to do nothing; waiting is purposeful and we are actively listening, present, learning, reflecting, journaling and providing a space for things to happen.

In Chapter 14 Maria O'Sullivan turns the modern concept of the word 'containment' in social care on its head, drawing heavily on Bion's theory. In this chapter she explores how an understanding of behaviour indicating need must not only be accepted by social care workers but persistently pursued in terms of what might work best when all hope of even any basic changes is slowly ebbing away.

Remaining with the therapeutic theme, in Chapter 15 Laura Behan describes the use of the therapeutic relationship in a residential care home in a therapeutic community. Laura highlights the daily challenges of using this approach in a sometimes chaotic world of care plans, challenging behaviour and our urge as workers to 'fix things'. Unconditional positive regard is at the core of this approach and through the example of Sarah's story Laura describes how the often challenging but always worthwhile journey of such a relationship can inspire healing and growth in the young people we work with. Laura stresses the importance of remembering that small shifts can lead to huge ripples of change for these young people and it is vital that we hold on to this in a profession that can so often leave us feeling helpless and disheartened.

The theme of therapeutic approaches to practice continues in Chapter 16. Helen Buggle explains the 'therapeutic alliance', describing a slow, painstaking process involving the bringing together of three separate elements. All three are necessary if the staff team, most particularly the key worker, is to be effective in addressing issues that are often deeply rooted, sometimes almost completely resistant to intervention. Her examples are interesting and indeed challenging, especially in today's work, where vital concepts such as touch and token, with all they imply, can be so easily misinterpreted.

Chapter 17, by Niall Reynolds, is challenging in many aspects, not least in exploring the task faced by social care workers as part of a multidisciplinary team dealing with a young person who might otherwise be on his way to a placement in another jurisdiction. The lengths to which the team was prepared to go may raise questions for some. One of those questions might well be: Could I or would I work in such a unique situation where tolerance and patience are tested to the limit and ingenuity is called for not only daily but sometimes from minute to minute?

Another unique situation is the focus of Chapter 18, in which David Williams shines the spotlight on his experience of working with young people who self injure in a residential setting. This chapter outlines key definitions of deliberate self harm and examines the implications of managing self-injurious behaviour for social care students and workers. The causes and functions of self-injurious behaviour are described, and David exposes his own personal fears when faced with a young person who self injures.

Chapter 19 presents an overview of challenging behaviour in a setting for adults with acquired brain injury. Here Marguerita Walsh describes her approach as cognitive in origin but developed from her practice experience of working with children with an intellectual disability. Dealing with challenging behaviour is difficult on a practical and personal level and using an ABC form can help social care workers understand more about the role they played in the incident, and how best to support people through these experiences.

In Chapter 20 Lillian Byrne-Lancaster begins by discussing how being both a placement supervisor on practice and a placement tutor in college kindled her interest in the role of placement in social care education. Placement is where students learn how to put theory into practice. They are supervised by a social care worker who has volunteered – or not, as the case may be – to invest their time and energy in this experience for the student. Agencies and workers understand the importance of placement but also acknowledge that the student learns in the real-life setting of the service user, and their needs are paramount. This chapter provides tips for the student on how to approach and secure a placement, and describes the benefits for the student if they are willing to engage, use their own initiative, listen and learn.

The importance of having the right placement experience is evident from the personal reflections at the beginning of Chapter 21. Here we continue to discuss the role and importance of the social care team, but this time in the disability sector. Claire Leonard describes how the team managed to change from a workshop model to a 'day activation unit' with a 'bottom-up' style of management. Claire also provides an insight into the personal and professional challenges faced by social care workers in management roles.

As mentioned in Chapter 21, supervision is essential as a support mechanism for staff and in Chapter 22 Fiona Doyle describes the process of supervision in social care. Supervision is relevant to all social care settings, and Fiona outlines the benefits effective supervision can have for the health and productivity of the team, evident in the two case studies presented.

Kathy D'Arcy's chapter, Chapter 23, provides us with an example of direct work with young people in residential care, looking at the challenges of teaching independent living skills and the importance of the 'small things'.

A whole range of areas are covered by Paddy Ormond in Chapter 24, in which he ranges from the impact of recent political and social upheaval, to acknowledging positive change, to the nitty gritty of pertinent examples and the devastation that can result when what goes on in dysfunctional staff teams is not addressed. Where does today's social care worker personally and as a team member stand in all of this and how can he or she maintain themselves as a *good enough* social care worker in the important context of that phrase? This chapter can leave no one in doubt about the ever-changing world of social care and the social care worker's responsibility in it. Paddy looks at what we can learn from those we work with and how those very people, disadvantaged and marginalised, can see through bluff, bluster and incompetency and recognise when they are being treated with empathy, care and compassion.

Fittingly, our final chapter complements Paddy Ormond's chapter, as Chapter 5 did with Keith's account. If *good enough* social care workers are needed, so are *good enough* managers. John Molloy's rather unique take on the management role in social care, based on over thirty years as a manager, leaves no one off the hook. Catching social care workers doing good work, he posits, is just as vital as detecting what they are not doing right. Moral discernment is his touchstone and, like Paddy Ormond's in Chapter 24, John's range is wide and varied.

A note on terminology: Throughout the book terms such as 'client' and 'service user' are used frequently. These may not be the preferred terms for many social care workers and may require further discussion by our profession.

Chapter 2
The Irish Association of Social Care Workers
Noel Howard

> *Those who cannot remember the past are condemned to repeat it.*
>
> (George Santayana 1863–1952)

A CHEQUERED HISTORY

Had anyone attended a meeting of the fledgling Irish Association of Social Care Workers (IASCW) in the early 1970s they would have been met by a sea of black. Why? Because, when what is now the IASCW was founded in 1972 as the Association of Workers with Children in Care (AWCC), nearly all of its members were religious priests, brothers or nuns. At a meeting in 1976 there were forty-three religious named – and three others.

What is now the IASCW was to have a chequered history, its members seeing and being part of extraordinary developments over forty years. There was progress and optimism, but also disappointment, and on occasion almost despair as the latter part of the twentieth century saw report after report bring the Irish child care system to world attention for all the wrong reasons. Much was gained and much lost, but the association, from its early beginnings to where it is today, managed to survive and at times flourish. Yes, on occasion its critics were many and its supporters few. 'Better to light a candle than curse the darkness' was often the only and best rejoinder to the critics, many of whom, in fairness, had the best interests of those in need and the profession itself at heart.

The history of the IASCW reflects the best of times and indeed the worst of times, when, to cull another phrase, shadows of madness, sadness and badness seeped into the consciousness of all those who worked with deprived children and those who over time were to be part of the evolving social care profession.

The association's origins had to do with children in care as the early 1970s brought a new sense of purpose and possibilities for change in that area. Today, its members work in a variety of settings which come under the umbrella of the term 'social care'. It is perhaps a natural progression that, whereas the association's members for many years worked with children, today's members also work with the disabled, homeless, migrants and the elderly.

INFLUENCES

The Kennedy Report of 1970 (DoH 1970) was a watershed report in relation to children in care. While not commenting specifically on the conditions in which children were kept in care, which is now seen with the benefit of hindsight as a failing in the report, its recommendations were challenging and far-reaching. Inter alia, it sought training for child care staff, a move away from old, outdated, large institutions to smaller group homes for children, raising the age of criminal responsibility, a new child care Act to replace the 1908 Children Act, and courts' regard for the welfare of children and assessments of children's needs. Other reports, notably the Carrigan Report (1931), Cussen Report (1936) and Tuairim Report (1966) had adverted to shortcomings in child care provision and legal and welfare remedies of various kinds were suggested. In view of what we now know, few advances were made and abuse and neglect were unenviable features of life for children in care.

Also not to be forgotten were Michael Viney's *Irish Times* articles from the 1960s, 'The Young Offenders', and Nell McCafferty's incisive articles from the mid-1970s, also published in the *Irish Times* and later collected in the book *In the Eyes of the Law*. Judge Kingsmill Moore and, later, Judge Hubert Wine were pre-eminent among the judiciary in demanding a better, more just deal for deprived children. Both endeavoured, like Judge Peter Kelly in the 1990s, to publicly articulate from the bench and at meetings, often out of sheer frustration, what was lacking in child care provision, giving a powerful boost to workers and a much-needed wake-up call to government. CARE, a campaign for the care of deprived children that was launched in 1971, was another strong force through its public commentary on general issues relating to deprived children, and its arguments for one Minister for Children. The CARE Memorandum of 1972 highlighted much of what needed redressing. One of its calls was for a Minister for Children but, as evidenced by the 1980 Report of the Task Force on Child Care Services, that call fell on deaf ears and was only to be addressed after more than thirty-five years.

With impetus given to calls for reform contained in the Kennedy Report and increasing public debate and media coverage around the plight of children in care, the emergence of an association representative of those who worked with those children was perhaps unsurprising.

Another development that aided the association's development in the 1970s was the Kilkenny Child Care Course, which began in 1971. Many graduates of that course, under the challenging tutelage of Mr Pat Brennan and Sr Stanislaus Kennedy, went on to become active members of the association. Where Kilkenny led, others followed, and the demand for training increased with Cathal Brugha Street College of Catering (now DIT) setting up a course in the late 1970s catering for child care staff in the old Eastern Health Board region. A course for managers was also held in Goldenbridge, Dublin in the 1970s. These much-needed courses eventually led to similar diploma and degree courses being set up by various institutes of technology around the country. There is a view that where once there was very little training available, perhaps we now have too much, with a proliferation of social care courses diluting the status of the academic award. Denise Lyons discusses this point in greater detail in her historical review of social care education in Ireland in Chapter 3.

PROFESSIONALISM AND 'THE UNION'

The foundation of the AWCC, then, can be seen as something that naturally emerged at a time of much debate around the Kennedy Report and other aspects of children's issues that new, increasingly focused groups and individuals brought to public attention. One unique feature of the association, which is seldom replicated, was that for a number of years its members were both managers and workers. This gave an interesting dynamic to proceedings and there were many vibrant, contentious meetings where workers crossed swords with managers. And this was in public! Inevitably, perhaps, such a democratic forum would have its critics on both sides and it was a matter of when, not if, the two constituents of the association would face challenges, which led the already strange bedfellows inexorably toward divorce. And that did happen.

A number of factors led to the managers eventually regrouping as a separate body under the banner of the former managers' association, the Resident Managers' Association (RMA). The workers retained the title AWCC. An increasing number of non-religious lay staff were being employed in the residential child care sector as religious vocations began a slow decline in the 1970s. This new breed and brand of worker opened up a debate around many issues, notably the concept of professionalism and terms and conditions of employment. The last nail in the coffin for the managers and workers remaining in the same association centred on discussion, often heated, and differences of opinion on trade union membership.

Such discussions and debates helped establish the distinction between trade union membership and membership of a professional body. They are not the same, though overlapping issues can to this day blur that distinction. It should also be understood that those who passionately argued against union membership did so from a belief that the inevitable consequences would dilute and fracture the attitudes and commitment of staff to the proper care of children, with all that was best being lost. On the other side, the argument was made that in many parts of the country, depending on what pertained locally, workers were being treated badly and unjustly. It should be noted that many religious saw merit in union membership and were helpful and supportive of the demands being made by those in favour of better conditions and salaries. In many cases their work situations were just as bad, if not worse, than those of their lay colleagues. The association newsletters of the time are peppered with different points of view, with one member writing in 1980 in response to a letter from sixteen child care workers from Cork: 'Comments on training, salaries, management, procedures and practice and child care workers' self image expose many a raw nerve in the residential care system.'

The then chairman of the association, Pat Brennan, writing in 1976, had the following to say, which brings to mind the expression, 'the more things change the more they remain the same'. The sentiments and the challenge apply today as much as they did nearly forty years ago:

> *So, events in the Association have meaning. The most obvious meaning to salaries is bread and butter and security. But there are other meanings – justice – not only by the State to workers, but justice to children; honesty – an honest day's pay for an honest day's work – and how honest are we to children? And Caring cannot be measured in terms of money – how is there to be full, sensitive commitment? And how do we witness to generosity, to the values that are at the heart of man, that are contrary to those of the rat race? What are our values anyway, and how do we enable children to discover values to themselves rooted in the value that they are in themselves; or do we condition, manipulate them, in a doctrinaire way?*

As early as 1974 the association urged the government departments to look at the issue of adequate salaries as opposed to capitation grants, in view of the increasing numbers of lay staff being trained (in Kilkenny), resulting in improved standards of care and greater professionalism. Unwittingly perhaps, the association in those early years, by advocating thus, hastened the debate around trade union membership, with the managers and workers eventually going their separate ways.

Following the publication of the Castle Priory Report in the UK (Kahan & Banner 1969), the association organised a ground-breaking conference in Dublin in 1974 with Barbara Kahan as the main speaker. (She was beginning to be a major influence on child care-related issues in the UK and eventually received an OBE for her contribution to children's services.) That conference helped also to establish the association as an important player in the general care field, though the emphasis was still on residential care.

In 1974 the Task Force on Child Care Services was established, and the association was consulted. Its report, published in 1980, was significant for a number of reasons, not all positive. (More on that later.) In 1978 the association published *The Athlone Papers*, which focused, in the main, on the child in care.

FICE CONFERENCE, DUBLIN 1979

The public image of the association was further boosted in 1979, designated the International Year of the Child. The association hosted the FICE (International Federation of Educative Communities) international conference in Dublin and requested that An Taoiseach, Jack Lynch, should open it. The Minister for Health, Charles Haughey, advised Mr Lynch to decline the invitation on the basis of the 'association's relatively minor status'. Mr Haughey himself seemed to be untroubled by this description of the association's status and he duly opened the conference himself. A highlight of his opening speech was praise for the work of the religious orders in the child care field. He noted that 'the dedication and endeavour of the religious has made easy the task of the state in discharging its constitutional responsibility'. Who would have thought that exactly thirty years later the Ryan Report (OMCYA 2009a) would excoriate the State and the Church for their failure not only to care properly for children in state care but for their collusion in perpetuating the neglect and abuse of those children? The conference itself was an unqualified success and enhanced the association's reputation.

TASK FORCE REPORT 1980

1980 saw the publication of the Task Force on Child Care Services report referred to earlier, which looked at the child and the family, child care services current at the time, alternative care and the child and the law. There was a huge response to the report, which continued for a number of years.

In the response to the report, and leaving much of what it had to say go unnoticed, reference was made to the fact that it was not a unanimous report; six members expressed reservations of one kind or another with the conclusions. Significant as all six are, it is worth noting that the Department of Education representative made his reservations known on the proposal that the Department of Health take over all children's services. In what was a very straightforward, quoted comment for a civil servant he declared that the Department of Health should not be allowed to proceed along the suggested path and he saw nothing that would indicate to him that Health 'are willing to take on the care, control and education of delinquent children, or that they have the capacity to do so'. Essentially, he wanted the industrial and reformatory schools, at that stage dwindling to what were to become 'special schools' or 'detention schools', to remain within the Department of Education. It would take nearly thirty years for that situation to be reversed.

Perhaps one of the biggest disappointments in the Task Force report was its failure to recommend a child care authority, akin to what CARE had recommended ten years previously, which would be a separate body with statutory powers, to replace the Departments of Health, Education and Justice, all of which had dealings with children. One the greatest and most frustrating difficulties the association and other professional bodies faced over many years was the 'buck-passing' between departments that was a feature of how children and their needs were looked at and decisions made. One of the most unedifying and scandalous aspects of this was that two and sometimes all three departments would have legal representation in court, at enormous cost, arguing about whose responsibility it was to care for children – despite their separate assertions that all they wanted was the child's best interests to be met. The proposal of a child care authority was probably too reasonable and sensible a suggestion to replace what was at times nothing less than a legal circus, with children, families and those who worked with them sitting on the sidelines aghast at how the 'care' of children was being decided. The association published a detailed response to the Task Force report in 1982.

EXPANSION

With the emergence of widening community services in the 1980s necessitating the involvement of child care workers, the AWCC decided to change its name to the Irish Association of Care Workers (IACW).

Aware of developments around calls for registration for child care and social workers in the UK, the IASCW, among other organisations, campaigned for a similar process to apply in Ireland. Who could have predicted that in 2014, the goal of social care worker registration has still not been achieved, despite continuing efforts by all parties involved?

In the late 1980s the all-party committee on the Child Care Bill (the 1991 Act to be) benefited from IACW input. The association, like many other interested bodies, stressed the need for a welfare-based rather than a punitive, legalistic approach to the problems many children were experiencing; and 1988 saw the association publish the *Ennismore Papers*, which resulted from an in-depth look at training. This was a valuable addition to the debate at a time when social care training was expanding. A code of ethics for care workers was also first published in 1988 (IASCW 1988a). The 1980s saw the organisation of an annual conference and care workers from all over the country met yearly to hear about and discuss the issues of the day, many of which were becoming more complex and demanding of attention as revelations of abuses and scandals from the past gradually became an almost everyday event as the 1990s neared.

IN THE EYE OF THE STORM

The association found itself in the eye of the storm and battled to preserve the good name of its members while facing the reality that not everyone who had worked with deprived children in the past had always had the proper motivation. That was to be proved beyond doubt in the following years. Emerging specific accounts of the lives of some children in care painted a horror story. The following years saw commissioned reports revealing a litany of criminal neglect and abuse, with Church and State clearly culpable in cruelly destroying the trust placed by children in the adults who were supposed to care for them.

A number of workers against whom allegations were made sought the assistance of the association and their trade union, and another frustrating process did little to help. This was because the different health boards took different approaches in dealing with allegations and the association found itself struggling to find time as a voluntary organisation to deal with increasingly complex, sensitive situations which clearly had legal as well as personal ramifications. Differences of approach also involved boards and committees of management and, indeed, individual managers themselves on occasion.

As report after report emerged the association struggled to maintain a professional attitude in the face of increasing fears among its members that they were open to allegation as never before. Over time, individual social care workers, totally innocent of any wrongdoing, would be suspect simply because it was easy to do. 'They were all at it' became a disingenuous, lazy mantra of the blame game for those who tarred all with the same brush. Men working in residential care were particularly vulnerable.

The year 1993 saw the publication of the Kilkenny Incest Report (McGuinness 1993), and the Madonna House Report (DoH 1996a) followed three years later. The association responded to the Kilkenny case by publishing a special edition of its magazine *Cúram*. The Madonna House Report covered many areas that were becoming more and more a feature, or suggested feature, of social care work: Garda vetting; reporting abuse; monitoring; social services inspectorate; and children's rights. The report indicated that the problems unearthed in Madonna House were not, in the view of the inquiry team, exclusive to Madonna House. The case of Madonna House, the jewel in the crown of the Health Board's child care provision, and the Kilkenny case received enormous media attention. Madonna House closed. Scarcely had the furore about Madonna House died down when the 'West of Ireland Farmer' case (*McColgan Report*) was published in 1998. In 1996 the RTÉ's *Dear Daughter* (Lentin 1996) documentary was broadcast and the Kelly Fitzgerald report (Oireachtas 1996) published. These cases were simply to preview what was to emerge – up to the present day – in many other reports cataloguing the failure of the Church and the State in carrying out their duty of care to vulnerable children either in the community or in residential care. It is worth noting that not all these damning reports were into residential care. Notable also were articles and books written by those who had suffered abuse, for example Paddy Doyle's *The God Squad*, published in 1989 and still available.

25TH ANNIVERSARY

Every profession and organisation searched for answers, answers which in many cases were not forthcoming. In an attempt to highlight the dilemma for the IACW and its members, the president of the association (the writer of this chapter), had the following to say on the twenty-fifth anniversary of the association's founding in 1997 at the annual conference in Killarney:

> *I would like to return, out of a sense of justice to those children whose lives were blighted when things went horribly wrong ... that too is part of our past and I don't believe I'm wrong when I say there are painful and disturbing questions here for all of us. The scandals and revelations of what was not child care have catapulted the care worker into centre stage at times and left all of us grasping for some answer to help us make some sense, if that were possible, of situations where trust was broken and innocence betrayed. ... What they suffered was at a time when, to quote an* Irish Times *editorial toward the end of last year, 'they had no voice and indeed they may not have had the words to convey what was being done to them.' What I'm going to say now is, I believe, reconcilable with what I have just alluded to.*

> *In seeking to redress the wrongs of the past let us be careful not to lose what was good in it. If that balance is not preserved then the very best of what we have to give, compassion, warmth, security and a sense of fun, all will be diluted and stunted, changed out of all recognition by a myriad of rules, regulations, section this and subsection that ... all in place, and rightly so, for very good reasons.*
>
> *It would indeed be sad and counterproductive if, in our modern child care system, we had everything ... legislation, inspectors, visiting committee, watchdogs of every kind, pages and pages of reports into every incident ... if we had all these and their only effect was a profession looking over its shoulder morning, noon and night. This is undoubtedly a challenging task but it must be addressed if our child care centres are not to become the very antithesis of all they are supposed to be. Such barren, regulation-ridden clinics, because that's all they'll be, will not respect personality or individual ability and will, in my view, as some would suggest is now happening, make child care a very unattractive and closed profession. And at the end of all that the children with all their needs may inherit another one from their time with us, victims of a system that has erected artificial, 'watch your back' barriers between adults who are supposed to care, but cannot, and children who need it but can't get it.*

Other important developments were afoot as the 1990s began, and the Child Care Act 1991 became law in July of that year. Its concentration was on the welfare of children. There was a view that the legislation did not go far enough in relation to the welfare of children, while others argued that it eroded the rights of the family. The association was represented on the group that drew up the 1996 *Standards in Residential Centres and Guide to Good Practice* (DoH 1996b) and the *National Standards for Residential Centres* (DoH 2001). It lobbied, with others, throughout the 1990s for the enactment of appropriate juvenile justice legislation, and the 2001 Children Act resulted. One of the results of that Act was the range of community sanctions suggested to avoid, where possible, detention being used. This led to community projects springing up around the country and care workers were moving into those areas and broadening their horizons.

NEW CENTURY: NEW CHALLENGES

A new century brought new challenges, new scandals, new legislation and an economic boom. Numbers in residential state care dwindled and private providers of residential and foster care began to gain a foothold in the provision of care. The term 'social care' had gained prominence as referring to a profession offering frontline services with a commitment to the planning and delivery of quality care and other support services for individuals and groups with identified needs. Training options became more widely available as the number of institutes of technology offering social care degree courses increased. This was one reason that the association decided, for the second time in its history, to change its name, becoming the Irish Association of *Social* Care Workers (IASCW).

The workload was spreading and the association, with its executive – all volunteers – found it increasingly difficult to give the level of attention and time that prevailing issues demanded. The association is represented on Health Information and Quality Authority (HIQA) working groups in relation to the development of standards and the Higher Education and Training Awards Council (HETAC) standards committee, which revamped academic and placement requirements for social care students. As noted earlier, since the mid-1980s the IACW has been at the forefront in calling for statutory registration. In 2005 the Health and Social Care Professionals Act, which provides for the registration of, among others, social care workers, became law. The IASCW has closely worked with CORU, the registration body, to move things forward in what has proved a very arduous and complex process because of the number of social care workers, the range of background experience/qualifications and the demands of the registration system itself.

While a number of Junior Ministers for Children had been in post from the 1990s, in 2005 Brian Lenihan, as Minister for Children, had a seat at the cabinet table. One of the first things he promised was a referendum on children's rights. The end of that long road came in November 2012 with the 31st amendment to the Constitution being voted in. Despite all the bleating and hand-wringing about children and the abuses of the past over the previous forty years, only 35% of the electorate voted. The IASCW (as part of Social Care Ireland) advocated a Yes vote and held a public meeting in Dublin as part of an information evening on the referendum.

Reference has been made in this chapter to the reports into abuse, but one cannot be accused of labouring that point by referring to the *Report of the Commission to Inquire into Child Abuse* (CICA) (OMCYA 2009a), more commonly known as the Ryan Report, and the publication in 2012 of the *Report of the Independent Child Death Review Group* (ICDRG) (Shannon & Gibbons 2012) into the deaths of children in state care. All the abuse reports are damning, but these two very clearly point out on the one hand the failures of the past (Ryan) and, perhaps more revelatory, what went wrong in the first ten years of the twenty-first century, during which period 196 children died in state care. This when there was no shortage of money, no Dickensian industrial schools and minimal, if any, involvement by religious orders. It was clear that there were many lessons to be learned. The IASCW submitted recommendations to the group set up after Ryan to come up with an implementation plan based on the Ryan recommendations, and that group eventually published a 99-point plan in the autumn of 2009.

SOCIAL CARE IRELAND

For a number of years there had been informal suggestions that the RMA and the IASCW should amalgamate, as many of the issues relating to social care were common to both. With statutory registration continuing to be a salient issue there was further common ground not just between the IASCW and RMA but also with the Irish Association of Social Care Educators (IASCE).

In 2010 the first steps were taken, and after much work over many months the three bodies were amalgamated under the umbrella title of Social Care Ireland. By agreement none of the three would have their distinctive roles changed, but it was strongly felt that one unified body with three important constituent parts made sense and gave a stronger, more cohesive focus on common issues. Furthermore, individuals who are members of any one of the associations are de facto members of the umbrella body. Minister Frances Fitzgerald officially launched Social Care Ireland on 20 June 2011 and this marked an important advance not only for the three individual organisations but for social care itself. A new executive took office in September 2012 and decided to explore the possibility of a closer merge; and details will emerge in time after consultation with the three bodies. (There is further discussion about the formation of Social Care Ireland in Chapter 3.)

Many of the issues that have faced the IASCW since the beginning of the recession began to face other organisations as well. With the Child and Family Agency part of the Department of Children from 2014 and a reconfigured HSE also imminent, with social care members drawn from at least three of the new proposed 'service areas', there will be a greater demand to professionally represent the views of members. After years of waiting and lobbying, 2014 may also see the establishment of a social care registration board within CORU. Thus will begin the practical process of ensuring that the interests of social care workers as well as those of the public are well served and that the title of social care worker is legally protected. That complicated process and other legislative changes will throw up many challenges and the IASCW's response, as part of Social Care Ireland, will be a further indicator of how far the association has come after forty years.

For many years the association has published a biannual magazine, *Cúram*, and a biannual newsletter, *The Link*. Various earlier versions of both have been part of the association's effort to keep in communication with its members. The scope and influence of material published in various forms since the foundation of the association may well merit separate consideration.

In an age of instant communication it is perhaps a sobering thought that through the letterbox of every member comes news, views and comments four times a year in written form with a copy of the *Irish Journal of Applied Social Studies* (IJASS) on publication. All this for a very modest membership subscription (currently €15).

The development of the newsletter and the magazine has mirrored the changing fortunes and influence of the IASCW and the archival material reflects the highs and lows and the face of social care since the first tentative steps were taken forty years ago. That material is testament also to the continuing struggle to maintain and further develop the association as a professional body. The dedication of the various executives and the continued commitment of its members from early beginnings to the present day have laid a strong foundation on which to face into the future.

Chapter 3
Social Care Education and the Irish Association of Social Care Educators
Denise Lyons

PATHWAY INTO SOCIAL CARE

My journey into social care was as serendipitous as it was for most contributors to this book. As a child I wanted to be an art teacher and after several failed attempts to enter the National College, I studied fine art and became an unemployable artist. A job advertisement for a Community Employment Scheme 'Arts Worker for People with a Physical Disability' in the Irish Wheelchair Association sparked my interest in the field of social care. I returned to college to study full time at DIT, and after several years working in residential care, I was given the opportunity in 2000 to lecture in St Patrick's College, Carlow, now Carlow College. I have spent the majority of my working life in social care education, a role that challenges me constantly, but as I am off the floor for such a long time I rely on my interactions with students returning from placement, and talking to social care workers, to maintain my link to practice. This need to communicate with both my academic and practice colleagues motivated me to become involved in the Irish Association of Social Care Educators (IASCE) and later Social Care Ireland (SCI).

INTRODUCTION

This chapter illustrates the foundation of our current experience of social care education from its inception in 1971. The first training course is of significant importance to current practice because of the emphasis on 'relationship' and the personal development of the student. To understand our education system we need to appreciate how it evolved and developed over time in response to changes in practice. This is particularly relevant as social care educators will be required to submit their programme for approval and demonstrate their 'fitness for purpose'. Under the Health and Social Care Professionals Act 2005 educators will need to demonstrate how the programme meets the needs of workers in all areas of practice. Fortunately, social care educators have a history of working towards best practice and in 1998 the Irish Association of Social Care Educators (IASCE) was established to increase cohesion between the colleges in Ireland. IASCE members have collaborated to produce core policy documents needed for practice, and have enhanced the overall quality of each programme. This organisation is one of the partners of the umbrella body SCI, and members of IASCE were very influential in the preparation stages of this representative group's development.

This chapter begins with a brief history of social care education and continues by exploring IASCE's role.

THE HISTORY OF SOCIAL CARE EDUCATION: FROM CHILD CARE TO SOCIAL CARE

In Chapter 2 Noel Howard introduced us to the first training course for child care workers in Kilkenny. This course ran for ten years (1971–1981) and was unique in that students learned to understand the lives of vulnerable people through time spent together in the practice environment, and also by deconstructing this knowledge through living with their fellow students (Lyons 2013). The exchanges with other students in a shared learning space encouraged the development of relationships in a safe environment, before the worker in training was released to the vulnerable public. This first course provided training for child care workers in residential child care, which then evolved over forty-two years to become the current generic programme of educating workers for a variety of services including physical and intellectual disability, homeless, elderly, addiction and family support, to name a few.

The National Council for Educational Awards (NCEA) was established in March 1972 to confer degrees, diplomas and certificates for students in non-university third-level institutions (Irish Times 1972), including students of child care. The first child care award accredited by the NCEA was the Diploma in Child Care of the Dublin Institute of Technology in 1974, followed by the National Diploma in Child Care at the Waterford Regional Technical College (RTC) (Lyons 2013). The next child care course was established in Sligo RTC to train prison wardens from Loughan House Juvenile Detention Centre for Boys (Reilly 2008). 'Between 1982 and 1991 a total of 600 awards were conferred in the six colleges including the Dublin Institute of Technology, and the Regional Technical Colleges of Athlone, Cork, Galway, Sligo and Waterford' (Courtney 2012). In 1992 the Open Training College began providing training for social care workers in the area of disability. In 2002 another social care programme was offered by Tralee Institute of Technology (IT), followed by Blanchardstown IT, Dundalk IT in 2003 and Carlow IT (both in the main campus and Wexford campus) in 2006. The final programmes to emerge included those at Letterkenny IT and Tallaght IT in 2008, and Galway-Mayo IT in 2009, bringing the total to fourteen members of IASCE at the time of publication.

What's in a name?

In 1989 a working group was established to look at the education of social and caring students (NCEA 1992; Courtney 2012). This working group, convened by Damien Courtney, introduced the title 'social care' to reflect the future need of workers in other care areas and the decline in need of residential care workers due to increased foster placements. In 2001 the NCEA was replaced by the Higher Education and Training Awards Council (HETAC), and the terms 'social care' and 'applied social studies' replaced 'child care' in the accredited programmes. The practice setting, and in particular the main employer, the Department of Health and Children (DoHC), were also considering a change in title. After a ruling by the Labour Court (recommendations 155515 and 17044), the DoHC established an Expert Review Board to examine issues relating to health and social professionals (JCSCP 2002).

This review group recommended that a subcommittee examine the terminology 'child care worker' and select a new title that was inclusive of the other similar helping professions, for example workers in the intellectual disability sector. The title 'social care' was also adopted in this context, and the practice of a social care worker defined in the report as the 'professional provision of care, protection, support, welfare and advocacy for vulnerable or dependant clients, individually or in groups' (JCSCP 2002:9). 'This is achieved through the planning and evaluation of individualised and group programmes of care, which are based on needs, identified in consultation with the client and delivered though day-to-day shared life experiences. All interventions are based on established best practice and an in-depth knowledge of life span development' (JCSCP 2002:9). The term 'social care' is now protected under the Health and Social Care Professionals Act 2005, thus restricting any person or educational institute from using that term without approval after the statutory registration is established. When finalised, the Social Care Registration Board will have a huge impact on all social care programmes.

STEPS TOWARDS STATUTORY REGISTRATION OF SOCIAL CARE WORKERS

In 1973 Pat Brennan, Director of the Kilkenny School of Social Education, submitted a letter to the Department of Education calling for the statutory registration of child care workers, to which the Department promised 'extensive consideration' (Courtney 2012:3). However, statutory registration did not appear on the political agenda again until Wednesday 4 June 1986, when during Dáil Questions, Dr O'Hanlon asked the then Minister for Health Barry Desmond to discuss a timeframe for the introduction of legislation for the statutory registration of health and social professionals.

On 14 April 2000 the then Minister for Health and Children, Micheál Martin, launched a consultation process with health and social professionals to discuss statutory registration. These consultations were published in a document entitled *Statutory Registration for Health and Social Professionals: Proposals for the Way Forward* (DoHC 2000). As discussed in Chapter 2, the Irish Association of Social Care Workers (IASCW) and the RMA represented social care practice in these discussions. The report presented a rationale for the introduction of statutory registration, mainly to protect the public and the professions, through legislative protection of the titles. The report also recommended a 'legislative framework for the appraisal and approval of education and training courses, examinations, qualifications and institutions, thus ensuring the proper development of education and training across the professions' (DoHC 2000:5). The report provided a basis for the structure and framework of the Health and Social Care Professionals Council (HSCPC), CORU, and the Registration Boards, evident in the Health and Social Care Professionals Act 2005.

As discussed above, after the Social Care Registration Board becomes established, social care educational programmes will have to apply to the Registration Board for approval. The main function of the Act is to protect the public, and social care is one of the twelve professions included in this legislation. A function of CORU, established under the 2005 Act, is to 'engage in research into education and training relating to the practice of the designated profession, including the formulation of experimental curricula and the evaluation of existing programmes and examination and assessment procedures'. In order to be approved by the Social Care Registration Board, institutes of technology will have to satisfy the board that the public will be protected, as indicated in sections 7, 27 and 38 of the 2005 Act, through the delivery of a 'high standard of professional education', that has suitably trained the designated professional to be a 'fit and proper person, able to engage in the practice of the profession, with knowledge of the language necessary for practice'. Educators are therefore gatekeepers with a responsibility to protect the public by ensuring that those graduates are fit and proper persons. This designated person will 'exercise skill or judgment' in 'the care of those in need of protection, guidance or support'.

In 2009 the Health Service Executive (HSE), as the main employer of health and social care professionals, published a report that aimed to 'support the improvement of services to service users through focusing on the development of health and social care professionals ... in terms of education and training' (HSE 2009:2). In this report the HSE outlined its responsibility to protect the public by ensuring that people are informed, guided and cared for by competent and qualified staff. The Health and Social Care Professionals Act 2005 defines the HSE as having a supportive and enabling role in the education of staff. However, the Act does not place a responsibility on the HSE to employ only social care workers, or other health professionals, with the appropriate qualifications. In current practice this has led to the introduction of another pay grade and title of 'social care assistant', introduced as a cost-saving measure. This new grade enables services to employ non-qualified staff, or pay qualified social care workers at the 'care assistant' rate, which has implications for the registration of social care workers, and this new category of worker. In addition, the HSE recruits social care workers under different titles, including 'project worker', a title that is not protected by the 2005 Act.

We must note that with the establishment of TUSLA, the Child and Family Agency, in January 2014, many social care workers will have moved from the HSE to the new agency. To complicate matters, however, it is worth keeping in mind that some social care workers will still be part of the HSE, for example the Child and Adolescent Mental Health Services (CAMHS).

IS SOCIAL CARE EDUCATION FIT FOR PRACTICE?

According to the Institutes of Technology Act 2006, section 5(2), 'a member of the academic staff of a college shall have the freedom, within the law, in his or her teaching, research and any other activities either in or outside the college, to question and test received wisdom, to put forward new ideas and to state controversial or unpopular opinions' (Government of Ireland 2006:8).

Throughout the years individual lecturers in social care have raised concerns over the future of social care education in relation to identity, increased numbers in classes, flooding the market with graduates, and the practice of setting no formal limits on repeat placements for social care students (Lyons 2013). According to Williams and Lalor (2001:86), 'Some commentators have expressed doubts as to whether social care courses are providing workers with the essential skills required for residential child care.' In my own education, the lecturers teaching on the programme were predominantly from the disciplines of social work, psychology and sociology. It can be argued that these professionals were selected because of the limited numbers of qualified social care workers in Ireland at the time. Until the recent economic downturn lecturers were hired on permanent contracts and on the basis of their practice or academic experience in areas relevant to social care. Most lecturers have specific areas of interest, and even the lecturers who come from practice have only worked in a few different settings. Therefore it is difficult for a team of lecturers on a social care course to design a programme that meets the training needs of an expanding and evolving profession. This can lead to a perception that there is a division between training and practice, leading workers and agencies to question the fitness for purpose of the programme to the different areas of practice. I feel we can reduce this divide by creating a structure that includes social care workers as practice tutors, not just within placement but inside the lecture halls. Like practice, education is constrained by budgets and management structures where changes can be slow, or in some cases not possible to implement.

O'Connor (2009) has described social care education and practice as having no identity, largely due to an un-integrated approach to education and practice. O'Connor (2009:101) performed an 'imagined SWOT analysis' of social care, arguing under 'strength' that 'social care educators provide in-depth courses that contain a professional body of knowledge and produce well rounded and well-meaning social care practitioners ... who are better trained ... due to diverse and flexible training provided.' However, O'Connor agrees that it is impossible to teach students everything required for practice because of the diverse nature of the profession. This is a problem for which we need to find a solution.

In a discussion with Ginny Hanrahan, CORU's Chief Executive Officer, at the 2012 Health and Social Care Professionals Advisory Group meeting, it was evident that CORU wants social care education to teach a 'generic programme' that will educate workers to be fit for practice in a variety of settings. In his concluding statements, O'Connor (2009) argues that if education and practice became more integrated we could collectively create 'a vision and blueprint' that could enhance both practice and education, and might help in the task of creating this fit. The journey towards increased collaboration between workers and educators began with the formation of IASCE in 1998, discussed in the next section of this chapter.

THE IRISH ASSOCIATION OF SOCIAL CARE EDUCATORS

Originally social care workers were called 'child care workers' and they worked specifically with children in residential care, or secure care. However, this title was destined to change, initially through the actions of workers in the disability sector who wished to receive the same pay and conditions as child care workers, then through the influence of the NCEA to meet training deficits in other helping professions.

As we saw earlier in this chapter ('What's in a name?'), the title 'social care' is now protected under the Health and Social Care Professionals Act 2005.

The *Irish Journal of Applied Social Studies* (IJASS) was established in 1998 by social care educators and the RMA (Courtney 2012). Later that year Kathleen Kennedy (formerly of Dublin IT) and Damien Courtney (Cork IT) returned from the Formation of European Social Educator Training (FESET) conference with the idea of establishing an Irish Association of Social Care Educators (IASCE). Point (2) of the IASCE Constitution proposes that 'the aims of the Association shall be to promote social care education, to co-ordinate the activities, to develop and maintain standards and to advocate on behalf of members.'

IASCE members include the institutes of technology, the Open Training College, and any other institution that delivers a social care programme approved under the 2010 HETAC standards. Unlike the two other representative organisations, membership resides in the member college, rather than the individual, and each college has one vote, although many educators can attend each meeting. The committee elects an executive comprising a president, vice-president, treasurer and secretary at the annual general meeting (AGM).

The first IASCE conference, held in Sligo in March 2001, was attended by thirty-seven delegates, and has grown since then into the shared conference of the three organisations under the umbrella title Social Care Ireland (SCI). I took over from Dr Áine de Róiste as Secretary of IASCE in 2008 and have remained in that position since then. Reading back over the minutes from 1998, it is interesting to review the issues that to this day remain unsolved, but it is also important to recognise all the work achieved by IASCE and the central figures who were involved from the beginning. The central themes that emerge from the discussions include Garda clearance, students' suitability for practice, placement policies, class size and placement supervision, to name a few.

Perry Share from Sligo IT developed the IASCE website, with a link to the Irish Social Care Gateway (Courtney 2003, 2012), and all the minutes from IASCE meetings are available online. Over the years IASCE became an essential communication forum, and a space to share ideas and collaborate on essential policy documents for social care education. Collaborative projects include, among others, the three editions (2005, 2009 and 2013) of the student core reader *Applied Social Care: An Introduction for Students in Ireland*, a manual for placement supervision and *Social Care in Ireland: Theory, Policy and Practice* (released in 2006).

IASCE plays an important role in the education of social care workers and this practice is coming under scrutiny with the forthcoming registration of social care workers. Under the Health and Social Care Professionals Act 2005 (part 2: 7), the main objective of the Health and Social Care Professionals Council (CORU) 'is to protect the public by promoting high standards of professional conduct and professional education, training and competence among registrants of the designated professions'.

In 2009, at the joint conference of IASCE and IASCW, Ginny Hanrahan of CORU presented a paper entitled 'Lead the Way, Follow, or Stand Aside'. In her presentation Hanrahan (2009) posed a challenge to the social care educators to identify if the 'hat still fits'. Hanrahan (2009) also stressed the critical importance of this for social care educators, as the HSCPC has the authority under the 2005 Act (part 5 (48) 1:b) to 'refuse to approve the programme if not so satisfied'. Thus within the process of registration all institutes of education providing social care training will be required to sufficiently meet the educational standards devised by CORU in order to continue.

IASCE has experienced changes in recent years. On a positive note, in 2013 it elected three qualified social care workers to the committee (Lillian Byrne-Lancaster, President; Vicky Anderson, Vice-President; Denise Lyons, Secretary), evidence of the development of the profession of social care. However, not all changes have been favourable, and the most notable is the loss of members at meetings. This may be due to the increased workload of lecturing staff and decreased budgets for the travel and subsistence costs required to attend, but it could also be due to IASCE's potential formation into the one representative body of SCI, and the loss of autonomy that this merger may bring.

AND THEN THERE WAS ONE

Chapters 2 and 3 have introduced the three separate representative bodies for social care workers, managers and educators (IASCW, IASCE and IASCM). Although separate, each organisation was formed in response to a need to connect and share ideas, and each has grown and developed in response to changes in the profession of social care. Over recent years certain changes began to bring the three bodies closer together, especially during the shared conferences, which enabled all members to see the value of collaboration. In 2005 the inclusion of social care in the Health and Social Care Professionals Act encouraged all three bodies to communicate with the shared aim of registration.

I first heard about SCI in the foyer of the Louis Fitzgerald Hotel, in the course of a conversation with David Williams and Kevin Lalor. It was easy to see the merits of having one representative body for all professionals involved in social care: workers, managers and educators. It was agreed that the executive of the three groups would form the first executive committee of SCI, which would be charged with the arduous task of bringing the three groups together. The original nine committee members were: John Molloy, Kieran Campbell and Sean O'Callaghan from the RMA; Noel Howard, David Power and David Williams from IASCW; and Pat McGarty, Kevin Lalor and Denise Lyons from IASCE.

David Williams was elected president and relevant executive functions were distributed among the other members. John Molloy did much of the work in drafting a constitution for the new body. Within the first year we created the website, established a bank account, and hosted a shared conference. SCI was officially launched in June 2011 by Minister Frances Fitzgerald in front of a packed audience. In September of that year the successful first term of the original fellowship of SCI came to an end. Three of the original members (David Williams, Noel Howard and Denise Lyons) remained on the next committee to ensure continuity in the process. The remaining six members were: Lillian Byrne-Lancaster and Vicky Anderson, IASCE; Paula Byrne, IASCW; and David Durney, Bernadette Manning and Caroline Cronly, IASCM.

At the 2013 conference the newly elected president, Denise Lyons, spoke of the aims for the next two years: the executive would try to promote SCI to students and workers in different settings. The core of the work of this committee was to progress SCI towards becoming one representative body rather than a federation of three.

On 4 October 2013 a total of eighteen members from the three social care representative bodies met to discuss the possibility of moving towards SCI as one working representative body. The meeting was chaired by Denise Lyons (President, SCI) and was attended by Karin White (IT Sligo), Miceal Burke (Student Representative, IASCW), Noel Howard (IASCW/SCI), Caroline Cronly (IASCW/SCI), Dave Williams (IASCW/SCI), Carlos Kelly (IASCM), Karen Sugrue (LIT), Lorraine Ryan (IASCW), Antoinette Behan (IASCW), Nicola Kane (IASCW), Perry Share (IASCE), Anne-Marie Keady (IASCM), Anne-Marie Shier (IASCE), Ann Morahan (IASCW), Fiona Walshe (IASCE), Martin Power (IASCW) and Catherine Byrne (IASCW).

The eighteen participants were divided into small mixed sub-groups, tasked with identifying the pros and cons of full unification into one representative body, SCI. Each group described the positive reasons for coming together, and the possible problems we might encounter, concluding with some suggestions for moving forward. All the participants were in favour of the three organisations coming together with one identity and a strong voice going forward. In the final discussion of the planning meeting there was consensus for a 'phasing-in' process which would address the aforementioned issues. The discussion also included the possibility of a paid position to assist with the phasing-in process, which could centralise the organisation of this unification. Several participants discussed the possible role in SCI of significant interest groups (SIGs) – common in many professional bodies.

In summary, the hurdles and disadvantages of coming together were described as the flipside of the reasons to move forward. They included issues on finance, administration, the nature of our smaller organisations, and how to deal with specific issues that might not involve all member groups. There will be challenges on practical issues, including membership fees, the constitution, representation, sponsorship, and control over publications. However, all agreed that this may be the right time to overcome the fears and hurdles identified.

The work of the SCI committee has not been without its own share of difficulties. SCI is not a financially independent organisation as all three representative bodies are still fully operational. SCI is funded through donations from IASCE, IASCM and IASCW, and has some income generated from the SCI conference. In reality this has slowed down the operation of SCI where extra funding is required from the representative bodies to conduct the business of SCI, for example to redevelop the website. The workload of each committee member has doubled as they engage in meetings for both the representative body and SCI. Cutbacks and increased workloads have impacted on some members' ability to attend every meeting, and this has slowed productivity from one meeting to another. SCI was criticised by Share (2013) for a poor public presence, especially during the Children's Referendum, and this is also a sign of the infancy of this organisation. A unified SCI will have an increased membership and a cohesive focus to target key issues, which will increase our public profile.

Stories from Practice and Management

Chapter 4
There's no Place like Home: Care and Aftercare
'Keith King'

'There's no place like home' is a quote from *The Wizard of Oz*. While the film portrayed a young girl caught between the realms of reality and a dream world, my experience was that of reality, not a fictitious dream or film script with second takes.

I was born into a large family that suffered physically, socially and psychologically through domestic violence and alcoholism. Growing up in an unstable home environment had many consequences that affected me directly and indirectly within my family and social systems. My role was supposed to be that of a child sheltered from abuse and offered love and security from both parents. However, due to the nature of alcoholism this was not the case as the roles of child and parent became skewed and reversed and I felt suppressed as a child, having to mature and develop rapidly before my time.

I recall finding myself doing my parents' jobs quite often as one or both of them would be out socialising or too intoxicated to function. I also took on this role in relation to preparing meals for my younger siblings, cleaning the house, advising and assisting my younger siblings, as well as protecting them from violence and danger in the world around them.

Even though it was not an ideal childhood of nurturing and security, and although times were difficult and harsh, we were raised with good family morals and values that have benefited me to this day.

Individuals may have a realistic or unrealistic view of what it is like to grow up in a chaotic environment that is entrenched in social disorder, violence and alcohol abuse. However, although this may be the situation, one has to remember that no parent desires to hurt or punish a child unduly or unfairly. Unfortunately, as addicts with a disease/addiction that consumes their very being, they are left with a distorted view of reality and behaviour that is reflected on the members within the home environment. I must state this part clearly: although my parents were, as I know now, functioning alcoholics, they were extremely loving when alcohol was not involved. However, sadly, alcohol use was quite prevalent in the home, which altered normal adult functioning, thereby impacting on social order and normal development.

The negative impact of alcoholism on me as a child took many directions. One major impact was that I never knew my identity, nor could I decide who I was, due to the effects of domestic violence and alcoholism. Why? I can only speak for myself. I remember sitting in the primary school classroom and always wondering at around 2.30 what I was going home to today. Was the alcoholic going to be drunk, sober, asleep, happy, sad or unconscious on the ground? Would the dinner be burnt to the pots again today? This was the reality of my growing up. You learn to exist more than live; you don't allow your emotions or feelings to flow naturally – my mood always morphed into that of the alcoholic on arriving home. It got to the stage as I got older that I could determine my parents' mood or mental state by observing how they dressed, stood, or even how my mother had her hair brushed. This is a state of mind in which one is hyper-sensitive to the environment and the individuals in it.

A recommendation I make to those who wish to engage on a professional level with children from chaotic backgrounds is to be very aware of this. As children who have lived through these experiences we become extremely attuned to observing people's body language. When depicting body language, I mean tiny, minuscule actions the worker may not even be aware of, such as frowning, rolling eyes and avoidance.

As a child living in this situation I would have to make choices, some good and some bad, to meet my needs and the needs of others. I wish to explain this further for a reason. When working with children who are labelled as deviant or aloof, be mindful as to why they may be that way. For example, as I entered secondary school, one parent had deserted the family, as had an older sibling; the other parent had been admitted to hospital, which occurred, in my recollection, on a number of occasions. These events left five underage children fending for themselves at home without any finances, support or adult guidance. During these times I would have to resort to stealing food and milk on a regular basis to provide for myself and other family members. This in turn led to me getting a reputation in the school and community as a thief and someone not to be trusted in friends' houses. I recall a couple of incidents in school where teachers and members of the community accused me of anti-social behaviour in the school and community. Although this criminal damage was nothing to do with me, I suffered from prejudice in school and the community due to previous behaviours. My teenage years made me feel worthless and damaged, due to living in an unstable home environment with no sanctuary, and feeling shunned by the community.

So what happened? When did my life change? I took up employment at fifteen years of age in the city centre. At this stage I was the eldest child in the home as my two eldest siblings had already left home and were in state care. As I was the eldest sibling it was now my responsibility and duty to offer support to younger siblings as well as doing domestic chores. At this stage the alcoholism was still rife with my parents who were – individually or simultaneously – absent at various times. If anything, it was getting worse, as was the violence and the alienation from my peers. When I refer to alienation I mean I was too embarrassed to bring friends to my house or too afraid that the alcoholic parent would start arguments with them.

As the drinking became progressively worse I knew that I had to leave the environment as it was affecting my quality of life. I had also befriended an undesirable group of friends in the community with whom I felt comfortable, as I was accepted by them, supported and not judged.

So I left home and moved into the city centre with the plan of maintaining my full-time job and obtaining a small bedsit. However, this did not happen and I ended up losing my job as I had no stable accommodation and was couch-surfing with friends. After a period of time, contact was initiated with the social services to source appropriate accommodation. At first I was put into a B&B on Talbot Street, Dublin, for approximately a week until more suitable accommodation was sourced. Eventually I was found emergency accommodation in a residential centre in Dublin city centre.

People have often asked me what my experience in the care system was like. I am aware that most young people who enter the care system appear unhappy, due to the stereotype of being in care, the shame associated with it and the loneliness and segregation from their family, friends and community. My experience ticked all the boxes in relation to these feelings.

Trust, or sometimes lack of it, became a key element in my experience of the care system. When you are young and vulnerable and placed into new surroundings with other children and adults, you don't know who to trust. Also, from previous social learning, all unfamiliar adults in authority can be frightening and come across as untrustworthy.

When I first entered this particular care centre most of my fears slowly trickled away. I recall that prior to admission I had to attend a drop-in coffee shop in the city centre to be assessed and meet with professionals.

I remember sitting in the café for hours and observing everyone in the place. However, one person caught my attention; a middle-aged man playing with a child. My first reaction was jealousy and envy as I felt that this is what fathers are supposed to do with their children – giving them attention and generally interacting with them in a playful manner – while here was I, alone, afraid and feeling I had no one. I assumed this middle-aged man was the father of that child. However, I soon found out this was not the case because when I arrived at the care centre, perhaps within the next couple of days, the same man from the café was there. For some reason I immediately felt safe around this person as I had seen him before and noticed how he appeared to be a loving and caring person. I was told that this man would be my key worker.

I remember my first day in care. I arrived at the centre that evening just before dinner time. I recall having the role of key worker explained to me and then I was brought to the kitchen for dinner. This moment I remember most. I remember dishes of food being placed on the table and everyone tucking in. However, I was painfully shy and took only a small piece of food, probably not even enough to feed a budgie. It wasn't the shyness that prevented me from taking more food from the table even though I was starving; it was more the fear of taking too much food and getting into trouble or depriving someone else of food. Remember that I had come from a disadvantaged home where food portions would have been basic and limited. You dared not try to take extra food or the repercussions could have been harrowing.

As my time in state care progressed, so did my confidence, social life, self-esteem, self-development and, most important, a sense of my identity began to emerge. This is why I always say that living in state care had a very positive impact on me as a person.

As I mentioned above, I was truly blessed in having the gentlest of men and the best key worker possible, and he made a massive impression on my life. In discussing this with him at a much later stage, he was very reluctant to take credit for his part in my success; but I do believe that he contributed greatly in my developing a moral code and sense of values.

Although we may have only been together for a relatively short period of time (five months), he – Maurice – made a massive impression on my life. During my time in care he was always there to offer advice and I knew I could trust him completely. He earned my trust because of what my observations of him told me. My trust in him grew because he always stood up and advocated for me. I remember him taking time to go for walks with me into town just to spend time with me and discuss events in my life. This simple reality would previously have been taboo for me at home.

It is ironic how small memories stay with us throughout our life. I often wonder if Maurice remembers the time we went into the city centre for a chat. On this particular occasion we went into Clery's on O'Connell Street. In Clery's there were two game consoles on display and we played a racing car game for a short period of time. At that time it was just great to be a child again and have fun with an adult without questioning their motives. This was my first experience of an adult man showing a genuine interest in me as a child.

When I was in care during the early 1990s one could not lounge around the centre in the way that seems to happen today. It was mandatory to be enrolled in an educational course of some sort to maintain your bed. I enlisted in a Youthreach programme in computers, even though I had no interest in computers – they were not a normal part of life as they are today. I probably spent more time out of the course walking around the city centre than attending it. One evening I returned to the centre and was called into the office by the centre manager. Maurice was there too. Well, I can tell you I got the riot act read to me for not attending my course. I remember the manager being furious with me and I think she was threatening me that if my course attendance did not improve I would lose my bed in the centre. I recall the tears welling up in my eyes and a lump in my throat forming. I was petrified. It revived memories of being screamed at by an adult without having any say in the matter. Even if I had been given a chance to speak I would probably not have been able to as I was so upset and on the verge of sobbing.

The following morning I attended the course without a second thought, due to the flea in my ear still ringing. When I returned to the centre that evening the centre manager called me into her office again and asked me to sit down. This time she could not apologise to me enough regarding the previous day. I accepted her apology graciously as I had never before experienced an adult apologising for their behaviour towards me. However, it was only later, when speaking to Maurice, that I realised that he had challenged the manager for the way she had spoken to me the previous day. After that I knew this man would always advocate for me and have my best interests at heart.

During the remainder of my time in this centre I felt secure and, most of all, I could discover who I was as a person. At home I never knew who I was as I was always living in the shadow of violence and being talked about as 'one of those'; at home or in the community I was never known as Keith. It was always, 'He's one of that lot.' I was tarnished with a preconceived notion that I must be the same as other family members.

Being in care had its perks and privileges for a number of reasons, but these privileges would eventually come to a bittersweet ending. As a child who came from poverty, I soon found that being treated as a child should be was phenomenal. I was given pocket money for the first time ever in my life and a clothing grant of £80 to buy Christmas clothes. Every Saturday and Wednesday evening we were taken on fun activities – go-karting, the cinema and trips to the beach and the mountains. This was true heaven for me: I had no worries, I felt safe and secure, plus I had a childhood again. For the first time in my life I longed to go home to the care unit after my computer course and spend time with some adults without worrying about it. This of course depended on which care staff were on duty. Although all the care staff had good qualities and attributes, some had a more nurturing demeanour about them, which helped positive relationships to develop.

The bittersweetness, however, came after five months. My time to leave the centre approached swiftly – it was only a six-month transitional centre – and now I had to get ready to move into semi-independent living (aftercare). I was uncertain about aftercare as I did not know what to expect. Before Christmas I went up to the new residence to meet the new staff team and have aftercare explained to me and what semi-independent living was. Maurice always accompanied me to these meetings, so I felt safe – I trusted any decisions he made on my behalf as I knew he always had my best interests at heart. I don't think I took these meetings too seriously, as it was prior to Christmas and I knew the move wouldn't happen until February. The reason I know these meetings were before Christmas is that I had a pair of runners that were falling off my feet. They were so bad my toes were talking to me. I remember people being more focused on my runners than me, which made me feel uncomfortable; and I had a new pair of runners back in the residential unit (Maurice having pointed out to the staff that I needed them), but I didn't want to wear them until Christmas.

That Christmas came and it was the most difficult Christmas ever. Though extremely anxious about going home, I was also excited to see the family. I ended up returning to the centre that night because, like every Christmas at home, too much alcohol was consumed and fighting followed. I remember feeling so bad leaving the home that night, not for myself but for my younger siblings, who begged me to stay. I couldn't as I had to protect myself and think of my needs.

When I returned to the centre, Maurice was on duty. I will always remember that Christmas night and the gist of the conversation we had; and every Christmas since I have recalled this memory.

I told Maurice that I just wanted to have a Christmas where no alcohol or violence was involved. Although I had no power to change this situation at the time, I remember Maurice giving me a glimmer of hope and a dream to hold on to. He told me that although things were difficult now, in time, when I had children and a family of my own I could give them all the Christmas wishes they and I desired.

The time came to leave the residential unit and move into aftercare. I was devastated and so sad to say goodbye to particular staff members and the friends I had met. I knew I wasn't going far, but it was more the loss of familiarity and the trusting relationships that had been formed. It felt like they were gone for ever.

Although I was eased into aftercare by doing a stay overnight once a week, I was still unsure and most of all completely unprepared for what lay ahead. I spoke earlier about living in residential care and it being a great experience, allowing me to be a child again and to develop. However, moving to aftercare at sixteen did not make me an adult. No matter how mature I thought I was, or how I thought I knew it all, I was still only a child.

In residential care there was a chef who made lovely homemade meals every Monday to Friday and the care staff made the meals at the weekend. We had a cleaner who kept the centre clean. I had pocket money, activities and a care team constantly around me, as well as recreational areas where I and friends could play pool or watch television, etc. We were nurtured and treated like children, as we should have been. But now the downside to care came crashing in. Now, in aftercare, all these luxuries had gone – and I mean gone completely!

If anything, I fell more into poverty and almost starved to death – at least that's what it felt like to me sometimes. As I was in a Youthreach course I earned £28 a week if I completed a full week. Out of this I would have to pay rent and save an allocated amount every week. A budget was set aside for shopping – if I produced a receipt for my weekly shop I would be reimbursed £10 per week. So realistically, I had to feed myself for one week on ten pounds, and this is without taking into account things like light bulbs and toiletries.

How unrealistic was this? I mean, you wouldn't buy much for ten pounds a week – maybe a pan of bread and a litre of milk which would sour within a few days. My diet had now turned from a homemade dinner every day to a packet of noodles and a couple of slices of bread and maybe a biscuit as a treat. This is no exaggeration. This was reality.

I recall starting to build bridges with my parents and I had to walk 12 miles from the city centre to visit them, hoping that they or a friend could lend me the bus fare back into the city. I do believe that what pushed me into building bridges with my family was the longing for a meal if I went to visit.

Unfortunately, and strangely, back then the rules of leaving care were that once you entered aftercare you were not allowed re-enter the residential unit for support or advice. However, Maurice was allowed to continue visiting me on a couple of occasions. Even though I had a new key worker in aftercare I just did not feel I connected with her as I did with Maurice.

I enjoyed these visits so much as I had a great relationship with him. The biggest struggle I had in aftercare was the loneliness, something which affected me in most of my adult life. When I moved into aftercare I was given a little bedsit at the top of the house. It had a bed, a two-ring cooker, a small fridge, a sink, a table with one chair, and a wardrobe. I will never forget the loneliness and the four walls. All I had for company during the night was a white Morphy Richards alarm clock radio with a lamp attached to it that Maurice and I bought as a going away present. Every night I would listen to Atlantic 252 for comfort and companionship. I remember feeling so lonely as I hadn't even a television to watch. All I had were my thoughts.

Although there were other residents in the building we were like passing ships as there was no common recreational area, and some of these lads had reputations and were older than me. So for a long time I just avoided the place and wandered the city centre and adjacent areas with friends.

I stayed in this unit for one year until an event occurred that caused my placement there to break down. The residential unit was broken into and all the residents' savings and petty cash were stolen. I was disgusted to be accused of this crime, but the staff didn't believe me. They were so adamant that I had robbed the premises that a meeting was called with my social worker. I will always remember how alone I felt in that meeting and how my voice was again lost over the adults' voices and their accusations.

I remained in the unit for a period of time after this accusation, but my relationship with all staff stalled and deteriorated, especially my relationship with my key worker – she was adamant I was involved. Maurice had always believed me and advocated on my behalf, but unfortunately I hadn't got a Maurice anymore.

SOCIAL WORKERS

I remember one meeting in particular when I was in residential care. I was informed that my mother and the social worker would be attending a meeting in the hostel and I would have to be present. I wanted the ground to open up and swallow me; the fear was so intense I can still remember it today.

Maurice assured me he would be there, so that eased my tension, but still I wasn't sure why I was to be there as the social worker had had no contact with me to discuss this meeting or what was expected. The morning of the meeting came and this is how I remember it.

I was called into the room in the residential centre and my mother, the social worker and Maurice were there. I don't remember if anyone else was in attendance.

I remember basically being asked was my mother an alcoholic. I remember the fear, the sadness of this question. I felt I was put in an impossible and traumatising situation. Yes, my mother was an alcoholic; yes, I hated her drunken behaviour; but I loved her deeply. I never wanted to go against my mother, nor did I want to embarrass her in front of these people. Plus I didn't know whether my statement might result in my younger siblings being taken into care. The weight of that question was so heavy for me as a child I would say it crushed me completely. I gave the social worker the answer he wanted and I remember my mother looking at me in disbelief, as much as to say 'How could you?', while at the same time giving excuses for her drinking.

More or less immediately after the magic question was asked and answered, the meeting ended. The social worker got up and left without saying anything else to me, and soon after so did my mother. I recall her leaving the building without even saying goodbye. I was left feeling so alone in that room after that meeting as I cried my eyes out. I cried because I knew I had hurt my mother for the sake of the social worker. I understand that the social worker had a job to do. However, the burden placed on my shoulders that day scarred me forever. Why? The social worker had been working with my family for years, knowing what was going on in the house since the eldest child left years earlier, with little or no intervention, yet he put me through that shame and torture for a reason I have yet to understand to this day.

My only grace at that moment in time was Maurice. I do remember him sitting with me afterwards until I stopped sobbing while every other adult disappeared. I suppose the reason that memory is etched into my mind is that I always had a close relationship with my mother, through thick and thin, while understanding she had an addiction. I hurt her so much that day and sided with the social worker and my mother never let me forget that scene all through my adult life until she passed away.

I suppose what I am trying to say here is that when we work with vulnerable people it is part of our job to ask questions and investigate abuse in the family. However, when asking questions one must be mindful of how the question or answer is going to impact on the individual at hand. Will there be repercussions for the individual? Does the question serve a purpose, and if so, for whom – the child, family, or social (care) worker? Most important of all, is the person supported afterwards? Although it was a terrible experience for me, at the time I was lucky in having a good, reliable key worker whom I trusted and knew would ensure my wellbeing in the future.

HOW DID KEY WORKING ASSIST ME THROUGH MY LIFE?

When I was in care, early on I could have fallen into abusing drugs and alcohol and loitering around the city, which was the culture of children in care who had no adult guidance or support. I do believe that it was the relationship with my key worker and family morals that helped me avoid these pitfalls. Maurice was always there for me to talk to when I needed assistance, and, more important, he took the time to get to know the real me. More often than not he knew when I needed guidance, even if I did not. It was Maurice who encouraged me to attend a course and take up counselling at an early age to discuss issues that had happened in my life. Although I did not want to attend the computer course or counselling, I did it for him because I trusted him and knew he wanted the best for me.

Just after my first Christmas in care – my first away from home – a family member who had left home years earlier returned to my social circle. With his return he brought a new trend – drugs. I remember vividly the effects alcoholism had on my family and now I watched this addiction consume friends and siblings. Although I did not get involved in the drug scene I felt I had no choice but to remain in this social circle, for several reasons. They were my friends and family and I felt safe in this group, plus I had a sense of belonging. Remaining in this circle did cause me a lot of stress as I ended up becoming known to the guards due to my association with these people.

This was the crossroads in my life; but when I look back, it was really Maurice who saved me and my future. I do truly believe it was Maurice who changed my destiny – I could have easily decided to bow to peer pressure. Most important, my relationship with Maurice was more sacred to me as this man had nurtured me in the most difficult times in my life and he believed in me. He also took the time to be honest with me, no matter how difficult the topics that needed to be addressed. He advised me about my brother and how associating with him and his peers was derailing me. It was probably easy for Maurice to have these tough conversations with me because we had a strong relationship.

From my experience of working with teenagers I find we sometimes do not want to approach tough subjects with them. But sometimes we need to be honest and direct and not beat around the bush when we have concerns about individuals who are in crisis.

Basically, what I am trying to say here is that family and friends were important to me but at the same time they also had an extremely negative effect on me. It was Maurice who pointed this out to me, even though I knew it all along in my own head. However, listening to someone else telling me confirmed my opinion. Maurice encouraged me and advised me to step back, away from my older brother, as he feared he would pull me down with him. I took this advice and did step away from my social circle. It was fortunate for me that I had a great key worker and took his harsh but correct advice as many of my friends from that social circle ended up in prison, deceased, addicted to drink and drugs, and/or with a range of diseases from hepatitis to HIV.

I returned to education at the age of twenty-eight. I obtained an honours degree in Social Studies and have worked in social care for the past six years. I am currently completing an MSW. I am still in contact with many of the friends I had when I was in care. It is unfortunate, perhaps, that I am the only person who appears to have succeeded in life so far. So why is this? I do believe a key part was down to Maurice having faith in me, believing in me and taking notice of my life inside and outside the walls of the residential unit and in aftercare.

I wish to conclude with a final piece of advice to current and future social care workers. Take the time to get to know the person in your care. Always show an interest in what is going on in their social circle. Have the tough conversations with them, if required, as you won't say anything to them that they are not already aware of or about which they have some understanding.

Chapter 5
The Impossible Task: Which Wolf will Win?
Maurice Fenton

Keith's is a remarkable story and I feel genuinely privileged to know him. He says I played a major role in his story and evidently I did, but to me, at the time, I just did the best that I could in working with him and other young people in care. Interestingly, at that time I was relatively inexperienced in social care and unqualified. I have subsequently immersed myself in academia, but my work with Keith had no benefit of academic learning or lengthy experience, just a desire to make a difference. This desire to make a difference is, in my opinion, the one essential element of relationship-based practice, which I believe underpins best practice in social care: experience and qualification enhance this fundamental motivation. Keith's story confirms that young people can identify those staff for whom this is the primary motivation and I hope that I have held on to this motivation throughout my career.

Keith's story encompasses many issues that are pertinent to young people in care and I will address some of these in this chapter. In talking with Keith about how he has made a success of his life, he describes how he chose to take responsibility for his own life and not blame others. Residential care, and my part therein, aided him in this but he had a caring nature and good moral compass prior to my meeting him. Also, and fortunately, I met him at a turning point in his life.

Keith has focused on the positive in his life rather than the negative, distinguishing the love from the harm – distinguishing his mother from her behaviours, which were brought about by her addiction. Similarly, we as social care workers are challenged to separate the child from their behaviour when working with young people who have experienced trauma. We need to constantly see the behaviours as a communication and a symptom of an underlying trauma, a communication of a need. We are tasked with seeking to understand the causes of the behaviour to better assist the young people we work with.

I choose to believe that human beings like to be liked and given the right circumstances people will choose to do the right thing. Our challenge as social care workers is to aid in the creation of the right circumstances. When I think of Keith's story I am reminded of the story of an old Cherokee teaching his grandson about life. The Cherokee tells his grandson: 'A fight is going on inside me. It's a terrible fight between two wolves. One is evil – he is anger, envy, sorrow, regret, greed, arrogance, self-pity, guilt, resentment, inferiority, lies, false pride, superiority and ego.' He continues, 'The other is good – he is joy, peace, love, hope, serenity, humility, kindness, benevolence, empathy, generosity, truth, compassion and faith. The same fight is going on inside you – and inside every other person too.' The grandson thinks about this for a minute and then asks his grandfather, 'Which wolf will win?' The old man replies simply, 'The one you feed.'

I will consider some of the key issues arising from Keith's story. These include:

Trauma	Hyper-sensitivity, hyper-vigilance, coping, re-experiencing and re-enactment of trauma, and developmental implications
Social exclusion	Prejudice, stigma, poverty, injustice, social isolation, labelling
Relationships	Key workers, family, professionals, peers, importance of the relationship
Power	Powerlessness, vulnerability, lack of voice, choice and responsibility
Residential care	The benefits, transitions, levels and types of support
Hope	Belief, trust, unconditional positive regard
Identity	Development, confidence and self-esteem
Aftercare	Loneliness, transitions and support

Keith's descriptions of growing up in a dysfunctional family and the need to act in socially unacceptable ways to survive gives valuable insight into how trauma affects a child's development and what underpins some of their behaviours. This affords us an understanding of why children in care sometimes exhibit a range of complex and challenging behaviours that, at times, appear to bear little relationship to their present surroundings. There is much research addressing the effects of trauma on children's development (Anglin 2002, 2003; Abramovitz & Bloom 2003; Hughes 2004, 2006) and we now know from neuroscience that children's brain development is altered physiologically following prolonged exposure to trauma (van der Kolk 2003; Twardosz & Lutzker 2010).

Keith describes how hyper-sensitive he became about issues of trust and threat and how confused his identity formation had become. His descriptions of the incident where the manager 'read him the riot act' and how this evoked fearful and painful feelings within him clearly illustrates the importance of being aware of children's pasts and being sensitive to the effects of trauma. For my part, I know this manager had no intention to cause him harm and was acting out of concern that he should maintain his placement, but she communicated this too strongly to him. To her credit, once she was made aware of this, she apologised genuinely, which had a significantly beneficial effect on Keith. He describes this as the first time an adult had ever apologised to him for their actions and thus it exposed him to adults acting in nurturing and responsible ways, challenging his previously held perception of adults. It has been my experience of care that we all, at times, make mistakes attempting to care for traumatised young people. As Einstein said, 'Anyone who has never made a mistake has never tried anything new.'

We have the opportunity to aid young people in evaluating their truths/ narratives/biographies. In this (re)evaluation young people can re-author some of these truths to more positive world views and expectations and/or less traumatic memories. This manager made a mistake but redeemed herself. She utilised reflective practice in her work and was open to constructive criticism. I respected her for this – respect is earned, not given by title or role in social care – and I think it fair to say she neither knew the harm she caused when she read the riot act nor the extent of the good her apology accomplished. This episode clearly illustrates the power of an apology when dealing with young people and encapsulates the accomplishment of the core challenge of social care work – what can metaphorically be represented as the completion of Bettelheim's impossible task set on the fairy-tale battleground, where hero children must prevail over villains such as the big bad wolf. The manager turned a poor beginning into a positive outcome; and every child in care came into care due to a poor beginning. At times our task in social care appears to be impossible, so great has the trauma been to the children, yet we persevere and sometimes we play key roles in aiding them to overcome apparently intractable adversity, occasionally unknown to ourselves. The willingness to show vulnerability and appropriately admit mistakes takes strength, confidence and self-awareness.

This approach to social care sits well within the child and youth care model as espoused by Garfat and Fulcher (2012), where an inquiring relational approach and collaborative meaning-making is fundamental to practice.

RELATIONSHIP IS THE WORK

Our epistemological position (typologies of knowledge – what we know and how we know it) is a valuable insight for each worker to be aware of as it is we ourselves who are our most valuable tool in working with young people, and therefore self-awareness is paramount.

> *An approach that is grounded in the belief that 'I already know' is one that is immobilised and is oblivious to context and perspective, which in turn pigeonholes experiences, behaviours, objects and other people into existing categories. In other words an individual's way of* knowing *predisposes a way of being and may obstruct learning.*
>
> (Bellefeuille & Ricks 2010:1237)

It is no coincidence that a key component of therapeutic crisis intervention (TCI) is the four questions, the first question being 'What am I feeling?'

Relationships and *key working* are central to Keith's story. If we accept, as previously stated, that each carer is themselves the most valuable tool they have at their disposal, their most protective and empowering factor, it is self-evident that the medium that most enhances and facilitates the use of self is the relationship between carer and worker.

Keith talks of the hope I gave him that Christmas night so many years ago, and clearly this had a profound effect on him. I believe that hope is integral to change. There is much to reflect on in the saying 'Man without hope is an animal', and I see a correlation between an enquiring stance, where many outcomes are possible, and hope, as opposed to a position of certainty where only limited outcomes are possible.

Trust and belief were fundamental to my key working relationship with Keith. One incident occurred at this time which I have long wondered about. Keith was accused of some misdemeanour in the centre and this came up for discussion at a team meeting. I advocated his innocence as he had told me before the meeting that he hadn't done it. Some time later, after he had left the centre, he told me he had in fact committed this misdemeanour and I sensed that there was something very important about this to him but until now didn't fully know why.

I believed him and he was able to manipulate me because of this, just as children do with their parents. We act 'in loco parentis' to children in care and while I extend unconditional love to my own children, doing likewise in residential care might not be deemed appropriate or indeed possible. Yet we know that children cannot thrive without love and even though we are acting as substitute parents, sometimes precisely because parents cannot supply these children with love, we are conflicted about this core issue in parenting and child development. Trust is key to positive relationship formation. In my key working relationships I always tried to extend what Carl Rogers termed 'unconditional positive regard' to my key children. This is evidenced by my actions, observed by Keith, which make clear that I genuinely like my key child and enjoy spending time in their company, in essence becoming invested in the relationship. Additionally, I communicate belief in my key child even though at times I might be proved wrong. We all fall short of the mark sometimes and, as with my own children, failings represent opportunities for learning, and trust needs to be re-established as quickly as possible. Sometimes we have to 'fake it till we make it' and encourage them to do likewise, as nothing succeeds like success.

It has long been my observation that social care staff are very good at identifying when children in care behave in ways that breach the expectations of living within the residential centre or social and legal norms. However, if we take a 'risk and resilience' perspective to some of these behaviours we can see justification for:

1. why the young person is behaving in this way
2. a rationale for 'filtering' which issues to address and which issues to allow to slide.

Clearly the crux here is identifying which issues are appropriate to let slide and which absolutely have to be addressed. In my practice with young people I have at times casually let them know I am aware of an issue but that I am taking no further action on the matter. Obviously, if they can completely fool me too easily this could equally have a negative effect on our relationship. There are so many factors at play in such situations that no single rule can apply and I have witnessed some excellent practice in this area over the years where colleagues have built trust with hard-to-reach young people yet maintained team consistency. This is a classic 'grey area' where so much relational work occurs.

All agree that it is normal adolescent development to test boundaries, including relationship and trust boundaries. Where do young people in care get this opportunity if not within the key working or other meaningful relationships with individual social care workers?

I now see from reading Keith's story the significance of my belief in him. Whatever the misdemeanour, it was trivial compared to the effect my belief in him had. I saw the positive in him and kept the focus on that, while always remembering when working with young people: 'Be prepared to lose battles every day in caring for young people; it's the war we want to win.' I am glad I unknowingly lost the battle over this misdemeanour as this helped Keith win the war.

THE ROLE OF KEY WORKERS

Key working is so central to both mine and Keith's dyadic story that it merits further examination.

> *Within the fields of policy and practice related to residential care services for young people, the recognition of 'key working' as a core concept associated with good practice with young people across a number of different sectors is firmly embedded.*
>
> (Holt & Kirwan 2012:372).

There is no clear definition of what constitutes key working or indeed evidence supporting the above quotation. Holt and Kirwan do undertake a review of international literature on the subject, which is worthy of readers' attention. They make the point that without clarity on the purpose and function of key working, 'it is possible, if not likely, that key working as a concept and as a practice means different things to different people' (Holt & Kirwan 2012:373).

Holt and Kirwan 'conclude that relationships are not only integral to key working but are also inextricably linked to successful transitions' (Pinkerton & Coyle 2012:305).

Keith's story authenticates this finding. Clearly our relationship and my key working role in his placement had a significant effect, which he articulates very clearly. But, as pointed out earlier, I had very little experience and no qualification at that time and, although I had a desire to make a difference, this alone would not necessarily have ensured that our key working relationship would have been so effective. There was a team around me supporting me in my work and indeed at a wider level there was an agency which, at that time, espoused values that placed the client at the centre of all services. I had a mentor who guided my practice in the centre and I remember clearly following the examples I witnessed of colleagues' good practice. I was empowered to develop my own style of key working, which facilitated the expression of my personality, rather than a prescribed or taught model of key working, and this allowed me to connect with Keith with more authenticity. I believe this played a key role in fostering his trust in me, as young people in care, by harsh necessity, learn to discern authenticity and intent in adults. This experience of a positive organisational climate and culture, in the absence of college placement, framed my inculcation into the professional culture of social care, which has stood to me since. A final point on key working is an excellent recommendation from Holt and Kirwan (2012) that young people have a voice in the selection of their key worker.

THE LONELINESS OF TRANSITION

Clearly the loneliness Keith experienced on transitioning to the aftercare service was severe. While this was twenty years ago – and today there would be two staff on duty and therefore more available to him – the same service still operates and caters for young people of his age. Keith was just weeks short of his seventeenth birthday when he made this transition. Research by Dima and Skehill (2011) and Anghel (2011), using the Bridges (2004) model, has identified that transition is composed of two distinct processes – the physical and the psychological; and has three distinct stages – endings, neutral zone and new beginnings.

What I have learned in regard to transitioning young people from one service to another is that ideally the levels of support need to be kept the same in the services to allow the time and space for young people to process the first two stages. Only when this has been achieved can the levels of support be reduced, as appropriate to the new setting, in the 'new beginnings' stage. This is especially important when dealing with step down-type services. There is more than one step in the transition and the one least allowed for in leaving care is the neutral stage, where the opportunity to 'space out' provides a time for freedom, exploration, reflection, risk-taking and identity search (Stein 2012:163).

> What we call the beginning is often the end
> And to make an end is to make a beginning.
> The end is where we start from.
>
> (T.S. Eliot, 'Little Gidding')

Loneliness is a major feature in the lives of many care leavers and current preparation for leaving care does not always address this area of young people's lives, their psycho-social wellbeing. I have witnessed much suffering for many young people who have left care where hardship, lost accommodation and crisis stem from loneliness. Loneliness can cast a long shadow on the life of care leavers (Stein 2012). Mentoring, I believe, offers a viable means of tackling this issue and I shall expand on this later in this chapter.

Keith's description of living in poverty in care highlights an issue that is unacceptable, then or now. We cannot dismiss this as being an issue from 1994; it has been my experience that today care leavers are, sadly, still marginalised and socially excluded. With the focus of aftercare support services shifting more and more to models of independence (mainstreaming into adult services) rather than interdependence (specialist services allowing for developmental work), increasing numbers of care leavers are experiencing poverty and homelessness (EPIC 2011).

MYTHS SURROUNDING RESIDENTIAL CARE

Keith also clearly identifies the benefit that residential care afforded him. This is significant because in my time working in residential care I have witnessed a negative perception of it being propagated, which I believe is inaccurate, and does a disservice to young people requiring specific forms of care. Residential care is compared unfavourably with foster care and non-residential care (Kahan 1984; Bates *et al.* 1997; Melton *et al.* 1998; Iwaniec 2006). It is portrayed as too expensive, with poor outcomes, providing unrealistic standards of living to children that they won't retain on leaving care, is associated with scenes of past abuses and with a confused theoretical base (Berridge & Brodie 1996; Jones & Landsverk 2006).

This has been exacerbated by two factors:

1. Residential care has been used as a placement of last resort and not used for children most likely to benefit from it. Rather, it is used for young people who cannot receive the support and/or safety they need from their own families or from foster families, or who pose a danger to others (Whittaker 2004).

2. There is a tendency for the problem under review to be associated with the child being in care rather than consideration of the factors that resulted in the child being admitted to care in the first place (McSherry *et al.* 2008).

Anglin and Knorth cite the following from the Stockholm Declaration:

There is indisputable evidence that institutional (i.e. residential) care has negative consequences for both individual children and for society at large. It is alleged that the UN Convention on the Rights of the Child includes an obligation of 'resorting to institutional care only as a last resort and as a temporary response'.

(Stockholm Declaration on Children and Residential Care, cited in Anglin & Knorth 2004:141)

A meta-analysis by Knorth *et al.* (2008) challenges many of these erroneous assumptions, now widely taken as incontrovertible, and particularly the Stockholm Declaration statements as outlined above. In contrast, Knorth *et al.* find that residential care in fact improves children's psychological functioning.

The failings of foster care are being identified on an ongoing basis in Ireland (Children's Rights Alliance 2010; EPIC 2012; RTÉ News 2013):

We have known for some time that many foster carers have not been subject to adequate checks and that large numbers have not been trained. This has proven a risk to the safety of children and recent proceedings in the high court have established that the risk is in fact a reality.

(IFCA 2012)

While internationally Jones and Landsverk (2006:1153) make the point that 'The empirical literature on foster care has not demonstrated that the presumed problems with residential care have been solved by foster care.'

The reality is that for some young people residential care is the best option and this has proved to be the case internationally where, just as in Ireland, there has been a concerted drive to minimise, if not eliminate, residential care (Iwaniec 2006). Therefore, minimising the use of residential care based on erroneous assumptions and fiduciary agendas has the potential to deprive such young people of being appropriately placed, thus weakening the care system. I wonder if we are now seeing residential foster care where the cost disparity with residential care is less pronounced and where the foster carers are so supported with teams of outside professionals coming into the home, and structures such as built-in time away, that in essence residential care has been recreated in foster homes.

I propose that a better way to consider what service is best for an individual child or group of children is the focus on practice underpinned by theory rather than a basic focus on the type of placement (foster/residential).

I have witnessed the stress care leavers are subjected to in Ireland and recognise it as a major issue they face when leaving care. Unfortunately, Keith was a case in point. This stress can be exacerbated by loneliness, isolation, fear of the unknown, pre-existing trauma, separation and loss. The behaviours I have witnessed over the years, at times accompanied with declining mental health, as care leavers approach their eighteenth birthday and overnight step into the unknown are, I believe, the symptoms of the underlying malaise of stress.

Legislatively prescribed aftercare support would require enhanced clarity of just what a care leaver would be entitled to, when and under what conditions, and this would reduce the stress associated with the fear of the unknown. It is not that they would necessarily get any more of anything, just that the uncertainty would be ameliorated. We must remember that they have no safety net of a family home to return to. Significantly, legislation would also benefit workers by standardising their role and employment conditions, with clarity on their purpose and function, along with ring-fenced budgets, and commencing the development of a positive professional culture for aftercare workers.

Finally, with regard to relationships, it is a cause of grave concern when the focus of the work increasingly shifts from relationships to bureaucratic tasks. We cannot forget that it is precisely in the area of relationships with adults that many young people experience difficulties. Consequently, the relationship focus holds the potential for young people to address life-changing issues through the medium of a safe relationship with an appropriate adult, thus enabling lost trust to be restored (Wilson 2000).

No social care worker I have ever met came into this profession to become a 'bureau-carer', and Keith's recollection, twenty years later, of the time we played computer games in Clery's bears testimony to the value of relationship-based work.

Keith returned to education in his twenties, completing his Leaving Certificate and thereafter honours and master's degrees in social care and social work. As a statistic he would have appeared as a poor outcome from age eighteen to twenty-eight, whereas from twenty-eight to thirty-six his is a remarkably positive outcome.

It is worthwhile considering the role mentoring can play in promoting resilience, as Colley (2003), Stein and Clayden (2005), Newburn and Shiner (2005), Osterling and Hines (2006) and Stein (2012) have done. They identified the importance of one significant adult relationship in the life of young people in the development of resilience and have identified mentors as ideally suited to fulfilling this role. The power dynamic between mentor and mentee is significantly reduced from that between worker/expert and client.

This promotes engagement and communication, while also generating an internal locus of control for the young person, thus promoting self-efficacy (Phares 1976; Clutterbuck 2002; Colley 2003).

Keith identified that the significance of our relationship was that it was the first time an adult male had shown an appropriate interest in his welfare, and the significance of this can be located in the context of this discussion on mentoring and relationships. Keith also recalls how his relationship with me was so sacred to him that he took my advice on matters that he was struggling with, deeply personal matters in which it is often difficult for workers to intervene effectively and successfully. This illustrates how behaviour can be changed through the power of the relationship. We are all more apt to listen to people we like and admire, whose company we enjoy, and particularly when they appear to like us too. In my experience, mentors have the potential to develop such relationships with difficult-to-engage young people and it is precisely this value of the relationship that can make mentoring so effective. Innovative behaviour change tools such as 'do something different' (DSD), utilising mobile communications technology, offer complementary programmes which, when coupled with engagement mentoring, have much to offer in the twenty-first century. But the relationship is key.

CONCLUSION

In conclusion, it can be seen that progress is being made in the area of throughcare since Keith left care, and his story is one of great positivity. However, there is also for me, just as there was for Keith on leaving the residential centre, a bittersweet reality. When I reflect on that time twenty years ago the memories of those young people I worked with but who tragically died before reaching adulthood live side by side with the positive memories. I attended my first funeral for a child in care at this time. Although this was twenty years ago we still have the situation where the legislation underpinning aftercare is permissive. Consequently there is a lack of clarity nationally as to just what aftercare constitutes and who is eligible for what and under what circumstances. As a direct result of this young people continue to leave care underprepared and without adequate support.

If social policies are to be empowering, equitable, effective and efficient they need to be based on firm foundations of social justice and participation. Services not so underpinned will always possess inherent flaws and will never truly achieve their intended purpose.

The world is changing at an unprecedented pace and this is impacting on young people more than any other age group. Globalisation, unemployment and ruptured pathways to adulthood have all added risk and uncertainty to the lives of today's young people that, as a young person, I didn't experience to the same extent. I am happy for Keith that he has found his career pathway in life in the social care profession and that he returned to education in his twenties to put himself on this pathway. Such is the pace of technological development that it has been posited by social scientists that today's children will have five different careers, two of which have yet to be invented. The search for security has become preoccupying yet elusive in an incessantly changing and risk-defined world with ever more porous borders, but for young people this is magnified (Pinkerton 2012). The impact on young people's search for identity, an issue at the core of all young people's development, but more so for young people in care who have had fractured family and community histories, is profound within such undefined futures. Here, as Stein (2006) has said, we must remember that care leavers are first and foremost young people and impacted by the same forces that impact all young people; but care leavers have the added disadvantage of having been exposed to trauma in their childhood, of being in care and, on leaving care, being at risk of social exclusion. Care leavers, who are already experiencing transitions that are 'accelerated and condensed' (Stein 1999), must also contend with these forces which, in their case, are both magnified and multiplied. They absolutely need our ongoing support beyond eighteen, just as parents now often support their children into their mid- to late twenties. By supporting them inclusively and in a manner any good parent would want for their child, with statutory entitlement to aftercare, we may get to the point where Keith's story becomes representative of the majority rather than the minority.

Chapter 6
Doing Small Things with Great Kindness

The Role of Relationship, Kindness and Love in
Understanding and Changing Behaviour

John Digney and Max Smart

> *Felt in the blood, and felt along the heart*
> *And passing even into my purer mind,*
> *With tranquil restoration: – feelings too*
> *Of unremembered pleasure: such, perhaps,*
> *As have no slight or trivial influence*
> *On that best portion of a good man's life*
> *His little, nameless, unremembered,*
> *Acts of kindness and of love.*
>
> (William Wordsworth, 'Tintern Abbey')

INTRODUCTION

As we reflect on our aggregated fifty (plus) years of social care practice at
various levels (coalface, clinical, strategic and management), we have drawn
many similar conclusions and formed many of the same opinions. At the top
of our list are the following:

- We (as a profession) need to avoid using rhetoric.
- We need to take time to learn from and teach each other.
- We need to respect and embrace our unique (experiential) learning.
- We need to *not* be afraid of speaking up about our beliefs.

As a profession, we are often buffeted by legitimate criticisms of past scandals,
but also by the whims and vagaries of politicians, policy makers and budget
holders. This professional 'hammering' can often sap confidence, deflate
morale and stifle proactive thinking. At a time of seismic change in public
services, this can add to the risk that our profession (social care) could return
to being reactive rather than proactive, allow abdication of our responsibility

to other professions and become complacent (content solely to 'tick the boxes'). Doing this would end in us giving up our very hard-earned professional status. However, we would assert that this is the very time we need to have faith in ourselves and our profession, take our specific 'body of knowledge' and broadcast the importance of concepts such as love and kindness.

Social care is about living in the life space of others; it is about understanding the complexities and individuality of each person. It is also about knowing the importance of understanding our clients' 'real needs' and it is about teaching through relationship.

As we mature, individually and as a profession, we have come to reflect on the cumulative experiences and knowledge we have acquired. As we grow in confidence, we begin to better understand things differently and the need to question the status quo (oftentimes the party line). In the past we have fixed our gaze on notions of 'care and control', where, more often than not, there was more control than care. When we encountered confusing or challenging behaviour it became the default position to attempt to merely 'control the behavioural excess' rather than responding to the needs the behaviour was communicating.

Contemporary thinking informs us that all behaviour serves a purpose, the purpose being to meet a need: 'our task involves working out what that *need* is – so we (the helping adults) can help the person find a better way of meeting the need' (Garfat 2011). If this assertion is correct, it assumes that challenging behaviour serves a purpose in the here and now. Making meaning about what needs are being met by the behaviour is vital if we are to design effective interventions that can meet those needs in a less destructive and, hopefully, a more constructive way.

Therefore 'challenging behaviour' is very useful indeed, especially if it has helped the individual survive past trauma. After all, behaviours viewed as 'challenging' by others may actually be an attempt to keep oneself safe by making others back away. People encountered in our care settings are often those who have been neglected, assaulted and often violated. To paraphrase Steve Van Bockern (in Brendtro *et al.* 1995), 'these are the folks who often bite the hand that didn't feed them'.

In an era of attribution that looks to apportion blame when things go wrong, we need to reframe our traditional understandings if we are to truly help make a difference. We must continue to use our greatest strength – our ability to form relationship and be 'relational' with those we seek to assist. Relationship must be seen as having its greatest value in 'being with and doing with other'; it must therefore, we assert, be about care, kindness and love.

UNIVERSALITY OF KEY CONCEPTS: DANCING A DIFFERENT DANCE

Where there is love there is life.   (Mahatma Gandhi)

Even though both of us have extensive experience in the field of child care, we bring generic experience and history from other 'care groups', including disability, elder care, ethnic minority, adult/youth offending, mental health and early years. The reason we say this is because the concepts we are writing about in this chapter draw heavily from the child and youth care perspective, but, we believe, are equally applicable across *all* care groups. We are talking about the universality of 'relationship', the complete necessity for 'caring' and the omnipotence of 'kindness and love'.

We do recognise as we write this that kindness and love as remedies for troubled and troublesome behaviours may seem a tad naive. Love and kindness are not concepts that have been massively explored in social care training or parlance, and as therapeutic interventions they are certainly not in vogue. However, we would argue that many so-called treatments, focused on fault finding and fixing, have clearly not been effective. Yet these techniques continue to be used.

This leads us to ask, 'Given that past techniques have been so ineffective, why are we still using them?' Brendtro and Shahbazian note, 'Emotional disturbance is not a solo performance but a dance with multiple partners' (2003:71). If this is the case, maybe it is time to dance a different dance.

A NEW HOPE

In social care assessments, reports and training we encounter references to 'challenging behaviour'. We also encounter the word 'relationship'. Both these words are bandied around with more frequency than most others at team meetings, statutory review meetings, multidisciplinary planning meetings and the like. But who stops to ask, 'What do these terms actually mean?'

There are a plethora of courses available that tell us how to 'Manage Challenging Behaviour', 'Build Meaningful Relationships' and even 'Manage Challenging Relationships'. However, before we go charging into someone else's ecology with a view to 'changing them', 'managing them' and imposing our values on them, we need to step back somewhat. We must take time to reflect and give deep consideration to the potential implications of our actions and how we act.

Fewster (2013) astutely notes that there is no pleasure in being around people who persistently abuse themselves and others, but here he is not arguing for control, rejection or isolation. On the contrary, he is arguing that we need to move beyond the theories and techniques provided by our friends in medicine, psychology and social work, which he refers to as outside-in interventions. Fewster suggests that outside-in methods identify the worker as the 'primary agents of change' (2013:28). A new hope in our profession is to refocus our gaze and move away from deficit or disability thinking, towards a belief that change comes from inside using inner resources and inner potential to effect growth. This thinking is inside-out, not outside-in, and the best way to bring the inside out is to connect relationally with those for whom we are privileged to care.

When we come to considering or reframing the concepts of love and kindness as a vehicle for inside-out change, and also how these (or the lack of them) can be linked to behavioural challenges, we begin to see that fundamentally 'challenging behaviours' are in fact very often challenges for us (the 'helpers' and also society in general). It brings starkly into focus issues of needs, and begs the question about what people need from us to grow up and to live well.

Brendtro and du Toit (2005) advised that if normal needs are frustrated, problem behaviour results. In fact, one could argue that challenging behaviours are inextricably linked, in the main, to breakdowns in positive connections to others; parents, family, peers and community. For our clients their challenging behaviours are coping strategies and learned responses to poor socialisation, lack of appropriate care and, quite often, an absence of the demonstration of love. Challenging behaviours are therefore adaptive responses to highly stressed and often overwhelming situations.

When we come to considering the words 'relationship', 'love' and 'kindness', we need to think of them as verbs – doing or action words – and not just nouns describing a process. Frances Ricks has said that the word 'care' is an action verb and it is true that if we care we will do. If we care, we will not sit silently off to the side, we will become actively involved – regardless of the task – and we will use the tools of caring, kindness and love. This is about being in relationship.

ENVIRONMENTALLY SPEAKING

Social care practice can be stressful; stressful for our clients, stressful for the carers and stressful for those with statutory responsibility for these most vulnerable groups. We would suggest that the antidote to this stress lies in having a good understanding of what actually makes a difference, what works in our profession. Thankfully, we are not alone and our decades-long shout into the wilderness is now being heard and even adopted by our colleagues in social work.

In an article by Juliet Rix (2013) in *The Guardian*, a social worker, Jenni Randall, talks about her approach with clients, her understanding of the importance of relationship, and her belief in the need for reform: 'The system needs a radical rethink that puts relationships at the core.' She questions the approach that is commonly taught and espoused, where people are demanded to have 'professional boundaries' and told, 'Don't get too involved.' Randall asks the question, 'I am the social worker, but that doesn't mean I can't have a human relationship. Why have we moved away from love, affection and caring being part of the social worker's role?'

WHAT WORKS IN SOCIAL CARE?

The table below, adapted from Garfat, Fulcher and Digney (2013) (original graphic supplied by James Freeman, Casa Pacifica, DLE trainer) represents the findings of a meta-analysis that has been ongoing over recent years. This analysis of research and writings from within the area of child and youth care speak to us about what leads to effective practice.

The table contains twenty-five central characteristics of effective practice (the twenty-fifth being the central characteristic – using 'daily life events' to facilitate positive change). These are split into three headings: Being, Thinking and Doing. Following the graphic is a brief description of each. When reviewing this comprehensive list, consider how each fits with the notions of kindness and love and ponder how any could exist outside a meaningful relationship.

Figure 6.1

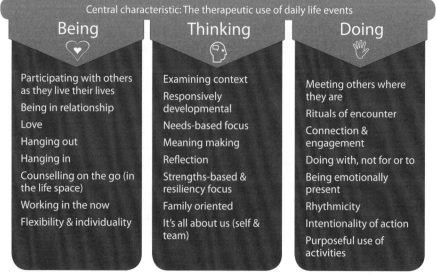

Central characteristic: The therapeutic use of daily life events		
Being	**Thinking**	**Doing**
Participating with others as they live their lives	Examining context	Meeting others where they are
Being in relationship	Responsively developmental	Rituals of encounter
Love	Needs-based focus	Connection & engagement
Hanging out	Meaning making	Doing with, not for or to
Hanging in	Reflection	Being emotionally present
Counselling on the go (in the life space)	Strengths-based & resiliency focus	Rhythmicity
Working in the now	Family oriented	Intentionality of action
Flexibility & individuality	It's all about us (self & team)	Purposeful use of activities

When we speak of 'using daily life events to facilitate change', we are referring to our ability and determination to use seemingly simple moments for therapeutic purposes. This requires us to be totally present and listening to and with all our senses.

1. *Participating with others as they live their lives:* This is 'exactly what it says on the tin'. Social care involves being with people, sharing in their everyday activities and moments. Good social care workers involve themselves in all aspects of the daily lives of the people with whom they work (Smart 2006).

2. *Being in relationship:* This is not the same as 'having a relationship with'. It means that we must value our ability to interact in an open, honest and responsive way, especially in situations where others have not.

3. *Love:* Thumbadoo (2011) argues that 'love must be present when real connections are made between self and other', and Whitfield (1987:133) states that 'love is the most healing of our resources'. Love is one of the most difficult concepts to define, but we know it when we see (or feel) it.

4. *Hanging out:* This again is exactly what it sounds like – hanging out doing apparently simple, everyday things, just as we do with our own friends and family. Such activities can be the best investment in developing trust and, with that, connection.

5. *Hanging in:* Quite simply, this means that we don't 'cut and run' when times get difficult. Rather, we hang on and hang in. This demonstrates our commitment and caring.

6. *Counselling on the go:* As our time is spent in the 'everyday' of others, we do not schedule times or sessions to meet with someone for 'counselling'. Instead, we use our skills of observation, engagement, reflection and communication in the 'life-space' of others to provide counselling in real time.

7. *Working in the now:* Like some of the other concepts, this refers to the particular relationship the social care worker has with the person they are working with. This is about having a focus on the 'here and now' and what is happening between us and the other.

8. *Flexibility and individuality:* In a world that is tending to seek 'standardisation', effective social care needs to maintain both a flexible approach to each person and also to ensure that all interactions are individual to that person and their particular context.

Case Study 1: Brian

Brian, at thirteen years old, like many other kids coming to our unit, arrived with two black sacks holding all his worldly possessions, and accompanied by a social worker. A young man who could be described as 'angry', Brian was now being delivered to his twelfth placement. Brian had had a history of parental rejection and abandonment and consequently was feeling lonely and relationally resistant.

Initially, Brian appeared impervious to any bid to engage him. Peer relationships were problematic – he did not want to be liked and pushed others away. With the staff team, he would initiate conflict and became aggressive at the slightest sign of disagreement or even limit setting.

It was possible to see why others found it very hard to care for Brian. Rejection had been his life and he seemed to have decided to take control of rejection by rejecting others before they ever had the chance to reject him.

The first eighteen months were the hardest. He pushed hard to end his placement, keeping staff at a distance and barely engaging with his key worker. Yet Brian's story is not one of continued rejection and pain.

When one staff member nursed Brian when he was unwell, his reaction was different – he accepted her tender kindness towards him, as she brought him soup, fluffed his pillows and sat talking with him for endless hours ('counselling on the go' and 'working in the now'). To everyone's surprise, Brian allowed her to be nurturing.

Gradually, Brian allowed other staff to tentatively engage him, beginning to trust, and rather than reject he started embryonic relationships with all staff. Brian lived with us for over six years and since then he has been to college and achieved an honours degree.

The turn in his life came from acts of kindness and tender caring when he was ill. He attributes success in his life to the relationship he developed with his carers ('being in relationship' and 'love') and the persistence of workers coming back repeatedly despite his hostility, when it would have been easier for them to reject him or respond with punishment or counter-aggression ('hanging in' and 'hanging out'). As with all kids in our care, we treated Brian as an individual and adopted our approach as flexibly as circumstances would allow.

Brian remains in deep connection with his carers ten years after leaving care.

9. *Examining context:* This requires that we are conscious that all things occur in specific contexts which are unique to each person. This requires that we make the effort to see things from other people's perspectives and from what is going on for them.

10. *Responsively developmental:* This demands that we give deep consideration to the appropriate developmental capacity of the individual and rather

than being reactive to behaviours, we are responsive to specific needs, consistent with their developmental stage.

11. *Needs-based focus:* Having such a focus assumes that everything we do is to meet personal or social needs. Our task is often to help others identify their needs and find appropriate and satisfying ways of meeting them.

12. *Meaning making:* We all 'make meaning' every moment of every day, interpreting the world in a particular way. An action occurs – and we interpret it according to our own way of making sense. We need to be aware of how 'other' is interpreting us.

13. *Reflection:* A reflective person is someone who is introspective and curious. They ask themselves numerous questions at various points of engagement. Questions such as: What should I do now? Why am I thinking this will work? Is this intervention going well? How can I improve what I am doing? Did that thing work well? What can I do better the next time? Reflection is a continuous process and ensures that we never rest on our laurels.

14. *Strengths-based and resiliency focus:* A really effective worker looks for and focuses on the often hidden strengths of the client. This focus on the 'positive and healthy' enables others to also experience themselves as competent and worthy (Brendtro & Larson 2006).

15. *Family oriented:* Not only do good and effective social care workers work with their 'client', they also focus on that person's family (and other supportive persons in their ecology). The skilled social care worker involves 'family' (where appropriate) in all aspect of care.

16. *It's all about us:* This is about reminding ourselves that there is an 'important interplay between the client and the helpers'. If we (or our colleagues) are not in the 'best of form', this can hugely impact on the people we work with.

Case Study 2: Helen

Helen was a thirteen-year-old girl from an ethnic minority group. She had lived with her mother, along with three siblings, all with different fathers. Her mother had limited parenting capacity and was very much ostracised by her community. Helen began to hang out with a much older group of young people and before long was engaging in all types of 'at risk' behaviours and getting into trouble with the police.

We took Helen for 'assessment'. Her social worker wanted her to be kept away from her home environment and her family. She was described as having an 'intellectual disability'; she also had a physical disability. Interestingly, though, Helen formed attachments very readily, some might say too readily. She had such a longing to be liked and to 'belong'. She spoke of loving her family but knowing she couldn't keep herself safe when she was living at home.

Helen was not without challenge. She would attempt to self-harm (cutting her arms, legs and face), she would become involved in any negative behaviours that the other kids were engaged in and she would leave without permission and take alcohol and possibly drugs. When we examined these behaviours within the parameters of what we knew about Helen, we came to realise that they didn't fit neatly into the usual boxes around why kids exhibit at-risk behaviours. What needs were being met? (A 'needs-based focus'). When looked at in the context of the living environment and what she gained from these behaviours, it became apparent (Helen was involved in this analysis) that she was looking to actually distance herself from the other young people's behaviours and trying to find sanctuary ('meaning-making', 'examining context'). An example of this was when she pretended to have taken a paracetamol overdose to get a hospital admission where she would have individual time with staff.

During the assessment stage, we quickly discovered that Helen was not in fact intellectually challenged; she was achieving scores in the above average range in many areas. When this was pointed out to her, she said it was always easier to play stupid and she didn't want to make her mother feel stupid. She was reassured that we would not be judgemental towards her mother and suggested that, if she wished, we would work with her and her family to help her mother take back more responsibility ('family-oriented') and create an opportunity for her to return home ('responsively developmental'). We also reassured her that she was well able to 'step up' and be a great support to her mother; that she had amazing ability and was a buoyant girl ('strengths-based and resiliency focus').

It took about eight months for the professionals involved to be reassured that Helen was ready to live at home. During that period, extensive work was done with Helen and her mother and siblings. It was a time of learning for all of us, a period that helped mould the ethos which stands to this day – one of respect, introspection and doing with young people and their family (where appropriate) as a team ('reflection', 'it's all about us'). After moving back home, Helen would visit for weekends. She was asked about this (statutory regulatory), to which she replied, 'Why would I choose to go back to a centre with rules and regulations? I'll tell you why. Because I felt safe there, because of the care that was given to me by each and every staff member, because of the way they understood me and my Mam. They treated us kindly and always seemed to know what I needed. I went back because I love the bones of my staff.'

17. *Meeting others where they are:* This refers to not only being involved with people where they live their lives, but also accepting people for who and how they are. It also refers to being able to respond to their developmental capabilities.

18. *Rituals of encounter:* This speaks to the conscious thought which must be given to the ways in which we engage with another and giving respectful attention to cultural protocols.

19. *Connection and engagement:* Given the belief that 'relationship' is the foundation of all good care, it is essential that workers are able to 'connect' with their 'clients' and 'engage' with them in a real and meaningful way.

20. *Doing with, not for or to:* This refers to how social care staff must engage with people, helping them learn and develop through doing things with them. It requires a constant focus on being and doing with.

21. *Being emotionally present:* This involves the worker making a concerted effort to be fully 'available' and intent on focusing with immediacy on the other. It builds on the notion of being fully engaged and interested to the extent that we take time to ask and remember things such as what people take in their tea (Digney & Gaffney 2006).

22. *Rhythmicity:* Being attuned to rhythmicity ensures a shared experience of engaging with other. Connecting with others at their pace and rhythm helps nurture our relationship with that person/family.

23. *Intentionality of action:* When speaking of the notion of intentionality, we mean that everything a worker does is done for a particular purpose. This also requires consciously thinking about the other person in a caring way. Of course this does not mean abandoning spontaneity – it merely means that we are truly reflective.

24. *Purposeful use of activities:* This links with the notion of taking the time to ensure that our activities are focused on creating 'experiences that promote the possibility of new beliefs for the people we support' (Phelan 2009). Consideration of the purposeful use of any activity can change a life for ever.

Case Study 3: 'Sarah'

We first met Sarah (not her real name) when she was fourteen years old. Her parents had already divorced and her mum was in prison for attempted murder. Sarah's father remarried and she struggled in this 'reconstituted family'. Her emotional pain and inner turmoil manifested itself in behavioural challenges for her father and stepmother. The result was a relational breakdown with the new family situation. Following a series of failed foster placements over a period of months, Sarah was referred to and admitted into residential care. She arrived with the 'usual' history of rejection and feeling of being unloved and unlovable.

The first months were fraught with difficulties and challenges (acting out, smoking, drinking, violence towards staff, other residents and indeed herself) as Sarah pushed staff to reject her ('rituals of encounter' and 'meeting others where they are'). Yet, to her surprise, she did not experience counter-aggression or rejection; instead she encountered the incongruence of being loved and not rejected ('being emotionally present').

Staff took the time to understand her behaviours, to reframe the negative emotion, and they rode through the acting out ('rhythmicity'). Sarah was constantly reinforced, provided with nurturing experiences as staff demonstrated warmth, sought connection and acted as emotional containers when things were in turmoil. Staff slowly but surely began to create relationship with her ('connection and engagement').

As time went on she began to enter into emotional work with certain staff members, allowing her to reflect on her life and situation. Alongside this intervention strategy were attempts to claim this girl's family, pulling them into her daily life and repairing the damaged bonds in her life. Sarah was able to grasp the many dynamics at play and able to quiz us on our intentions ('intentionality of action'). While in our care, she had once asked, 'I've grown to know you care about me, and us [the resident group], but do you love us'? Thankfully we had the confidence to answer her honestly!

Shortly after leaving our care Sarah had a child of her own. Key staff continued their relationship with her and continued to provide advice and support, helping to set up her new flat and staying involved in the transition from care. Indeed, a female staff member with whom the girl has a close relationship was very involved in the birth of her child and supported her in early motherhood ('purposeful use of activities' and 'doing with, not for or to').

Sarah continues her relationship with us, being in regular contact and receiving nurturing support in helping to bring up her child. She has grown into parenthood and become confident in her parenting skills. She is now a wonderful young woman, interconnected in a community of caring and support. She is independent and also, just like the rest of us, interdependent.

In October 2013, at an important function (with government officials present), she informed the audience, 'I know I'm loved, I know my wee girl is loved [by staff] and I love them too.'

LOVE AND KINDNESS REMEMBERED

Staff kindness, as an important therapeutic value, has been neglected and disregarded in reclaiming troubled students. (Long 2007:242)

Over the many years we have practised, we have become convinced of the potency of all of the above notions and we recognise that when they are distilled a little further, they represent the fundamental concepts of 'being relational', 'showing kindness' and 'providing love'.

We have found that kindness and love in the context of relationship, even in the midst of strife and rancour, can facilitate the very healing required for troubled and troublesome clients. Mother Teresa once noted that we cannot do great things on this earth, only small things with great kindness; and most people have experienced at least one kind act in their lives that impacted hugely on them, possibly changing how they viewed themselves or others.

Putting kindness at the heart of what we do may sound a bit gooey and sugary sweet, but kindness is at the core of healing and development. Tiny acts, imbued with meaning and derived from human instincts, can promote care and caring.

Care environments have always been busy places. People come and go and caring continuity can be hard to establish and maintain. Amid the day-to-day hubbub of schedules and activities, one thing is essential to caring and healing. It could even be considered the life blood of care work. Relationships that support and enable development are at the heart of all effective 'social care'.

Relational caring comes from the heart and to be most effective it requires that skilled social care workers interpret the many complex situations that arise and 'respond to the needs' being communicated through behaviour. Gaining these skills is essential to responding effectively, sensitively and appropriately to even the most challenging of situations.

While again asserting the need for all social care workers to create trusting relationships (with a focus on continuous small acts of kindness and love), we also need to remind the reader that both kindness and love are areas of practice that have long been neglected and undervalued in our field. At times and probably because of a child protection paradigm framed by past abuse scandals, writers and social care workers have edited out discussions on love and kindness and relegated topics of this nature to the whispered corners of our profession.

This neglect of crucial areas of caring has not served the profession or our clients well. It has served to cast a shadow of suspicion upon acts of kindness and tarnish the sentiment expressed by those daring enough to speak of love. So how do we as a profession reclaim these aspects of care and caring?

COMING FULL CIRCLE

Caring relationships are the cradle needed for positive change and resilient healing. The weight of evidence from twenty-odd years of the 'what works' debate in our profession has shown that 'healing' relationships start at a place of risk and end up unleashing the effects of the often hidden resilience within those for whom we care. People evolve through caring actions involving kindness and generosity.

Paraphrasing the findings of the *Making not Breaking* inquiry (Care Inquiry 2013), relationships are the 'golden threads' in children's lives. So, if relationships are the golden threads used to knit together all positive aspects of care and healing, we should rest assured that they are of crucial importance in helping all who struggle and need our presence.

Seligman (2002:11) advises that 'love includes kindness, generosity, nurturance, and the capacity to be loved as well as to love' and Long (2007:242) states, 'Kindness is envisioned as a vital force to our well-being and in our therapeutic work ... just as sunlight is the source of energy that maintains organic life, kindness is the source of energy that maintains and gives meaning to humanity.'

Let us learn from what we already know, from what is normal and natural:

- Look at all challenges and challenging behaviour as opportunities to learn more from and about our clients.
- Toil over forming relationships – it pays dividends.
- Demonstrate love through 'being there' and performing small acts of kindness.
- Recognise that showing kindness is not showing weakness – it is showing strength of character and conviction.
- Take the time to truly care.

For, as an old Hindu proverb states, 'Help thy brother's boat across and lo, thine own has reached the shore.'

Chapter 7
The Language of Social Care
Why Use Many Words When One Will Do?
Pauline Clarke Orohoe

There she sat, a twelve-year-old girl with her future being decided by a number of professionals discussing her 'assessments, needs, and possible interventions'. A language that is so far removed from her world that if and when asked what she thinks, she merely nods in agreement. This is a small example of the type of language used in planning services and supports for families and young people in need. These are the same young people and families we as professionals pride ourselves on having involved in this decision-making process.

In my practice we discuss family needs as a means of creating a picture of the family's world. This allows staff to develop a plan for interventions to support and facilitate these service users to achieve positive outcomes. When introducing these concepts to families, however, our language has to be altered, which takes us as professionals out of our comfort zone. It challenges us as workers to be creative about how we introduce and explain our services to families in language they can understand. We can at times take for granted that service users are familiar with terms such as 'needs', 'interventions', 'assessments', 'outcomes', 'self-esteem' and 'support'. In the discussion to follow I share some of the alternative strategies for engaging meaningfully with families that I have found beneficial in my practice.

I entered the field of social care with a blind desire to make a positive difference to the lives of those with whom I came in contact. A naive aspiration, some may say, but one that developed from my own experience of a relatively stable and happy childhood, and a belief that surely this could be attainable for all children. My initial contact with the reality of this work came through working in residential care and community childcare. From there I moved to a service providing support to vulnerable families who were considered to be at risk. I presently work as a manager in the field of social care, and together with a dedicated and committed team we are striving to actively engage with families so that they can meaningfully agree to and participate in a work plan to support their needs.

Throughout my practice I have engaged with families who may be experiencing difficulties in their lives by focusing on their strengths and previous successes. The work is based on supporting these families to make positive changes in their lives so as to address specific needs that have been identified. From there a support plan can be developed that sets out the type and duration of services that can be offered by those involved.

In order meaningfully to engage families, children and young people in this process, as a team we are challenged to explore alternatives to the language with which we as social care workers have become all too comfortable. Too often when families are referred to new services there is a sense of entering the unknown, where they are often unclear about why they have even been referred to the service in the first place.

Take the case of a family who are attending a number of local support services. A lengthy discussion takes place with the family regarding their 'needs' and the possible 'interventions' that can be provided. On meeting with the family afterwards it is evident that they are unclear as to what decisions have been agreed, and what the future holds for them.

So following such discussions, whose needs have actually been met? The professional jargon and descriptive terms may merely serve the purpose of keeping reports concise, and asserting the position of social care workers. The language which we as professionals use so readily is lost on the very people it was intended to support and empower, and while well intentioned it can leave families feeling isolated and unclear on what is to follow.

It is worth noting and remembering how the word 'jargon' is defined. A web definition of 'jargon' is 'the specialised language of a professional, occupational or other group, often meaningless to outsiders' (www.askabout.com), while a definition in Webster's dictionary is one we might sometimes identify with in the workplace: 'obscure and often pretentious language marked by circumlocutions and long words'.

We need to be mindful that prior to our training in this field, this was a language with which we were equally unfamiliar. There were times when I sat in lecture halls and was unsure of the meaning of some of the language being used. As a first year student, terms such as 'family support' and 'professional supervision' held little meaning for me. While there were lecturers who would explain these terms in detail, in some cases it was only with research, time and experience that I became aware of the broader meaning and implications of the terms discussed. I was in the happy position of having this time available; but bear in mind that the parents and young people whose lives are being discussed and critical decisions being made concerning their future often do not have this luxury.

We are keenly aware of the need for professional and accurate record keeping and reporting systems. To take just one example, we only need to look at the *Roscommon Child Care Case* report (HSE 2010) to be reminded of the destruction that can be wrought in children's lives where this type of good practice has not been implemented. However, we must keep to the forefront the young people and families we serve, and ensure that when parents, carers and young people have to sign forms they truly understand what they are agreeing to.

The National Adult Literacy Agency (NALA website) has published figures stating that one in four adults in Ireland have difficulties with literacy, and a campaign has been launched to promote the use of plain English across all sectors, with a Quality Mark being awarded to those organisations who meet the required standard. This issue is not unique to Ireland. There are campaigns throughout the USA, the UK and Canada to promote the use of plain English in various government departments. The European Commission has also embraced this campaign, and has launched a set of guidelines on writing clearly (EC n.d.).

We have all experienced situations when, following a meeting with a doctor or financial institution, we are unsure of what the basic conversation was about. It is these very situations that make plain English campaigns so important for workers in social care. A proportion of the families we work with will fall within the 25% of people who have difficulties with reading and writing. The groups who have been identified as being most at risk are early school leavers, those who are unemployed, older adults and non-English speakers (NALA website). So surely there is an onus on organisations that work with families in need of support to strive to achieve a Quality Mark for the language they use to convey their message?

Our work as social care workers is based on the basic principle of relationships: family relationships, worker–client relationships, inter-agency relationships. In these relationships it is often what is not spoken that has the greatest influence. I can recall situations where I sat with families who were awaiting important decisions regarding their future. To a stranger walking past we were merely sitting waiting, but what was taking place within that interaction was of a greater significance. It was the presence of a consistent adult who was available to that parent or young person to acknowledge the uncertainty of the situation for them while maintaining calmness in an utterly chaotic environment.

What families and young people want most of all is honesty and consistency. While some of the families who come into contact with services may have little routine in their lives, as workers we must not mirror this chaos. The significance of simple tasks such as returning phone calls in language that will be clearly understood and carrying through on plans as agreed cannot be underestimated. Families who are operating in highly stressed environments become increasingly frustrated when they are unable to make contact with relevant services. And while, with the demands of increasing caseloads, reduced staffing levels and service provision, it may not always be possible or appropriate to discuss issues at that time, families appreciate such honesty and availability.

While attending meetings, I have often been curious about the interactions between various service providers and the families they engage with. I have seen situations where a worker has been regularly engaging with a family member, and yet while they are waiting for a meeting to commence, there has been little or no communication. This is the same service user and worker who have been meeting over a number of weeks and will be meeting in the weeks to come. Basic interactions can be utilised as tools to strengthen the relationship between the worker and the client, or, as in the example above, they can highlight the need for increased self-awareness on the part of the worker.

We work with highly emotive issues and situations. It is fair to say that family members can at times feel powerless when engaging with support services. Too often families feel that they are not being heard and so need somebody to advocate on their behalf. This has highlighted for me the power imbalance that families can perceive and sometimes experience when engaging with services. Workers need to be aware of how they might be perceived by the families with whom they work, and reflect this awareness in the language they use. Language can be used as a force to control and intimidate, or as a tool to empower and encourage families to work towards their desired goals. Surely our role as social care workers is to facilitate this change through our practice, and in turn through the words we use so that families fully understand the message we are trying to convey. The benefit is twofold: the family clearly understand what is being communicated, and because they feel they can trust the worker they may be more committed to actively engaging with the service; and hence the worker is facilitated to progress with their interventions so as to address the identified need.

In considering the impact of our work on the family, Ruch (2005) points out the need for staff to be aware of the impact their work has on family members as individuals. This takes into consideration their values and belief systems both as a worker and a person in their own right. Workers should be facilitated and supported to reflect on their practice by communication through supervision. Increasing caseloads and time constraints can impact on the quality of supervision frontline workers receive. At a time when casework is becoming ever more complex, supervision needs to be given priority in teams. This ensures that workers are receiving appropriate support to manage the potential impact of their work. Such reflection and support lends itself to more constructive and open communication with service users without the use of unnecessary professional jargon. It also helps staff to have those difficult conversations with families, with which we are all too familiar, in clearly understood language.

We are in the business of family support, and by its very nature this entails having conversations with families that can lead to heightened emotion and reactions from all parties. As social care workers, over the course of our careers there will be times when we have to have those difficult conversations with families about concerns for their situation. While initially such sessions may be complex, families appreciate openness and clarity in these discussions. Families are reassured when they understand clearly why the matter is being discussed. It is for this reason that workers needs to use clear, concise language to ensure that families understand what is being said. It often comes down to keeping in mind not what we say but how we say it. As one example, parents and young people are sometimes unclear on the differences between psychology and psychiatry services. An explanation of their differences can lead a family to be more open and accepting of a referral to these services.

The use of language and conversation in our field is closely coupled with the need to listen to the families and young people with whom we have contact. But what exactly are we listening out for? As workers we need to have a genuine curiosity about the person as a whole. When meeting with new families I explain to them that their current situation has developed over time, and to know where they are coming from we need to hear their 'story' and the life events and hurdles they have had to overcome that have brought them to their present situation. Within this dialogue we are carefully and attentively listening for how they have survived or successfully overcome a situation in the past, because this can point to where future success may lie in relation to problems they face.

Sharry, Madden and Darmody (2001) discuss the benefit to clients of highlighting the positive aspects of their lives in terms of what's working well, and the potential resources they may have within their family and community. This changes our conversation with clients from being problem-focused and technical to clearly highlighting their skills and strengths. Families often find this unusual, particularly if they have had a lengthy period of involvement with services, as the conversation does not continually and clearly focus on what is going wrong in their lives.

Take the situation of a young person where there are issues regarding non-attendance at school, leading to increased frustrations and stress within a family. By using solution-focused therapy techniques, we can as workers form a picture of how such a young person would want their future to look. If we ask the young person about their ideal future, where they would like to be, what they would like to do, we can support them and their family to develop realistic goals for their future. We can then begin to discuss the steps a family needs to take to achieve these goals. Gradually, attendance at school can become a means to an end, and can thus become more tolerable. As workers we could focus on what the problems are in attending school on certain days, though this merely serves to hold us in problem talk and keeps us focused on the deficits of the situation. Through using tools such as the 'miracle question' (de Shazer 1984), we can help service users to think of where they would like to be in six months, in twelve months and beyond. It is a language that is understandable, and can facilitate families to visualise a future that they may have felt was unattainable. It allows us as social care workers to develop realistic goals with the family, and so develop realistic outcomes which are practical and achievable.

This is particularly relevant when trying to engage young people and children who may not have the vocabulary to let us know what their life journey has been so far. This requires the worker to be creative and use additional tools to gather the required information. In my experience as a social care worker, I have found that art-based activities can facilitate young people to communicate their feelings in a language they are comfortable using. These activities have helped me develop a sense of a young person's perception of themselves, their self-esteem and the people in their world who are important to them (Jones 1998). Using sessions based on activities such as art and baking, rather than trying to communicate using technical terms, can allow the worker to build a relationship with a young person. These normal, interactive activities can help gather significant information that can be used to enrich the service that is being provided to address that young person's needs.

As workers involved with vulnerable families we must be their advocates at all times. This places a responsibility on us to involve them meaningfully in the process of change from referral to closure. One of the key learning points from my experience is the importance of reflecting information back to the family to ensure that both parties have a clear understanding of what has been discussed. In preparation for formal meetings, which by their very nature can be intimidating experiences for parents, carers and young people, it is vital that we ensure that the family is aware of the information we will be sharing. I have also found it useful to agree with service users a method of communicating within a meeting if they are confused by, or do not understand something that is being discussed. This may be as simple as an agreed gesture or word to let you, the worker, know that there is a problem.

As we know, best practice in record-keeping reminds us that we should record in clearly understood language as if the family member was standing beside us. Therefore, when preparing reports we should ensure whenever possible that the family have seen the report before it is submitted. This practice ensures that a worker is mindful of the language being used, and that the content of the report is evidence-based – from observations made and discussions conducted during sessions. While professional language, jargon and acronyms are commonly used in the helping professions, we must remember that it is a language which is unfamiliar to the wider community. I recently read a document that contained some unfamiliar acronyms; and this reminded me once again of the need to be aware of how we speak with, gather and share sensitive information with the families and young people we meet throughout our careers.

The stories we tell and the vulnerable people we encounter are real. We must never forget that our interaction with these families has the potential to influence lasting positive change. We must not take for granted the families who allow us into the most sensitive and often difficult aspects of their lives. It is for this reason that we must be respectful and aware of our position as professionals within this dynamic. If what we request from families is true engagement, we must also, as workers, adhere to that same principle by way of the language we use.

Even the most conscientious among us must examine how we communicate and not lazily fall into the trap of assuming that the vulnerable people with whom we deal always understand what we are saying.

Chapter 8
An Approach to Family Assessments
Angela Feeney

INTRODUCTION

Family assessment is a developing area of social care practice. This chapter examines the concept and practice of home-based systemic ecological assessments, with particular emphasis on the issues encountered by professionals engaging with vulnerable families. Family assessment is an opportunity for both professionals and families not only to gain extensive insight into any existing problematic dynamics and experiences but also to identify family strengths and potential for further change and development. Meaningful engagement by families is dependent on their understanding of the referral issues, motivation to change and capacity to modify behaviours. The approach of such family assessments and interventions ultimately determines the level of engagement. The view that a crisis can be an opportunity for change can in some cases be very true; however, there are more far-reaching complex factors to consider, as will be discussed in this chapter.

My interest in writing this chapter came from my experience and knowledge in the field of family work, specifically in the area of home-based systemic ecological assessments and interventions. After completing a BA in Applied Social Studies in Social Care at Athlone Institute of Technology in 2002, I worked in a children's residential centre on the north side of Dublin until 2006. I then became involved with the establishment of what was then a family outreach and respite service; it has since evolved to become a specialised family assessment and intervention service, in which I hold the position of Deputy Manager. (In order to protect the anonymity of its service users I will not use the full title of the service in this chapter, but I shall refer to it simply as a family assessment and intervention service.) I have furthered my education in the areas of introductory family therapy and conflict resolution and mediation techniques, and in 2010 I completed an MA in Child, Family and Community Studies at Dublin Institute of Technology. My thesis, entitled 'Family Service

Coordination: A Case Study', examined the experiences of various family work professionals with regard to the challenges of inter-agency co-ordination.

THE FAMILY ASSESSMENT AND INTERVENTION SERVICE

The family assessment and intervention service from which practice examples for this chapter originate works with families who require assessment and specific family interventions and who are referred by local social work departments. The service model is based on prevention, for example the prevention of children being admitted to foster or residential care. Referrals generally involve families who are experiencing problematic and difficult circumstances, for example mental health concerns, learning disabilities, addictions, behavioural problems, domestic violence, relationship difficulties, parenting issues or impaired parenting capacity, environmental and safety concerns. Typically, families who are referred have already reached levels three and four of the Hardiker model (as cited in Howarth 2002) of service intervention. Levels one and two relate to early intervention services where families generally self refer; level three is where social services are required to intervene; and level four is the stage where children have been placed in care. Reunification services for families at level four, for example the reunification with their families of young people from foster and/or residential placements, are also a core function of this service. For the purpose of this chapter, practice examples will primarily refer to engaging families in the assessment phase.

HOME-BASED SYSTEMIC ECOLOGICAL ASSESSMENTS

Systemic ecological assessments are a process of collecting information to determine levels of overall family wellbeing and to identify existing family dynamics. According to Thomlison (2010), family assessments have a number of aims, for example:

1. to determine the functioning of family systems
2. to identify areas for change or development
3. to assess the positive attributes of a family and to highlight overall strengths
4. to identify further interventions required, in collaboration with the family.

'Home-based systemic ecological assessments' is a term used to describe assessments that encompass all aspects of family life to create a comprehensive overview of environmental factors, social integration, childhood development, family dynamics and functioning, and parenting capacity. Assessments are intensive by design, working inclusively with all family members within the family home. Home visits, which are observational, are undertaken as frequently as four times weekly for four to five weeks, and each lasts for two hours. This approach utilises an ecological framework where further information is gathered from meetings with extended family and services/schools/community supports that the family avail of. The main components of the assessment are analyses of:

- safety
- environment
- family functioning/wellbeing
- communication/interactions
- parenting capability.

Completed assessment reports are used to inform decisions about future interventions, to determine parenting capacity and in some cases to make recommendations for care placements or the reunification of children and young people with their families.

HOME-BASED SYSTEMIC ECOLOGICAL ASSESSMENTS AND SOCIAL CARE

The family assessment and intervention service is staffed by social care workers who are referred to as family workers. These family workers are all suitably qualified and have experience of working in residential care. The rationale for recruiting staff with residential care experience was that these workers would have particular expertise in dealing with challenging behaviour, along with various diagnosed conditions, for example attention deficit hyperactivity disorder (ADHD), oppositional deficit disorder (ODD) and other behavioural and developmental disorders. Considering the practice of home visiting, it is paramount that family workers comply with the staff safety policy, which provides mechanisms for support and strategies for the protection of staff in their workplace, which is in effect the family home. Family workers must practise specific interpersonal skills to avoid potentially dangerous situations while working in the community. Service provision extends into unsocial hours, as a move away from traditional clinic hours of Monday to Friday, 9a.m. to 5p.m. These working hours are not especially unique to the contracts and working arrangements of most social care workers in practice. Again, this highlights the suitability of having qualified social care workers with experience of working in residential care to fill the role of family worker.

ECOLOGICAL THEORY OF HUMAN DEVELOPMENT

The ecological theory of human development, first proposed by Bronfenbrenner (1979), has provided the foundation for family intervention design as adapted by family therapy theorists Minuchin, Colapinto and Minuchin (1998) (cited in Bryant and Wasik (2001)). Ecological theory views people as being nested within layers of various complex environments: the family is at the centre, surrounded by layers of community: neighbourhood, schools, employment, family resources, religious/spiritual institutions, health and social services. State policies align at the outer layers of the nest and exert influence directly or indirectly. Bronfenbrenner's emphasis on the influence of community variables on families had already been voiced by home visitors as early as the 1900s. The theory states that positive or negative changes in social conditions, for example childcare policy, transport and employment, influence family life. Social support in the family and community also has direct influence; for example, in families where social support is low, mental and physical health is affected. In my experience social isolation and low or no social supports are features of the majority of the referrals that have come through the service. Families can in turn become the victims of antisocial behaviour, with some family homes being targeted. Families can be intimidated and harassed within the community, which serves to further isolate them. In some cases professionals are the only source of support, and family workers are sometimes the only visitors to extremely marginalised families in a community.

Chaskin (2006, cited in Dolan *et al.* 2006) values the contribution of community in the context of family support, identifying the community as a context that needs to be 'taken account of', informing the planning and provision of support services:

> *The lives of all family members are interdependent. Hence, how each family member reacts to a particular historical event or role in transition affects the developmental course of other family members, both within and across generations.*
>
> (Bronfenbrenner 1996, cited in Bryant & Wasik 2001:31)

Viewing the family within an ecological framework can help to recognise behaviour as interactions between protective and risk factors. According to Fraser (2004, cited in Thomlison 2010), an ecological assessment can identify 'points of entry' for planned interventions to reduce specific risk factors. These 'points of entry' are essentially where services need to intervene. It is not uncommon for families who meet the threshold of the service to have had several previous interventions offered with various aspects of their difficulties having been addressed in some way. The assessment can identify the level and intensity of service required. Interventions may target situational experiences, for example nurturing childhood development. The knowledge and skills of the social care worker in relation to childhood development is especially relevant when assessing milestones and childhood behaviours. Home visiting in the context of ecological theory provides optimal observation opportunities of ecological and developmental interactions between family members and their communities.

FAMILY SYSTEMS THEORY

According to Minuchin (2002, cited in de Róiste & Dinneen 2005), with respect to systems theory the family can be conceptualised as a system in itself. It consists of family members who are interdependent and co-ordinated elements that are influential both directly and indirectly. The assessment and intervention service works with all family members, including both those living in the family home and those outside it. The views of all parents, carers, adult children and young people are gathered in the assessment process so as to compile a comprehensive overview of difficulties and to establish clarity about the relationships, attachments and familial supports. Working with a young person in relation to poor school attendance in isolation from his or her parents/carers, in my experience, will not effect change. Joint work between parent/carer and the young person will offer greater chance of success as they can come to a common understanding of issues and work out strategies to move forward. Grandparents are often an extremely helpful source of information as presenting difficulties can often be intergenerational. This is where the assessment and intervention phase can explore parenting experiences and the subsequent impact on current parenting practices. A family systems approach is therefore a less individualistic model of therapeutic intervention; it treats the family as a whole unit with a family-centred ethos as its theoretical foundation. It is based on the assumption that 'Family relationships are sources of the most intense emotions in people's lives; they are both the source of joy and happiness under positive circumstances' and 'great distress and sorrow when things go badly' (Thomlison 2008:185).

According to de Róiste (2006), the family is viewed as a system that is more than the sum of its components. Attention is required to examine the degree of closeness and the power structures in family relationships. Referrals to the service often detail chaotic homes in which parents have no power over daily living, for example school attendance or curfews. Imbalanced power structures can exist in cases of domestic violence or where grandparents, parents and children are living together.

Family workers taking a systems approach often employ the use of a genogram, or life graph, which can not only assist the worker but also help the family in piecing together their family and social history. For some families this may be the first time they have analysed and explained their own family system while making connections with their intergenerational family patterns. Generally, through the use of a genogram families share information about bereavements or abusive experiences which remain unresolved. These unresolved experiences are often causal factors of low mood, mental health difficulties and the subsequent impairment of parenting capacity. This type of discussion again identifies possible points of service intervention. A genogram is especially helpful and can complement 'family tree' or 'life story' work with young people who may have been separated from their family.

Minuchin (1985, cited in Bryant & Wasik 2001) describes subsystems within the family unit, for example parents as a subsystem and siblings as another. Overall family functioning is determined by positive or negative interrelations between subsystems, with critical, non-supportive interactions contributing to family dysfunction. With respect to home visiting, the family worker needs to interact with all family members because change is most likely when all residents in the home are included in interventions. Along with this approach, Thomlison (2010) states that it is not only family members who shape behaviours; so too do family friends, teachers, childcare providers and community systems. A single intervention conducted in isolation from other services is not likely to be hugely beneficial. Family interventions need to be co-ordinated with all other essential services so as to afford the family an opportunity to grow, develop and in some cases rebuild their lives.

THE STAGES OF CHANGE THEORY AND ENGAGING FAMILIES

According to Buckley, Howarth and Whelan (2006), family assessments should be a dynamic and interactive process. There are, however, many other factors to consider in light of the integral engagement process of family assessments. When I began my career in family work I was introduced to the concept of 'engagement' and quickly learned that families were more often than not defined by how they 'engaged'. Being new to this area I soon realised that it was this topic of engagement that would become the most thought-provoking and time-consuming element of my work. Ideals of completing informative assessments and designing problem-specific interventions were well within the scope of this new service, but without the engagement and participation of the family, nothing could essentially happen. Professionals exchange information about how families engage, for example 'they are very good at answering the phone', 'the only way to get in is to visit unannounced'. Families may or may not be ready to engage in a process of change. One may consider Landy and Menna (2006), who detail the stages of change theory. Prochaska stated that services are required to adapt interventions to the client's 'readiness'. Services come into contact with families at various stages. For example:

- The first stage is the *precontemplation stage* – the family are not intending to take action soon.
- The *contemplation stage* indicates that the family intend to take action in the near future.
- The *preparation stage* indicates a possibility of immediate action.
- The *action stage* indicates that change has already commenced.
- This is followed by the *maintenance stage*.
- Finally there is the *termination stage*.

This clear-cut theory and ideology that services adapt their interventions to match readiness is logical and client-centred, but in the reality of child protection and welfare-oriented family work it is not always possible.

Families may be at any of these stages when they are referred to the service. The initial meeting between the assessment and intervention service and the family can bring about interesting experiences, both for the family and for the worker. As part of my role I introduce families to their family worker and to the assessment process. Notwithstanding the information recorded in referral forms about a family's readiness to change or pattern of engagement, the actual introduction to the service and what occurs after this can vary. Families can present in a variety of ways: for example, they may be distressed and in a crisis cycle; they may appear uninterested and resistant to the service; they may appear willing to engage and, in some cases, overly eager to get started. The family's perception of the service can be affected by their previous experiences of service involvement, which must be taken into account. The intense nature of the assessment can be overwhelming for families and much clarity is required at this stage. Some families realise that the assessment process may be their last opportunity for intervention; they are often referred by child protection case conferences as care placements and supervision orders are being discussed. In light of what may be going on for a family, it is crucial that the initial meeting serves its purpose, which is to inform, afford clarity and engender a sense of collaboration with the family, a sense of working honestly together. As a professional I must acknowledge the power imbalance in such instances and I reassure families that the assessment is an opportunity for reflection and exploration of family issues with a view to resolution through the use of specific interventions.

Case Study

In relation to the change process I will note one particular case where the foster placement of a male teenager had broken down, and because of a lack of foster placements, and his age, there was a possibility that he might be placed in a residential unit. The teenager's father had a long history of problematic alcohol misuse. This hadn't improved since the placement of the teenager in care two years previously; however, the father gave an undertaking that he would address his difficulties and the teenager was returned with in-home support offered by the assessment and intervention service. The placement at home was fraught with difficulties as neither party had been prepared for this unexpected transition. The father didn't engage with an alcohol treatment service and the difficulties that had been apparent prior to the foster care placement quickly resurfaced. The family clearly hadn't been at the precontemplation, the contemplation or the preparation stage. This example illustrates the reality of the demands on families to engage and the reliance of services on families 'playing their part'.

When engaging a family proves challenging, the family can as a result be labelled 'hard to reach' or 'difficult'. It is important to note that expectations for families to engage with services can be high. Attending appointments (e.g. counselling, child mental health services, speech and language therapy, family centres) can be extremely time-consuming, placing parents/carers under pressure to be in several places in any given day or week. Although these appointments are necessary, they can overstretch a family and impact on actual family time. In this case services must shift from perceiving the family as the obstacle to questioning what it is about the service or volume of services that families find hard to accept.

BARRIERS TO ENGAGEMENT

Notwithstanding the stages of change theory, there are further pragmatic and attitudinal factors that may hinder the participation of families (Clipsham 2006, cited in Landy & Menna 2006). Language barriers may result in confusion about the purpose of the service involvement. The use of interpreters can be difficult and often makes the assessment experience more invasive or uncomfortable for the family. Family workers with particular language skills are encouraged to use them where appropriate. In my experience I have been fortunate enough to carry out an assessment through my own knowledge and use of Irish Sign Language, which greatly assisted the process of developing a relationship with the family, who were deaf. Other barriers include literacy difficulties, safety concerns for workers entering family homes (for example in unsafe neighbourhoods or the perceived threatening behaviour of family members). Scheduling, and the co-ordination of home visits with family schedules and other service providers, may prove difficult.

There are also attitudinal factors that may prevent families engaging with services. Clipsham (2006, cited in Landy & Menna 2006) describes many reasons for parents to hesitate about participating with interventions; for example, families may fear involvement from child protection services because they are worried that they might lose their children or are reluctant or resistant to taking parenting advice. Parents often have expectations that they will be criticised, and isolated parents are especially vulnerable to these feelings. This can lead to feelings of rejection and a sense of not being 'good enough'. Parents can fear losing control and this can be due to past disempowering circumstances with agencies or even their own life experiences. Families may have experienced chaotic functioning, which prevents them from being consistent or reliable. This pattern of engagement can frequently be found in families experiencing addiction and who struggle to conceal drug or alcohol misuse. Such families have often experienced a disorganised history, which then translates into their current state as adults, and maintaining predictability is an unknown experience. Working with parents with learning disabilities brings its own challenge, for example how services balance the rights of parents against the rights of children in relation to good enough standards of nurturance and care. Families can be reluctant to share information with non-family members, maintaining that they can solve their own problems: this is frequently experienced with the Travelling community and people of African origin, who have a tradition of 'looking after their own'. Families sometimes feel that the service is not relevant to their needs, for example a service including all family members when a parent views only one child as having the 'problem'. Families may decline home visits due to embarrassment about lack of resources or the appearance of the home, for example where there is extremely poor home hygiene. In one instance I had an initial meeting with a family who were due to be evicted the next day. It had been difficult to schedule this meeting because of the family's resistance. I encountered a situation where my agenda was at odds with that of the families: while the family said that they wanted the service, the reality was that purposeful engagement at that time would have been an expectation too far. The referral was held back until the accommodation issue was resolved.

VOLUNTARY AND INVOLUNTARY FAMILIES

Ferguson (2011) writes about two types of clients in social work and child protection, and this typology is also applicable to family work.

Voluntary or co-operative clients are those who seek out and receive support and assistance. The voluntary client often has their own agenda, for example to avail of services that will help the family or to develop their own skills or to secure the return of their children to their care. The family assessment and intervention service engaged with two similar cases where children had been placed in care due to investigations of non-accidental injury. These families demonstrated full engagement and participation with services. One may argue that of course these families who had a common goal desperately wanted to prove to services that they could care for their children and would do anything to secure their return home. However true this view, from my experience these families had something else in common. The ecological assessments informed me that regardless of their predicament they were functioning at a high level and, more important, had the capacity to learn, engage and change, thus enabling them to engage fully in the process.

Involuntary or unco-operative clients actually pose problems for themselves and/or others and can be dishonest in their dealings with services. These clients can be in denial or are in a pattern of manipulating services to stay away by engaging in closed or even threatening behaviour. Approaches such as empowering families and working from strengths-based perspectives can be complex in these cases since the involuntary client may not demonstrate their positive features or feel that they need to be further empowered. Involuntary clients are often under supervision orders. Supervision orders are granted by the courts when a social worker has made an application for a parent to fulfil various responsibilities to their children as listed in the order. Engaging with the family assessment and intervention service may be one recommendation of a supervision order, and in this instance families may feel they are being forced to engage in an assessment. Again this highlights the stages of change process and families' readiness for change being in conflict with those who have a duty of care and their duty to ensure the wellbeing and protection of children under *Children First*.

Reder (1993, cited in Ferguson 2011) describes three types of control conflict – attempts by the family to control or maintain social isolation. The first is *closure*, where a family is threatened by those outside the family boundary and the response is to tighten the family circle to prevent contact with wider systems. This closed behaviour has been widely experienced by family workers, with many assessments not moving past the initial introductory meetings with families. In my experience families who demonstrate 'closure' generally have had little previous history with services and decline any offers of assistance from early intervention services, for example public health nurses and crèches.

The second control conflict is *disguised compliance*. This becomes apparent in cases where families initially agree and appear co-operative but withdraw when interventions become intense. Disguised compliance often comes to light at the end of an assessment. I can recall many cases in which families complied with assessment tasks, even completing all in-home observations, only to decline an intervention offered at the end of the assessment phase. The assessment phase is the information-gathering phase, so families are usually not challenged to make major behavioural changes and can therefore appear to be compliant with all they are asked; but when the goals and aims of family work are identified and families subsequently withdraw it becomes apparent that they did not have any intention of engaging meaningfully in the work. Many families will allow you through the front door; however, it is their understanding, motivation and capacity to change that that enable them to meaningfully engage.

The third control conflict is *flight* and this occurs when families completely close off contact with agencies and move to live in another area or even another country as a means to avoid further intrusion. This has also occurred in my experience of family work, and where it is suspected, families must be informed that relevant social services in the area they have moved to will be notified. This may help families to realise that the concerns are ongoing and perhaps they can re-evaluate their difficulties about receiving assistance. When dealing with a family in 'flight' mode, family workers must analyse carefully their own agenda, the needs of the family and also any immediate child protection concerns. This is one of the more challenging times when engaging a family and concern for children can be escalated. The challenge to be open and honest about what may potentially happen, while not threatening or frightening vulnerable families into destructive decision-making, takes considerable skill and case management. Family workers in this situation require high levels of support and supervision to manage their own feelings and frustrations about the case.

BALANCING FAMILY ENGAGEMENT AND FAMILY WORKERS' SAFETY

As mentioned above, working in unsafe areas or homes may pose risks to family workers and be a barrier to engaging with families. The previous section focused on how families receive and engage with family workers, but it is important to note that not all engagement issues are purely with families. The practice of 'lone working' in the community can pose all kinds of hazards and risks to workers, and requires careful research and preparation in advance of any home visit. Ferguson (2011) writes about undertaking home visits, detailing the process with reference to professionals feeling anxious or unsafe in the course of their duties. The family assessment and intervention service has, as mentioned above, its own staff safety policy. The safety of family workers in the community is of the utmost priority, and staff safety is continually assessed. Along with standard practices such as a pre-visit phone call, observing the immediate surroundings of the home for any suspicious behaviour and, on entry to the home, keeping your mobile phone with you at all times and positioning yourself close to the nearest exit in case a quick departure is required, there are often further measures to be taken. In one instance the family were living on the thirteenth floor of a mainly unoccupied tower block. The family were awaiting new social housing; however, the assessment was considered a priority and needed to be completed as soon as possible. The parent and child involved only left the flat when necessary because of the troublesome behaviour of gangs of youths, drug users and homeless people on the stairwells. The lift didn't work and the family worker used the unlit stairwell to gain access to the flat. Gangs at the base of the tower block watched out for activity or cars in the vicinity. All of these factors posed risks for the family worker in question. However, a solution was found through community resources: a social care worker working in a nearby residential unit who was familiar in the area, and to some of the youths loitering in the tower block, accompanied the family worker on home visits. This inter-agency co-operation enabled the family worker to gain access to the flat and the assessment was completed. Late night visits are a component of the systemic ecological assessment and are used to observe bedtime routines and adherence to and parental management of curfews.

Some communities and neighbourhoods can be daunting and even threatening after dark. In one case the neighbourhood was particularly unsafe and a social worker was mugged on the doorstep to the family home. The building was frequented by drug users and used syringes had been found in the communal laundry facility. In this instance two family workers were allocated the case and always visited the family home in pairs. It is important to note that it wasn't the family who posed a threat, but the environment they were living in. This raises the question that if it is unsafe for workers, how can it be safe for children?

There are also cases, however, where family members can be threatening and intimidating in their interactions with professionals. One case involved a middle-aged couple and two young children. The father's aggressive and threatening behaviour posed a serious risk not only to his family but to professionals as well. The family assessment and intervention service was required to assess parenting capacity; however, the case had reached crisis point, with various professionals being intimidated out of the family home. Arrangements were made to meet the father outside the family home so as to prevent any conflictual situations that might occur in the home in the presence of the children. The assessment was completed in due course. What was achieved in relation to this issue was that by naming the threatening behaviour and possible consequences for the family's engagement with services the family were informed and could decide to co-operate or otherwise. The power the father had to intimidate professionals was reduced as he realised that he had the power to engage and make changes for the overall safety and wellbeing of his children.

CONCLUSION

The knowledge and skills of social care workers in the area of family assessment and intervention are extremely valuable. The depth and value of home-based systemic ecological assessments is determined by the engagement of the family, which, as discussed above, can often be impaired by various complex factors. A home-based service eliminates one of the most common barriers to service engagement; for example, if the family cannot attend clinic-based appointments, the service comes to the family. Considering systemic and ecological theories, home-based services are essentially best placed to fulfil the remit of systemic ecological assessments, given that a family home is placed at the centre of most family systems and families can be viewed from within their immediate and extended environments. Families may be in continual crisis, repeating the same cycle several times before they recognise the need to change. Families may be court-ordered to engage in a process of change, which demands compliance with the courts, as opposed to voluntary engagement, which in turn achieves authentic maintenance of long-term change.

Family engagement is ultimately the most common challenge for services in child protection and welfare, and where these families are most vulnerable is often in their unsafe communities and homes. Workers must overcome these potential safety barriers to gain access and afford opportunities to families who are otherwise enclosed within an unsafe community. In my experience this calls for a shift in the view of why families can't engage to what is it that services can do to engage families further. Hence our role of home visiting and promoting engagement within frameworks that ensure the safety of vulnerable families involves ongoing risk assessment throughout the course of home-based practices.

Chapter 9
Achieving Independent Living for People with Disabilities
Aoife Killeen

INTRODUCTION

At the Social Care Ireland Conference 2013, it was notable that my presentation 'Our Right to Independent Living: Your Choice or Mine?' (Killeen 2013) was scheduled after a presentation outlining the necessary, essential and ideal components of person-centred plans. My presentation subsequently highlighted the stark realities faced by people with disabilities, the main one being a lack of choice in their own living arrangements. What resources are in place to meet the so-called person-centred plans? This is where the value of the practising social care worker and, indeed, this publication lie – highlighting the realities of care and securing the needs of the people we work with.

This chapter outlines the current policy for people with disabilities, with a particular focus on the Congregated Settings Report (CSR) (HSE 2011). It also highlights some of the many issues faced by people with disabilities and social care workers in choosing a place of residence. It provides a model of supported accommodation that, as a social care worker, I feel is a cost-effective measure to fill the perceived gap of need in independent living options. This chapter gives a broad overview of the advantages and disadvantages of such a model, while redacting any specific details to protect the confidentiality of people living there.

INFLUENCES FROM THE PAST

In the eighteenth century, before the Industrial Revolution, people with disabilities lived at home and in the community. Following increased urbanisation, institutions, including workhouses, became more common and people with disabilities were increasingly segregated from society. From the 1920s, religious orders came to the fore in helping and accommodating people with disabilities. According to the Department of Health:

During the 20th century, a well-established service infrastructure existed for people with physical and sensory disabilities provided by religious orders, such as the Christian Brothers, Daughters of Charity of St. Vincent de Paul and the Vincentian and Dominican Orders. Their services were largely educational, but they quickly, in many instances, became lifelong institutions, with people coming in at an early age and remaining into adulthood.

(DoH 2012:12)

Such 'lifelong institutions', now termed 'congregated settings', still exist in Ireland today. The government (through the Health Service Executive (HSE), Tusla), voluntary organisations and emerging private organisations are responsible for the provision of health and social care services. Such services now increasingly cater for distinct, individual needs, thus emphasising the need for choice in accommodation options. As social care workers, we aim to facilitate needs.

MY STANCE ON SOCIAL CARE

To trace it back to its origins, my interest in care was ignited from witnessing a grandmother who acquired Alzheimer's disease and gradually required increasing levels of care. In preparation for college I considered psychology and social work, but the practical subjects and grounded hands-on approach appealed to me more and I chose to study social care at Cork Institute of Technology. Since then I have worked in Ireland in rehabilitation/training, day care, providing assistance in the community and in residential care. I have also worked in Western Australia and had the opportunity to work in many areas through agency work and a home care organisation. This chapter is based on my experience of working in supported living accommodation for people with intellectual disabilities in Ireland.

Having worked in the field and discussed everyday practice issues with students on professional practice placement and with social care professionals in the field, I assert that, even with all the theory in the world you cannot meaningfully discuss social care practice without having worked in the area, which is the crucial advantage of institutes of technology (IT) courses. At the same time I am, and possibly will always be, an academic at heart and so I pursued a PhD. Although practice experience is crucial, as I am interested in policy I feel a sense of duty to link theory to practice and highlight the reality on the ground. Like Heaney, I take my pen and dig with it!

So what guidance does policy provide and what reality does experience show?

'POLICY': HOW THINGS SHOULD BE

There are various policy documents and legislation in place for people with disabilities and they generally read wonderfully, being both positive and empowering. Social care workers in the disability sector should make themselves aware of these:

- National Disability Strategy 2004 (Government of Ireland 2004)
- UN Convention on the Rights of Persons with Disabilities (UN 2006)
- Health Act 2007 (Government of Ireland 2007)
- HIQA Standards (HIQA 2013)
- Congregated Settings Report 2011 (HSE 2011)
- National Housing Strategy for People with a Disability 2011–2016 (DECLG 2011)
- *New Directions: Review of HSE Day Services and Implementation Plan 2012-2016* (HSE 2012)
- *Value for Money and Policy Review of Disability Services in Ireland 2012* (DoH 2012).

Particular attention needs to be given to Article 19 of the United Nation's CRPD. This definition of independent living focuses on choice as it recognises that a person should be able to select where they want to live. Article 19 states:

> a) *Persons with disabilities have the opportunity to choose their place of residence and where and with whom they live on an equal basis with others and are not obliged to live in a particular living arrangement;*
>
> b) *Persons with disabilities have access to a range of in-home, residential and other community support services, including personal assistance necessary to support living and inclusion in the community, and to prevent isolation or segregation from the community;*
>
> c) *Community services and facilities for the general population are available on an equal basis to persons with disabilities and are responsive to their needs.* (UN Enable 2013)

Inclusion Ireland gives an overview of these in its *Information Pack: A Guide to Disability Law and Policy in Ireland* (Inclusion Ireland 2013). I warn that these policies and human rights imperatives should not be read with too much optimism, as progress in realising their aims has been frustratingly slow. There are also a number of reports on current plans to integrate health and social care (see O'Connor 2013). On paper, while there are valid objectives for supporting people with disabilities in their right to independent living, on the ground there is disarray.

The Health Information and Quality Authority (HIQA) (created under the Health Act 2007) has generated a positive shift of change in conducting and monitoring registration/inspections of the organisations that provide care. Social care standards are currently set for children, disability and older people services. On the other hand, while such oversight is long overdue, this couldn't have come at a worse time since services are experiencing staff embargos, cutbacks and budget overspends, which, in some cases, can make it impossible to reach set standards. The government appears to have no policy in place for funds to meet standardised outcomes. For example, the *Value for Money and Policy Review of Disability Services* (VFMPR), while not a policy (but a report specifically on disability services), explored the current set-up of services to pave the way for the future and for best practice design. This report uncovered the varying degrees of service provision, highlighting that there is no standardised assessment of need or method of calculating resources and outcomes for people with disabilities. Added to this is the fact that the lengthy necessary recommendations for reform suggested in the VFMPR were to be 'considered in the light of the national financial position and the funding available to the health sector' (DoH 2012:xvii).

The HSE published a long-awaited report, *Time to Move on from Congregated Settings: A Strategy for Community Inclusion*, in 2011.

It stated:

> *As a society, the supports we now provide for people with disabilities are driven by values of equality, the right of individuals to be part of their community, to plan for their own lives and make their own choices and to get the personal supports they need for their independence.*
>
> (HSE 2011:3)

The report marks a welcome recognition of need for change in housing options for people with disabilities. The future will be bright: 'there will be no more need for congregated settings'. (A 'congregated setting' is defined as one with more than ten people resident.) Although 'choice' is alluded to, there are strict conditions in the report. People with disabilities are to be 'dispersed' into the community with a maximum of four other people, even though the report asserts that 'people should make their own life choices'. Apparently people with disabilities can look forward to an 'exciting future within a welcoming local community'. While this is just a report, it is also the underlying policy framework for the positive future of social care practice.

The following encapsulates my issue with the practical realities arising from the report: it very briefly acknowledges the concerns of staff, stating that they are apprehensive regarding the needs of certain service users – 'Many staff feel that the proposed model will not meet the needs of their clients' – with ensuing recommendations that staff who work in congregated settings be retrained. It also states: 'Supported living means providing the range and type of individualised supports to enable each person to live in the home of their choice and be included in their community' (HSE 2011:8). To be supported involves resources (as discussed later in this chapter), but there are no signs of these being provided. Also, the working group for this report based the recommendations on the premise that congregated settings are not suitable places of residence for people with disabilities. Yet, as my PhD research (Killeen 2014), which focuses on the differential treatment of people with physical disabilities over and under the age of 65 due to the divide in disability and older people services, highlighted, 6% of the population aged over 65 years were living in communal establishments in 2011 (CSO 2012). Contradictorily, an older person with a disability going into long-term residential care is part and parcel of policy, which is evident in the government's 'Fair Deal' nursing home scheme, which supports this.

In 2002 the National Disability Authority noted, in a report on health service provision, that in the UK the Disability Rights Commission argued for an enforceable right to independent living for all disabled people and quoted the following:

> There should be a basic enforceable right to independent living for all disabled people. Policy objectives for social care need to include guaranteed minimum outcomes, backed by a right to independence. ... All social care support services should be based on the principles of independent living.
> (NDA 2002:148)

This is mirrored in Article 19 of the CRPD, where the key to attaining independent living recognises that each person should have the right to choose whatever living arrangement they wish and the necessary supports to facilitate this. Both Article 19 and the NDA acknowledge the intrinsic importance of social care in independent living and service delivery. While the significance of the principle of independent living for people with disabilities is unquestionable, the challenge of realising this aim on a practicable level is only beginning to be scrutinised. What is the point in having policy, standards and person-centred plans, etc. in place if social care workers do not have the power, resources or time to act upon the wishes of the person?

'PRACTICE': BEING REALISTIC ABOUT INDEPENDENT LIVING

Back in 2011 the HSE's CSR report stated that:

> *All those living in congregated settings will move to community settings. No new congregated settings will be developed and there will be no new admissions to congregated settings.*
>
> (HSE 2011:28)

Thus far, cutbacks in services have had a direct impact on the ability of people with disabilities of all ages to live at home independently and this appears to contradict the policy on moving people from congregated settings, as well as the policy of maintaining persons in the community. There is currently no standardised domiciliary care support for people with disabilities living in the community (Killeen 2014). The home support services and housing options that are available are limited. Service users currently in crisis have no other option but to enter large group homes, as I have witnessed from working in residential care, even though limitations on new entrants are now contained in service level agreements. The following views of social care workers in the field mirror this view.

Social Care Worker One

'In my opinion it's all about the money, when I first started work in the residential area we were in recession but it was only the tip of the iceberg, there was still money in the pot. Due to dedicated staff I believe clients' interests were taken on board. Frontline staff more so than managers went to great lengths to put compatible people together for the big move into community living and it appears no expense was spared in doing so, whatever they wanted they got.

'As time went on and the recession took its toll and all the budget cuts came about it was a very different story. Although staff did their best still (whatever staff was left after all the cutbacks) the needs of the service users became bottom of the list. Compatibility didn't seem to matter anymore, anywhere where money could be saved, it was! Often undoing overnight what may have taken years to set up ... and from what I can see it ain't getting any better.'

Social Care Worker Two

'Many Service Users moved from their institutional homes where they may have been living the majority of their lives to community living. Due to cutbacks and employment embargo, cutbacks within the organisation were needed to be made. Service Users were being moved to residential units that did not meet their needs and some Service Users were being moved back in to the institutional type living they had previously lived in many years before.

'The organisation claims to empower people with intellectual disabilities to live the lives they choose. From a social care worker's viewpoint this is untrue. The organisation gave people the opportunity [of] community living and then retracted that without the Service Users' or family of the Service Users' input. The people that made the decisions for the residential moves were not working hands on with the Service Users. When the social care worker and key workers advocated for the rights of community living for the Service Users their opinions and voices were in my opinion unheard.'

LIFE IN A LARGE SUPPORTED HOME

I have experience of supporting independent living as a social care worker in a setting with two two-storey houses, separate buildings but connected by a one-storey flat, both linked by a hallway to the front door of the flat, which also links up the two houses. Seven residents live in each house and by definition it is a congregated setting. Both houses are equipped with a kitchen, sitting room and bathrooms. In the flat there is an office area, some presses for storage and a bedroom with an ensuite bathroom. One member of staff is available at all times from 8a.m. until 11p.m. and can be called during the night if required. There is a line of management over the organisation and funds are allocated for food and household bills. Each resident has a key to the house and to their bedroom and there is a secure gate.

So what works? The truth is that 'what works' in social care differs in every single situation because every single person is different.

This example of supported accommodation, in my view, provides a happy medium between large institutions and housing four people in the community. As we saw in the comments from social care workers, it is all about the current environment – which calls for cost-effective measures to provide care. The fact remains that the only people who can say whether this works 'well' are the people who live there. However from observation, experience, conversations with the residents and a knowledge of the rights of the individual to choice and independent living, I argue that for the most part, a model where two houses are joined by staff quarters does work and has many advantages (but some disadvantages too).

The good bits

- **Integrated flexible support:** The person is supported based on need and their person-centred plan.
- **Living life how you choose:** The person chooses where they would like to go, what they would like to do and when they would like to do it.
- **Routines:** When it comes to shopping, meals and medications there are some set times in place for the provision of certain aspects of daily living (which are flexible). While people have choice, on a practical operational level there needs to be some level of timing so that things 'work' in the kitchen, etc., so that cleaning tasks and other chores are attended to by each resident.
- **Medication supports:** People are assessed and may administer their own medication using a blister pack, which is stored in a secure location in their bedroom. For those who need monitoring and assistance with medication, the staff member present administers their medication.
- **Practical provision of basics:** Both houses are allocated funds for food (certain residents go shopping for food provisions, staff balance the receipts/costs) and bills are paid.
- **Cost-effective model:** One staff member at a time must be on duty and they sleep over at night: 14:1 is a cost-effective model of support.
- **Assisted trips away:** Holidays, weekends away, day outings, etc. Residents are given the option to go on many trips at home and abroad. The staff help and accompany residents if, when and where required.
- **Money management:** Some residents manage their own funds. Others who require assistance have the support of staff.
- **A sense of community and support:** One of the strongest advantages of this model, in my view, is the fact that friendships have grown, residents support one another when needed and there are many connections with the community and elsewhere.

Other benefits are:

- supported health and wellbeing
- support with appointment monitoring, making and attendance
- support with bereavements

- support with occasions – birthday parties, etc.
- support with Christmas
- fire safety
- qualified, consistent, supportive and trained staff
- independent living skills and training.

The bad bits

- **Incidents happen, stepping back and stepping in:** Verbal disputes between residents, difference of opinion, anxious behaviours, emotional outbursts, among other issues, can require intervention by staff at times.
- **Difficulties with supporting high dependency levels:** This unit cannot accommodate people with high levels of disability. Another problem is that if a person acquires an injury or health issue that requires 24-hour care, the facilities are not in place to provide that care. This creates problems when a person who is happy living in this type of accommodation is left with no choice but to move on. In the current climate the only option is to move to a congregated setting that provides 24-hour care.
- **Loss of family connections and local area:** From speaking with residents it is evident that many miss their original homes (although contact is maintained) and some have little or no family connections, which can be difficult – but it makes the fostered sense of community in this model of care all the more important.
- **Personality clashes/resistance to change:** Not all residents get on with one another (even those who are the best of friends have disputes). Also, as new people enter the accommodation, some of the longer-term residents struggle to adjust to a new resident in their home. I have found, from speaking with them, that some of the residents who have been there for some years, while they are welcoming to those who come in, feel a certain connection to the people they know longer.
- **Routines:** While routines are important, they can be restrictive.
- **Lack of solitary space:** Because people are living in groups there is a certain lack of space, although all have private, good-sized bedrooms with their own sink, TV, etc.
- **Lack of available options for independent living:** This will be discussed later in the chapter.

Another theme worth noting is that some service users do not wish to move and could experience deep fear and upset at the prospect of moving to a small unit that is 'dispersed' and cut off from others. Some would jump at the chance – and I would love to see them provided with the opportunity to move on; others, however, have lifelong friendships with staff and residents and may fear such an enormous change. The voice of each service user needs to be heard on a *case by case* basis.

What the model means for the service user

How does this work in practice for the residents? When a person is considered for staying in one of the units, a gradual process of introduction is involved. Initially the person comes to visit and is shown around. Then they may stay for a meal and with time they may stay overnight. Transition and change are often difficult for the residents, whether they have moved from home or from another unit. Often there is a trial before the person officially moves in.

This can also be difficult for the people already living there, with some being quite resistant to change. Furthermore, there is a certain paradox in regard to accepting more residents, as giving someone the opportunity to move from residential to supported living simply serves to increase the number of people in the houses, thus creating more of a congregated setting-type situation. On saying that, while a congregated setting is defined as ten people or more, this model is two separate housing units, which, although interlinked, cannot absolutely be defined as a congregated setting.

On a day-to-day basis the routines are, as far as practicable, based around the wants and needs of the service user. People often rise between 7a.m. and 9a.m. during the week and at whatever time they choose at the weekend. Some go to work, some go to day services; others visit friends, do shopping, go for walks, go swimming or whatever chores or appointments they may have that day. Everyday cleaning tasks and chores are assigned to different residents. On evenings and weekends people who are friends meet up, others go out, do laundry, clean their rooms, rest, watch TV – whatever they wish. Those who rely on staff for support in accessing the community are accompanied wherever they would like to go. The full-time staff member and the residents living there monitor day-to-day issues such as room decoration, maintenance requirements, help with clothes shopping (where required), etc. If there are any birthday parties these are celebrated with family and friends, if the person wishes to do so, with the staff helping to put preparations in place.

What is my role?

The greatest thing that I must remind myself as a social care worker is that the less you do, the better opportunities you afford to those living there. This is something of a struggle – social care work is not about providing care, it is about enabling people to do what they can for themselves as this is their own home environment. Of course there are always duties in this type of model – report writing, medication checks, stock checks, cleaning and so forth – and the residents who require assistance are facilitated. I must ensure that all residents are accounted for every day.

Administratively, there is a communication book to leave notes for other staff, a diary of appointments, an address book of relevant contact numbers, fire safety records and other information necessary (person-centred plans, etc.) aimed to maintain the wellbeing of the residents. There are monthly meetings and links with management of the service as required. The residents pop into the office on a very regular basis: some tell me when they are home; others wish to discuss their day or inform staff of various upcoming events.

On the whole I have found this model of supported living to favour the service user, with staff present when and where required, facilitating people to live independently albeit in a relatively large setting. Fourteen people live there and for that to 'work', staff need to ensure that everything runs smoothly and that the health and wellbeing of those living there is monitored where essential. I should also add that the dedicated full-time staff in place have greatly influenced the success of such a model of care, as their priority is each individual resident and, from what I have seen (albeit on a part-time basis), no need has gone unmet.

The key point is that some people would wish to continue with this model of community, with this level of support. Does removing this option really facilitate choice?

'It's not for everyone'

I have argued that as a model of care such supported living in two houses linked by an apartment with a staff member present has many advantages. To be realistic, we must acknowledge that it is not for everyone. As in any situation where people live with one another, personalities can clash, which can make it difficult for the persons involved and for others living there. There can be a certain lack of space; although, that said, in this set-up, with two sitting rooms, residents often sit together in one of those sitting rooms, while other residents prefer some alone time in their bedroom, which has a TV. For people who prefer time alone, it is not a model of best practice. But others appear to thrive on having company, the staff to link in with and speak with regularly, and have made lifelong friendships with others.

So what about people who wish to move on to a smaller housing unit?

A MODEL OF TRANSITION FOR INDEPENDENT LIVING IN THE COMMUNITY?

Contrary to the CSR, which states that people should be able to 'make their own choices and to get the personal supports they need for their independence', there is a lack of available options. People who have not worked with people with intellectual disabilities might read the CSR and presume that it is an easy path to follow – and, indeed, that we should give people the choice to control their own life and living arrangements.

Nevertheless, it takes a large amount of work and time to support a person with an intellectual disability to move on to a house of their own. Depending on cognitive function, it may be challenging, as although independent living skills are encouraged in a model of housing such as this, it can be hard for each individual to learn and perform all tasks. Also, you cannot train people to improve their intellectual abilities; it may be difficult for them to learn independent living skills or deal with certain situations, and they may need staff present. As staff you can only endeavour to empower, to teach and encourage life skills so that people can lead self-directed lives. From experience as a social care worker I know that many unexpected issues arise from day to day that may require intervention by staff, for example verbal disputes; misunderstanding labels/instructions; fear of change or of the unknown; filling out application forms such as that for the medical card; a lack of knowledge and understanding of health issues – even, for example, anxieties over upcoming blood tests. The list is lengthy and differs with each person.

One person who moved on in recent years fully achieved, over time, independent living with the support of staff and management and maintained contact with the service. While they could self-reliantly deal with day-to-day issues, this person in due course faced isolation and loneliness in their new accommodation and as their health deteriorated they chose to move to sheltered accommodation. The benefits of sheltered accommodation (just as in the model outlined) are numerous, with security and having a person to call for support being two of the key characteristics. The fact that the CSR recommends 'dispersed housing' may result in a worrying trend of isolation and loneliness, which is what some older people are fighting against – as the ALONE campaign's posters say, 'Old age isn't a problem – loneliness is.'

While I was preparing this chapter I spoke to a co-worker who, along with management, has taken on the role of providing training to those who currently wish to move on to their own living arrangements and require an extra layer of support. Given the plans outlined in the CSR and Article 19 of the CRPD (which Ireland has signed), it would appear natural to expect a certain level of training and support to be made available for people with disabilities who wish to live independently. From the experience of my co-worker, this is not in the case. Her biggest challenge has been to source information and training on independent living. The only course she could apply for was specifically for people with physical and sensory disabilities, and so the applications put forward were denied. As she said:

Social Care Worker Three

'Having worked within the intellectual disability services for a number of years I believe that a shift in ethos towards independent living is very positive. But on a practical level during the current economic downturn there is a serious lack of housing options available for those with intellectual disabilities. There is an extremely long waiting list for council housing and the social housing option seems equally unattainable.

'I am currently attempting to complete an independent living programme. But I have come across many obstacles along the way. There is no national structured independent living course available. Each disability service seems to have compiled their own course. And trying to access information from other services is very difficult. Services are reluctant to share information. A more cohesive attitude needs to develop where all services need to work more closely together to ensure that independent living becomes a more viable option for the future.'

My co-worker also noted that some people who require training may not be able to read and write confidently, thus posing a greater challenge to support than those learning through text, and more picture-based learning may be required. She also acknowledges that no one standardised training programme should exist per se, as individual requirements are different in each case. However, it would be helpful if there were adequate training resources and housing options easily available for those who wish to move on.

CONCLUSION

This chapter has outlined a model of supportive housing with background on policy/practice to offer social care workers an idea of the issues in the field. My advice is to keep up to date with publications such as those listed earlier in the chapter, as we should be fighting against policies that are not given the resources for implementation. We also need to remind ourselves of the importance of human rights.

We should remember that we are not nurses and that the greatest strength of a social care worker is to stand back and discover what a person can do for themselves. This is no easy task, as behind it all there is a duty of care involved. One must gain experience and knowledge and the ability to risk assess, manage and intervene in situations; we must learn reflection and reflexivity. This is why social care courses often emphasise personal development to facilitate a greater awareness of one's self.

It is only by working in the field of social care that we become aware of the practicalities and realities on the ground. At times we need to challenge the government-set agenda when policy does not link to practice. As a social care worker I've realised that this is 'my thing'. You too will find your own 'place' in social care – this will influence what area you wish to work in, who you would like to work beside and your level of satisfaction with the job.

Presumption is lethal. This chapter has taken only one example of a setting that works, but we still need to acknowledge that individual needs are never the same. A positive change is coming, in fully recognising the rights of people with disabilities, but a lot needs to be done and, more important, resource options and support need to be made available if we are going to fully achieve Article 19 of the CRPD and the plans for community living outlined in the CSR.

Chapter 10
The Stranger in the Mirror

Dealing with Dementia in the Intellectual Disability Sector

Iseult Paul

PATHWAY TO SOCIAL CARE

My path into social care is a strange one and it kind of happened by accident. I remember being asked in school what I wanted to do when I grew up. My reply was 'An air hostess'; this always makes me laugh now, because I do not like flying and avoid it when I can.

I left school at an early age without any formal qualifications. I had sat some of my Intermediate Certificate exams (the equivalent to today's Junior Cert). I was not surprised that I failed and I still remember that on the day I collected my results, the principal held out the envelope to me, and as I went to take it from her she let it fall to the ground. I still remember her words: 'I never expected any better from you.' At the time I was fifteen years old.

The only way to describe secondary school is that it was an 'experience'. The three years I spent there taught me a lot: unfortunately, though, very little of it was academic. As a result of my experiences there I became more resilient regarding how I allowed others to treat me. It was not all bad – I made new friends and I did enjoy some aspects of it.

So I was fifteen and had finished school with no qualifications. I had signed up to do a secretarial course, but while I really enjoyed learning to type I did not enjoy the rest of the course, so I left. My employment career began and social care was far from the equation.

I grew up in a family of printers; my Dad used to say that we all had ink running through our veins instead of blood. Everyone in the family had been involved in some way or another in the printing business. I guess as soon as I could reach a table I had been involved too. By the time I left school my father was doing some work for a relative who owned his own printing company and he brought me to work with him. I think the rationale for this was to ensure that I would have something to do during the day, I would earn money and then (Dad being Dad) I would get a trade. So I began training as a small offset lithographer, and my Dad became my instructor, mentor, trainer and colleague. It was a wonderful experience working with him as I got to know him as a man, not just as Dad. I trained and qualified as a small offset printer and moved on to another printing company.

In 1991 I gave up working full time as my one-year-old son had become very ill. We were told that he probably would not see his first birthday, and we were lucky to share ten birthdays with him. Most of those ten years were spent in a Dublin children's hospital. What an experience that was. The staff and children of the hospital became family to us and the time spent there was a valuable lesson. The children, particularly those with long-term illnesses, were often dependent on the staff, not just for their medical needs but for their social, emotional, educational and spiritual needs. Every staff member had a role to play in meeting the needs of the children, from the kitchen staff on the bottom floor all the way up to the top surgeons and consultants, and the priest.

Many people who work in health and social care come into it as a result of their own personal life experiences. Life experiences can shape our attitudes and perceptions, our values and beliefs and as a social care worker this can influence the approach taken to practice. For example, my life experience as a service-using parent of a vulnerable child provided me with an approach to practice from the individual and from the family perspectives.

Life experience has taught me that vulnerable people can rely, either somewhat or totally, on others, and those who support them are very influential and important in their lives. The children who spent long periods of time in the hospital were very resilient, considering what they had to endure; they were also very resourceful, for example finding out what staff were on night duty so they could phone them and get them to bring in their favourite food.

During those ten years I became involved in a voluntary capacity in my community. A friend got me involved in running some activities for the local children during mid-term breaks. This then led to us forming a committee and organising an annual children's summer project. As a result of an identified need in the first year we re-opened a youth club in the local community centre.

When my son passed away I considered returning to work, but I did not want to return to printing and did not really know what I wanted to do. I applied for a course as a legal secretary, and when I told a friend she laughed, and gave me the number for a day care centre that provided support to adults with physical disabilities. I contacted them and soon after began working there on a part-time basis. On my first day I met a gentleman who was sitting in his wheelchair, and I noticed that there was a computerised communication device attached to the chair. I was familiar with these types of communication device, known as AACs (augmentative alternative communication), as my son and some of his friends had used similar devices. The first thing this gentleman said to me was, 'My name is Michael. My body is disabled but my mind is not.' This reminded me that it is so important to see the person first and the disability second.

During the two years I worked there, I did a lot of training; I even learned to drive a minibus. It was while I was working in the day centre that I returned to education, nearly thirty-two years after I had left. It had never been my intention to go back to education and it sort of happened by accident – needless to say my family were in shock when I told them. One of my colleagues had been given a place on a FETAC accredited community care course but had declined it. I was asked if I would like to avail of the course and I thought, 'Sure, why not?' I did the course part time over two years and surprised myself when I passed with distinction. I guess I wasn't stupid after all. One of the tutors in the college suggested I go on to college to study social care. I was not too sure of this but went to Blanchardstown Institute of Technology for an open evening and subsequently became a student in the very first course in social care at the Institute.

I had considered asking for a part-time job in one of the local shops and the centre manager at the time laughed and gave me the number of an agency. This agency sent me to do a six-hour shift in a private nursing home and I continued to work in the nursing home for a number of years. The nursing home was a private facility and the patients were all male.

In my second year of college I went on a three-month practice placement to a residential setting that provided a service for individuals with an intellectual disability. The residential home was part of a larger organisation that provides a range of services to people with an intellectual disability in Dublin. A couple of days before I was due to go on placement I had doubts and was pretty nervous. I had spoke about this with one of my lecturers and told her that I did not think it was for me. She advised me to try it as it was only for three months and at least I would be able to make an informed decision about career choices by the end of the placement. When my placement finished I joined that organisation's relief panel.

My first shift as an employee of the organisation was in a day service that provides support to over sixty men and women with a mild to moderate intellectual disability. While I completed my degree on a full-time basis, I worked relief there, at the same time continuing to work in the nursing home. A short time later I secured a permanent position and have worked there for eight years. This chapter is based on my work in the day service and in particular working with the challenges of an ageing population. My approach to working with dementia has evolved over time and is based on my previous experiences inside and outside traditional care environments.

DON'T MENTION THE D WORD!

In my current work environment we do not like to mention the 'D' word – dementia. We generally refer to it as 'memory loss'.

It would seem that there is not just one illness or condition that is called dementia. According to the Alzheimer's Society, 'dementia' is generally an umbrella term that can describe a number of conditions that affect the brain. The condition people are probably most familiar with is Alzheimer's, but other conditions are dementia with Lewy bodies (DLB), Pick's disease, Creutzfeldt-Jakob disease (CJD), vascular dementia and frontal lobe dementia. Dementia is a progressive and terminal condition and it affects individuals differently.

My first ever encounter with memory loss was when my friend and I used to 'ditch' school to go and visit her granny in hospital – I guess I was about twelve or thirteen at the time. We would go and sit with her and give her soft jellies to eat and basically keep her company. I did not like where she was; it was an old building with lots of patients sitting in large chairs on their own. Sometimes she seemed happy to see us, but it was clear that she did not know us. Initially I did not understand why she called her granddaughter by the wrong name, but my friend explained that she thought she was her daughter. My friend would talk to her and tell her all about the family and give her lots of reassurance, comb her hair and hold her hand. Sometimes we just sat with her in silence.

When I began working in the nursing home nearly twenty years later I still did not know an awful lot about memory loss. When I first began working there one gentleman would talk about his life growing up and about his father who had taught him to swim. This man was very quiet and reserved but he loved music and would play the harmonica. There was a piano in the lobby and the two of us would spend some time on a Saturday playing some of his favourite songs.

I noticed that when I brought him from his room to the bathroom he would always stop at the doorway, put his foot out and tap the ground. This would happen when he went from any room to another and when leaving the building to go for a walk in the garden. It was strange because once he was through the doorway he would walk around without too much difficulty. I thought he had a problem with his eyesight and I always ensured he had his glasses on. I was told he had been diagnosed with dementia. Over time he started to need more support with his daily living and he spent more time alone. When I assisted him with his shower he would become very rigid and it was difficult to help him wash and dress. I would chat and offer gentle encouragement to him but he looked as if he had been scared half to death. I would constantly talk to him about the things he had shared with me about growing up, which I thought would help his memory and give him reassurance. One morning I was chatting away to him and he said, 'Will you ever shut up?' I had performed a miracle, according to some of the other residents, as he had not spoken for weeks.

He eventually stopped playing the harmonica but I continued to play his songs for him. Sometimes he would sing some of the words; other times he would just listen. The music seemed to bring back memories for him because on occasion I would see a tear in his eye. Over time he became more isolated and fully dependent on staff for support. I continued to reminisce with him in a gentle way, being conscious not to overload him with too much information. Sometimes we would look at old photographs or listen to his favourite music.

The next encounter was with a gentleman who was ninety-three. In the evenings before he retired to bed he would ask if his mother was coming to visit him. Some staff would tell him that his mother was dead and remind him of his age. The man would get terribly upset, almost go into shock, get agitated, wave his walking stick around and refuse to go to bed. I am not one for telling people I work with untruths, but I never saw the point of telling a ninety-three-year-old that his mother was dead. The man was having difficulty with his memory and each time he heard this it was as though he was hearing it for the first time. When he asked if his mother was coming in, I would tell him that I would check the book when I finished helping him to get ready for bed. I would return with his cup of tea a short while later and he would have forgotten all about his mother. On the rare occasion he asked again, I would tell him that his mother's name was not in the book, so she would not be in that evening. This always seemed to satisfy him; it prevented unnecessary stress, and it also reduced the need for medication.

When I began working in my current place of work, the 'D' word – memory problems – was not really an issue. As previously mentioned, the people I work with have a mild to moderate intellectual disability, and a large group of them have a diagnosis of Down's syndrome. As with the general population, anyone with an intellectual disability can develop 'memory loss'. However, it would appear that someone who has Down's syndrome can be more vulnerable to developing Alzheimer's disease and the progression through the different stages is usually much quicker. Diagnosis can also take longer, which may be due to communication difficulties or because the current assessment tools are not sensitive enough. According to the Alzheimer's Society's website, studies have shown that the number of individuals with Down's syndrome who have Alzheimer's disease are approximately one in fifty aged 30–39 years, one in ten aged 40–49 years, one in three aged 50–59 years and over half aged over 60 years.

I work as part of a team where many of the members have a long-term relationship with the men and women we support. More recently, as a team we have become very sensitive to 'memory loss'. We have experienced the loss of several people in our unit in the last two years who had developed Alzheimer's. We have a small number of people who have recently been diagnosed, a number of others who are experiencing some issues and we are very aware that we have a large number of people in their late forties to mid-fifties with Down's syndrome as well as an ageing population in general.

As a team we have had to educate ourselves about how to support people in a different way. This also involves supporting families and the other people attending the day service who are watching their friends lose their memory, and naturally wondering if they are next. We have also had to learn how to support ourselves emotionally as a team as we lose people to this terrible disease.

The place where I work is a large building with many rooms, and a large number of people, which means a large volume of stimulation and noise. People with 'memory loss' can become easily disorientated, lose interest in activities that they would have enjoyed in the past, develop difficulty with depth perception, develop changes in their sleeping pattern, experience isolation and a general deterioration in their daily living skills (see the Alzheimer's Society's Fact Sheet 401 for further symptoms).

These changes are what we as a team watch out for and there appear to be some similar patterns in the people we support. For example, small issues began to emerge for a number of individuals who travelled independently, such as one man leaving the building early, and returning a short while later because had forgotten a bag. Now, anyone can be a bit forgetful at times, but when this is a recurring issue it raises concerns. Another concern is when someone begins arriving into work much later than normal and cannot account for where they have been, or when others report that there were safety issues.

When this occurs there are a number of interventions and strategies that we use. Naturally if someone is travelling independently and there are safety issues they must be addressed immediately. No one wants to stop someone travelling independently, as this has wider consequences for their participation in the community and social life, so it is important that we don't jump to conclusions; and we are lucky to have a multidisciplinary team as support. We aim to take a holistic approach to dealing with any issues. Gaining information is important and it can help to investigate or rule out other factors that may be contributing to changes in behaviour. Maybe people are not sleeping well and are a little tired, or maybe there is a physical problem that is causing confusion, so a full medical is conducted. The psychologist conducts an assessment with the individual but also with the staff and family members to identify any changes. The psychiatrist will also get involved and the social worker will do a home visit. As assessments and diagnosis can take time, the staff team assesses the individual's safety. One member of the team will shadow the individual concerned on a number of occasions, put in training if required and then re-assess by shadowing again. Where there are safety issues and the individual is no longer safe to travel independently, alternative arrangements are made.

DAILY PRACTICE ISSUES

Some of the issues we have are environmental, such as the floor coverings throughout the building. For example, the canteen is tiled with two different-coloured tiles and this caused a problem for one person in particular who was experiencing difficulty with depth perception. She would stop when the colour changed, and she would go around the tiles. Then, when she reached the doorway of the bathroom, the floor covering was entirely different – it is non-slip covering and is a different colour. Going from the main room to the exit, the hallway is carpeted; then the doorway to the minibus caused great difficulty. She required lots of reassurance and support. One way of doing this was ensuring that members of the staff team with whom she had a long-established relationship and whom she trusted would assist her. They would walk with her, hold her hand, and talk her through the different transitions. Staff would speak to her calmly and offer clear direction. It was important that she was allowed the time to test the changes with her foot and feel confident. Initially one staff member supported her, then two, and eventually health and safety determined the need for transfers on and off her minibus by wheelchair. Following an assessment with an occupational therapist and physiotherapist, it was then determined that she required a wheelchair while she was in the unit, to reduce her anxiety and also for her safety.

Another concern is that some individuals have difficulty when eating lunch, for example eating out of sequence, eating at the wrong time, or forgetting they have eaten and as a result constantly feeling hungry. Others have problems with feeding themselves as they cannot distinguish between the plate and the tablecloth. Designating a staff member every morning to support the individuals with memory issues is how we try to ensure that they are having their needs met and are engaged in activities, but also that they are safe. An individual with memory issues can put themselves in danger, for example if they are unable to recognise a potentially harmful situation. They can also create difficult situations for themselves, for example clearing tables when others have not finished eating, eating food that does not belong to them, telling others to go away or being physically or verbally abusive to others.

Being aware of what the individual liked in the past is a way of helping them to engage in previously enjoyed activities and keeping to their routine. However, if the activities become stressful for them they should not be put under any pressure to participate. Someone who enjoyed doing an art class in the past may find group work too stimulating and distressing, and one of the ways of overcoming this is for the individual to do art in a quieter space, perhaps at the other end of the room or away from the group altogether.

Orienting people in the morning is a way of creating a sense of awareness of surroundings; in the hallway we have a large board with the day, the month, the year and the season on it so that people can check it on their way into the building. Visual symbols and pictures that people are familiar with are an excellent way to support people with memory loss. Placing a photograph at the table where a person sits, or on a locker, can help them and it can also help unfamiliar staff or their friends to support them. Having a small visual timetable that a person carries with them can help them remember what they are doing that day. Taking a picture of the person doing the activity is a good way of helping them remember that it is something they like.

Creating life story or memory books is an intervention that can prove useful for people with memory loss. It is important that these are done as early as possible and they should ideally be made before people start experiencing memory problems. Participation in the creation of memory books ensures that favourite pictures, words, and special memories for the individual are included. The books should have pictures of the person, family members and friends, important people and events that have occurred over the person's life. It is important to include pictures from when they were young as the person with memory issues may not see themselves at the age they are now; they may see themselves as much younger. I recently met a lady with memory issues who had a photograph of herself and her father. She could point out her 'Daddy' in the photograph, but did not recognise herself in the picture. She carried the picture with her everywhere and it was obviously very important to her. It is a good idea for support staff to make a copy of important photographs in case anything happens to them. Included in the books should also be what the person likes or dislikes. For example, one lady I made a book for wore false teeth and carried a handbag, and these were very important to her and she would get very distressed if she misplaced either of them. The same lady loved a glass of Guinness and liked to have a glass while she was watching the television or if she went to a party. This was information that other people needed to be aware of. Another lady liked the colour pink, and trousers with a stripe on them; she loved music and had a favourite artist. When she was no longer independent this information was important for those who were supporting her to help her dress and put on her music.

REFLECTION

Schön (1983) talks about reflection *in* action and reflection *on* action. Sometimes situations require us to draw on our previous experiences and we do it almost without thinking. This may be because we have experienced something similar before and used strategies that worked for us at that time. Reflection on action comes later, when consideration is given to interventions that have or have not been successful. Kolb's experiential learning cycle is similar in that reflection and analysis occurs as a result of experiences and then action plans are created (Morrison 2001).

Before I started my degree course a friend of mine said to me, 'You are the tools you bring to your job.' This is something I try to pass on to the social care students I supervise on practice placements. Social care workers are not like other tradespeople who might take the necessary tools from their toolbox to solve a problem: we *are* our toolbox. We rely not only on our academic knowledge but also on our experiences.

My first encounter with memory loss taught me the importance of knowing what the person likes, but, more important, sometimes it is fine just to be present and not say anything. It is upsetting for families and loved ones to be forgotten, so they need support. It is also important to remember that they are the people who have important information about what their loved one likes or dislikes.

THE MIRROR

Listening to people is vital in social care as it is how we form relationships with those we work with. Understanding what is important, either past or present, in people's lives can help individuals to reminisce. Playing favourite music or talking about old photographs can help people to remember and it can also have a calming effect. I recently watched a video that showed an individual with dementia looking into a mirror and what was looking back was unfamiliar to him; and I realised that when I assisted the man in the nursing home to shower he may have become rigid because of the mirror that was directly facing him in the shower room. The poor man was probably terrified that there was a stranger in the room with him. When a person with memory loss looks into a mirror they may see a familiar face, such as a family member, or they may see someone they do not recognise at all and become afraid. If I were to go back a few years to when I worked in the nursing home, I would cover that mirror. It is something I consider in my current practice as all the bathrooms have large mirrors in them.

Having empathy and understanding that memory loss is just that will help prevent unnecessary stress to individuals. Reassurance and distraction are tools that are very useful in supporting individuals with memory loss. If an individual with considerable memory loss asks a question and you know the answer is going to cause distress, it is best to be a little bit creative with the answer.

Environmental factors can cause a great deal of stress: for example, people with poor depth perception and who have difficulty with different-coloured flooring may not visit the bathroom because it is too stressful and they may be incontinent as a result. Unfortunately, where I work the building is so large it would cost a fortune to change all the flooring, but it is definitely something to consider.

Loud noises, too much stimulation and large environments can be distressing for people with memory loss. Too many people talking at once, or being approached from behind can be distressing. Approaching people from the front and speaking in a clear, calm and concise manner is more efficient. Smiling at the person always works well.

Adapting the environment to the individual can be difficult, but there are small things that can be done that can have a big impact. Making sure there is finger food around the room can help with eating. Using visual prompts can help with orientation and memory. Memory books, life story books and other types of book can help share important information as well as helping with memory. Knowing what the person likes or dislikes can help support them in a creative way. For example, a person who likes pink and is not drinking can be encouraged to drink if the drink is put in a pink cup. It is difficult to adapt a situation to everyone's needs, especially in a large day service, and no one solution will be suitable for everyone. Solutions or interventions need to be person-specific, for example having a clock with large numbers may help when orienting a person regarding time, but it might be unsuitable for someone who never had the skill of reading time, and can cause more distress.

One of the most important things to consider in social care is the relationship you have with the people you support. When you have a good relationship with the person, you can identify any changes that occur, so when people start to isolate themselves from their peers, or when they start behaving a little strangely, forgetting things and getting disoriented it will be noticed and the correct supports and interventions can be introduced.

It is also important to remember that looking after people with memory issues can be stressful and emotional for staff. It is important that staff teams provide support to one another as well as the individuals they support.

My Dad always said, 'The school of life teaches us many things', and I have learned much from all my different experiences, but does that make me a better social care worker? I hope so – otherwise I should reconsider my career choice. I have learnt from personal and professional experiences and I use them in my daily practice. I continue to learn and develop my knowledge and experience, and I guess that will continue throughout my life.

Chapter 11
It's All About The 'I'

Self-understanding in Social Care Practice

Frank Mulville

LEARNING FROM A CHILD

We can only change ourselves, and part of how we do this is by understanding our reactions to the projections of others. The children and young people who are cared for in various care settings by social care workers have been dreadfully hurt, neglected or both. The experience of abuse can be physical, sexual, being uncared for, taunted, traumatised by seeing people important to them being hurt, being blamed or held responsible for all that was going wrong for the adults in their lives. And it is in these settings that social care workers operate, often as part of a multidisciplinary team. It goes without saying that such work is really difficult and at times very painful, with the children and young people in care having very confused, unrealistic, anxious and fearful expectations of us, the adults who are charged with looking after them.

I know that all this is self-evident; however, it is not always in the forefront of our minds as workers. Understandably, at times, when some young person is talking about how painful their life is and recalling the events that caused them that pain, we are listening with our ears and our emotions, paying as much attention to them as is possible. Yet again, when another young person is screaming abuse at us and threatening physical hurt, spitting, or threatening self-harm, our hearing is mixed with anxiety and the question quickly arises, 'Is it to be fight or flight?' Or maybe something else is possible.

> This struck me when I and a very supportive colleague were walking to the cinema with a small group of children. We were walking on a public street in Dublin and one of the children walked about five paces behind us, spitting at me, calling me names, and every time I tried to calm him down, and keep calm myself, it was in front of an audience of hundreds. He taunted me and got the upper hand. The child's behaviour

was much more offensive and angry than usual. I was embarrassed, angry and feeling revulsion at the spitting (he got me with one of them). I felt some people on the street thought I looked like a useless father – but how were they to know who I was? – so I had to deal with shame as an emotion as well as everything else. I wanted to go back to the children's centre, but the other three children and my colleague wanted to go to the cinema, so we carried on. This continued until we got to the cinema and as the children really wanted to see the film, the agitated child calmed down just in sight of the 'pitchur house', and in we went.

I was left exhausted and carrying all the feelings of the journey. I didn't enjoy the film, but they loved it. I was thinking of the journey back and the child in question was engrossed in a cartoon. The journey back was full of the film, and I spent every step waiting for the whole thing to start again, but it didn't.

I felt angry, disempowered, silly, to name a few emotions, and relieved that the group had settled for while in the cinema. My colleague spoke with me and wondered how I had kept my cool. She told me I had been quiet, calm and hadn't 'risen to the bait'. This was not at all what I thought I was. Thinking of this years later, I wondered how really distressed that child must have been in his life to have managed that walk to the cinema like that, feeling he had to control me all the way there. That was what it was – I felt controlled by the child needing to be in charge of the journey on terms he understood. But what did it elicit in me, the powerless adult, embarrassed in front of people, feeling inadequate, feeling punished? If fight or flight are normal reactions to distress I could do neither, would do neither, so simply had to manage myself through it. What did the child get? The cinema? A discharge of aggression and frustration?

In later years I got to understand that any person who needs to behave in the way he did really has suffered, and my job was to survive the attack and not behave as the child (unconsciously) expected me to. What did I get from that experience? I got to know that what is done to me by some of the children I have worked with tells me what may have been done to them. Most important, I need to know what I am feeling, why I am feeling it and, if I am fortunate, have the support of good colleagues who can help me.

Experiencing being bombarded or blamed is difficult and painful. We do not relish that pain or discomfort and so we can close down. For me, the thought of having to go back to a young person who had berated and shouted at me for an hour is not one to relish. Yet that is one of the responses children in care may need, to know that they did not annihilate the adult. The proper response can change their sense of self-worth and reduce their sense of omnipotent destructiveness.

LEARNING FROM COLLEAGUES

Yet again, we can become defensive, self-protective and cautious, with colleagues from within and without our service having conflicting or rejecting opinions of our work. This can happen at team meetings, multidisciplinary team meetings or case conferences. Our reactions in such situations can close down the openness needed to actually work effectively with the children and young people in our care.

Watching a colleague, and a very skilled one, fall into a defensive outburst in a meeting (at which there were professionals other than social care workers present), my defence was to just go quiet, to become 'invisible', as they lost their clarity and focus. This was really difficult for me. More difficult was not being able to support that colleague, help them out. Looking around the room at the group and seeing the power dynamics, I realised that we too can return to a childlike state, to a stage in our lives that we are reminded of by a current situation. It is important to know that this does not just happen with the children in our care – it can happen with ourselves.

One of those in the room had made an angry critical comment about a piece of work. The person criticised said they felt undermined. The other person said that was not what they meant, but the music behind the words was angry. The atmosphere felt unsafe and my colleague and I really felt undermined. Then a sophisticated conversation of diverting away from the core issue of conflict left everyone fighting to find a 'safe corner'. We, the social care workers present, felt like the lowest-status people in the room as others in the group focused on our practice, because it was the easiest thing to do. There was, as it were, an unintentional 'curve ball' thrown and we, the social care workers, took it and we left the meeting without challenging it.

Afterwards, we discussed it with our team's consultant and realised what had happened. So instead of the usual angry blaming of 'others' we got to understand what had happened and the reactions to it. We learned that if you feel attacked or put upon, pause, look where it is coming from, pause again, and choose your response. Put back into the room the feelings that are floating around, and maybe name them. Phrases like 'I think some people are unhappy about something', 'Can we look at that again?', or 'I think something really important is being said here' can be helpful and non-aggressive.

Group work is a key skill in social care and we use it all the time. Maybe we can use that same skill in multidisciplinary meetings, to address the tasks and help manage the emotions that may be projected into the room or onto us and which may affect us deeply.

In our work we focus on the change needed for, by and in the young person or child, and this is a valid hope. However, I do not believe we can change anyone else; imagine deciding that our manager, the JLO, teacher or social worker should change their behaviour or actions and that it was a compulsory requirement for continuing in their role. We may well feel that to be the case at times, but we cannot and would not attempt to enforce it. The vulnerable people with whom we work are no different.

LEARNING FROM ONE'S 'SELF'

We can only work to change ourselves. This includes caring for and valuing ourselves, and part of that caring is understanding our reactions to others; seeing where the feelings originate, maybe in our family, school, etc. Separating what belongs to us as opposed to what belongs to those we are dealing with, whether children or colleagues, can be very helpful. We need to keep asking ourselves questions and this can help us focus. I didn't feel angry before I met them ... I wonder were they angry? Did I act out their anger? I came into work today in great form; why did I feel miserable or powerless after the handover meeting? Did that interaction with the young man or woman spark off an old distressing memory, something unfinished or unresolved in me? What happened to me during the conversation? Why did I become quiet and subdued, and is that why the young person became angry? Did they pick up on my discomfort? Was a parent sometimes like that and they had to defend themselves from attack because the discomfort turned to drink and then violence?

On many occasions we are faced with an immediate situation that needs sorting out: 'He has to understand that he can't do that ... he needs a sanction.' Rather than a reflective approach, this can at times be the last resort of the offended and powerless worker. Not at all easy, but this is the daily reality for social care workers.

We need to go back to the beginning. The children and young people are in care because the world, their community and their family cannot care for them, and they have poor skills of understanding and expressing their hurt; some may never develop those skills. We as workers are in the centres they live in because we applied for a job, convinced an interview panel to employ us and are paid a salary. Not just that, though, hopefully: we want to care professionally for these children and make a difference in their troubled lives. We are the people who make the adult choice.

In the context of the above we need to look after ourselves, and so do our employers. Here, as I hope I've made clear, I think a key piece is understanding our own behaviour and reactions. And from that, learning what happens to us while caring for confused and hurt people. We are also hurt, and I do not mean this in the philosophical/spiritual sense alone. Most of us have been hurt or damaged in some way in our lives and this leaves residues of distress within us. These distressing elements are more visible to people who are very hurt because they have to be on their guard constantly and will see, sense or expose our vulnerability for their own protection. They do this, not for any vindictive reason, but in order to be able to manage and understand their relationship with you or me. Most likely, this will be on an unconscious or subconscious level. So they may not even know they are doing anything. Hence 'What the fuck did I do?'

In social care safety is a key concept, and I think it is Bowlby who says that adventures begin from a safe place. So this also applies to workers' development and reflection. We need safe places and safe relationships to explore our own hurt and how it impacts on our work.

So why should we open up old areas of hurt, remind ourselves of being bullied in the yard, embarrassed in front of our friends, seeing our parents row, or losing our mother or father too young, or being assaulted by a so-called trusted adult? The list is long and varies from person to person.

I think there are two main reasons. First, professional: we are all working as therapists/healers of some sort and use relationships as one of the means to help young people grow through distress and realise their dreams. If we clutter up these relationships with our own pain and with the way in which we defend ourselves, we may be blocking the healing we seek to offer. Because of this, the young person enters into a confused relationship with us, where our focus might well be defensiveness. As a result they may lose the chance to gain useful insights into themselves by having an open and attentive adult who knows their own 'buttons' and is able to contain them, a worker who is not to be diverted into anxiety or judgement and has the capacity to tolerate the young person's pain, blame or whatever else. In other words, to stay with them, and help them feel safe enough to think as well as feel. We must be clear on the work of the moment.

I would suggest that two or three in the morning at the end of a long day is not a good time to do this. We often say more than we should, because of tiredness and maybe a sense of camaraderie, grown of a crisis well managed.

I worked as part of team of four men, and our 'self care' after a very long shift was one of the best experiences in my early career. After the young people had settled to sleep, we would gather in the office, with tea or coffee, good sandwiches, the occasional cream cake, a deck of cards and an irreverent sense of humour. We grumbled for the first part of the conversation, then joked, then played cards (25s); we cheated, laughed, sometimes played table tennis and generally let go of the day's hassles. We supported each other when things had been difficult; we did not invade each others' private lives, open old wounds, or get into blaming.

In reality, we played – and we needed to; we had been in the company of very distressed young people; we were tired, overloaded by the work and we needed to clear our heads. We looked at the next day's work and then headed off to our rooms, with less stress and no regrets about having said too much.

The second reason, I believe, is that we all can benefit from learning more about ourselves. Most people love talking and when there is a good listener we can talk about ourselves with enthusiasm. (I realise I may be talking about myself here.) Working as we do with young people who are hurt and being exposed to their distress, anger, tantrums, violence, screaming sessions, etc., we can become tired and irritable. In some senses this is at times inevitable. However, we can reduce the impact on us of other people's issues and become more effective in our work, if we address our own needs and distress. If we know some of the ways in which we can be hurt, and learn how to deal with them without becoming overly defensive, they may have less of an impact on us. Why? Because we can differentiate between what is ours and what belongs to others.

I used to find anger a most difficult emotion to deal with in others, and still can find it difficult at times; but as a way of defending myself from it I developed the defence of laughing when I felt anger was present in a situation. This sometimes distracted the person who was angry and they were able to laugh with me about something neutral; at other times they became angrier (and maybe rightly so). While I can't think of a specific incident where it went wrong, I think that when we are caught up in a situation we find difficult and the person we expect to be sensitive to it makes an inappropriate response we can feel disappointed, annoyed or hurt. When we do this with a young person whose world is raw, and who has a tendency to act out rather than think, it can bring a very angry reaction. If we are going to laugh and introduce humour we need to think of the consequences, and pick our moment. Some are better than others at this.

As for me, I used laughter unconsciously; I didn't plan to do it. Supervision has been a safe place for me. Over the years I talked about this and learned that if I acknowledge that the desire to laugh is present, I may well be picking up anger (or at times not), but I have that split second to make an informed judgement. This meant that I could name the anger, be more appropriate with the young person, and by naming the presence of anger allow the young person the opportunity to speak their anger rather than act it out by, for example, throwing something. This has been very useful for me.

Another situation, and an area of great importance, that could cause me anxiety was visiting the homes of the parents of some of the children. I used to feel that they disliked me for somehow having taken their children from them, that they were angry or embarrassed in my company because of my role. Here again, in discussing this, I was helped to realise that it was a projection of my ambivalence at visiting them that was at play. It took time, but with that awareness I could begin to reduce my anxiety and pay more attention to the parents and begin to focus and be supportive; perhaps about plans for their son to return home, the purpose of the visit in the first place.

In our own lives away from work there can often be situations similar to those we encounter at work, whether that be with families, partners, spouses, parents or children. I do not believe that residential care is family life – it is not – but at times the dynamics can be intense in both and can have similarities. In our work teams we can fall into the roles we had in our family or with our childhood friends, in school, etc. Our teams can add to this too by encouraging us to continue to fulfil a role on the team, e.g. 'Best at writing reports – always has to write them'; 'Has a special rapport with a particular young person – he'll do it for you'; 'The minder'.

We need to separate our actual personality from that put on us by others. In teams staff members talk at times about the 'good relationships' or 'poor relationships' they have with children and young people, and this can be a source of competition and conflict in teams. While young people put expectations on us, or describe us as no good, or amazing, in most cases these are just 'transferences', misplaced expectations placed on us because we remind them of somebody in their lives. If we don't know this we are in danger of carrying these expectations with us and behaving in a way that is a mixture of the young person's expectation of us and our own defensive reaction to them.

> A young person I worked with told me in the company of another staff member that I reminded her of the teacher who used to hit her, and that she didn't like me because of that. I had only met her ten minutes beforehand. The other worker had the insight to say, 'But you know that is not him', to which the young person replied that she did. In that one sentence the other worker saved me months of grumpy comments from her and allowed us to get on with the work.

When we go home we have earned our time off, for ourselves, not just to be refreshed for the next shift, and we benefit from not having to carry the expectations of our work with us. Our partners and those we live with want to have time with us that is not always blurred by work; our children want the energy needed to play, to be listened to and minded. We need to be able to enjoy our home life by understanding how working relationships impact on us. Being less confused or exhausted by the sad expectations of the young people in our care; and being more in charge of our own emotions helps this. Home is home, work is work.

It is difficult enough work without making it more difficult by not knowing how our own biases impact on others, and how others impact on us. As workers we are entitled to good supervision, and when it is working well it is a really effective form of support; it allows us to examine our work, see what is happening to us. We would be missing the opportunity given to us by the people with whom we work if we did not learn and grow from our experience.

Chapter 12
Precious Cargo

Focusing as a Practice Approach

Derek McDonnell

INTRODUCTION

This chapter will reflect how I work as a social care worker and how I have utilised a process called focusing to help children to listen to their own inner wisdom and find their own answers and steps forward.

I have been working in the social care profession for twenty-two years. I spent fourteen years working in a child and adolescent mental health service in Lucena Clinic in Dublin, first in a residential treatment unit and then at St Peter's Special School on a social care team that helped young people address their own issues and stories in a therapeutic way.

I am currently working as a community social care leader in a child protection social work team in the Child and Family Agency (Tusla) Laois/Offaly area and my role is to offer therapeutic intervention to children and young people who are at significant risk due to their life stories.

Before discussing specific case studies, I wish to share a story that symbolises to me how I see my role as a community social care worker working day in, day out at the coal face.

PRECIOUS CARGO

The most precious cargo we have in our society is our children. They are the next generation of parents that will shape and form the elements of our society. On a lighter note, they will be picking our nursing homes for us in our old age, so beware!

Consider the analogy of a ship out on the ocean. On this ship is a precious cargo. First, it sets sail and all is well. As time goes by the climate changes, the atmosphere changes to the point where the storm comes and waves crash all round it, battering it from left and right. It survives for a time, until one day the storms become too powerful, too frequent. It crashes against the rocks and it is scuppered.

We all know that the external elements of the storm are beyond the control of the precious cargo. Often it is during the storm that our service is called upon to redress the situation. We attempt to board the ship, to stabilise it through this stormy period by offering various forms of intervention. Other times, though, with the ferocity and duration of the storms, the precious cargo gets thrown overboard, out of reach, and is lost.

However, the cargo may remain in the wreckage for a long time until it is so damaged that it needs to be removed from the shipwreck. The ship is no longer a safe base for the precious cargo and it needs to be rescued, taken to a safe place. For our damaged, shipwrecked children a care setting is and should be the safe place. This can sometimes be a relative's family home or an alternative care setting.

The children who have experienced the voyage on the ship have their own unique stories to tell. They experience trauma, a sense of loss, separation, abandonment, confusion, insecurity and uncertainty about their future and, indeed, their past. They head into the unknown, not knowing how things will unfold for them. And of course they can and will display many challenges in this safe environment. The damage and impact of the lived, deprived experience is still contained within the child as they arrive at their new living space. They board this new ship that sets sail and endeavours to offer a secure base, giving stability and hope. It is now paramount that the child is provided with the space and appropriate support that allows healing and recovery to unfold. Of equal importance is that the social care workers are given the support they need to manage, hold and nurture the child.

At any stage of the child's voyage, as a social care worker I can be asked to intervene and help them to journey with it, either within the family home or, often, in the transition into relative care/foster care or, less often, residential care.

This is where the process of focusing, which I have incorporated into my skill base, comes into play. Focusing is all about listening to children in a fresh and new way, and to their lived experiences of life. It opens up this possibility of listening for both the child and social care worker. It's not about huge changes; it's about small steps that help the quality of daily living to be somehow different, in a better way, for the children and for those with whom they share their living space.

WHAT IS FOCUSING AND WHAT DOES IT DO?

Focusing was discovered and developed in the late 1970s by Eugene Gendlin, who was a student and later a colleague of Carl Rogers. He carried out research into why it is that some people do better in therapy than others. From this research he discovered a process and developed a way to teach people to gain access to this natural process, which he called focusing.

There are a few key elements that are important to mention about this process that Gendlin developed (2007). It is an experiential process, whereby one pauses and pays attention internally to what he called the 'felt sense'. It is a process where you develop an inner dialogue with what is happening inside you in relation to any aspect of your life.

The images below show how you form a dialogue between yourself and your felt sense.

Figure 12.1

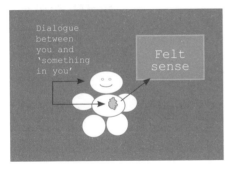 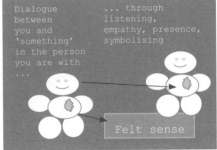

The felt sense is making contact with a special kind of internal bodily awareness.

1. It is usually vague at first: *fuzzy, unclear, indefinable, not immediately recognisable.*
2. It is not just there, but has to form. This usually takes thirty seconds or more.
3. It feels meaningful but not known.

To access a felt sense there are at least four entry points, starting with how 'it' feels in the body, what is the feeling or emotional quality that comes with that. An image or story will bubble up that helps the felt sense to form more fully. It will have connections with aspects of one's life.

4. To let it form, one must grow quiet and pay attention. If the answer comes too quickly it may be your mind talking, i.e. what you already know about

it – nothing wrong with that, but there has to be congruency, a match between thoughts and feelings. If not (e.g. the mind says: 'This really isn't such a big thing, you know', and the body says: 'Ugh, this feels terrible'), pay attention to what the body is saying. That is focusing.

Figure 12.2

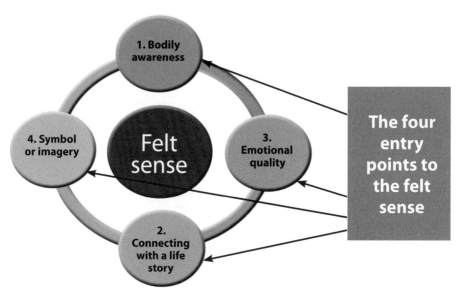

It is about connecting to:

1. **The body's felt sense** of a particular problem or issue (rather than the mind's interpretation of the same thing).
2. **Something in your life**.
3. A definite **quality** that fits, checks out, resonates with the feeling you have about it.
4. The **whole thing**: not just an emotion. It is always bigger, a holistic sense of the totality of the problem or issue.

For example: You are angry that you had a fight with John.

- Anger is an emotion.
- There's *more* to the anger, i.e. *a quality* of the anger. It includes all the fights you've had with John in the past about this very same thing, how it's always left you feeling, and how it feels right now – *all that, everything*.

You take time to check the quality behind the emotion (in your body). Is it: *tight, constricted, explosive, jittery? Like a squashed bug?* These are felt senses.

Can you see how much more there is to it than just anger?

It was Carl Rogers who developed the concept of positive unconditional regard, a quality that he encouraged therapists to hold for their clients. Following his research, Gendlin (2007) took this a step further and encouraged his clients to hold this quality, a caring presence inside, around whatever aspect of their life story they were processing.

It is a fundamental element of the focusing process to bring a sense of caring presence to whatever unfolds inside, holding the felt sense with a quality of compassion.

Figure 12.3

Creating this inside climate with and around your feelings somehow releases the potential energy that is contained within the felt sense to move towards rightness in the body. This allows the next step to emerge.

In creating this inner climate, you are allowing the flow of life within your inner places to unfold. Our inner experiences are contained at the edge of awareness. When our awareness is brought here, the 'more' of the story begins to unfold.

Figure 12.4

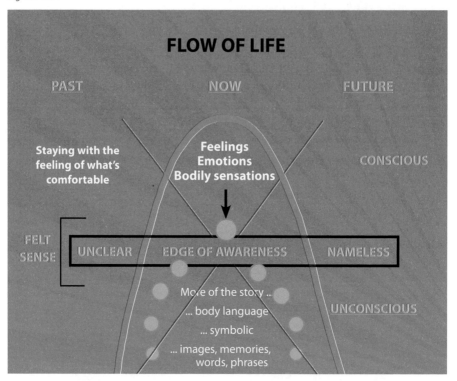

The 'more of the story' comes from our unconscious and begins to bubble up and up via the entry points: symbols, images, memories, words, colours, phrases, connections to one's life. It is the language of the body that the mind can understand; it has a sense of new insight or understanding contained within it. The possible next steps forward begin to emerge.

The six steps map

Gendlin (2007) developed six steps for the process, as a means of teaching it. In 2012 Marta Stapert and Erik Verliefde developed these specifically for children. I call these steps the six pointers, and this is the map I use when listening to children and young people.

I have developed a way of using art as a medium to help young people express their stories with their felt senses. It's important to mention that this is not necessary to experience the six pointers; it can happen in a simple conversation and with teenagers I have found that they can process their stories during telephone conversations. These pointers are useful when learning to incorporate the technique into everyday situations.

Figure 12.5

Before sharing some case studies, I want to bring to mind a reflection from Gendlin that I remind myself of with every young person I am working with:

> *What is true is already so. Owning up to it doesn't make it worse. Not being open about it doesn't make it go away. And because it's true it is there to be interacted with. Anything untrue isn't there to be lived. People can stand what is true for they are already enduring.*

(Gendlin 2007:1)

In the following case studies I will highlight some of these elements of focusing while emphasising the heart of the therapeutic process.

Case Study 1: Listening session

I arrived to complete a home visit with a family and siblings I was working with. The relationship between mother and daughter had become strained. They were not talking and had had a serious exchange the previous evening.

So I had a discussion with the daughter about what her sense of the situation was. She explained how everything was 'coming in on top of her', to the extent that she just didn't wish to live at home. She was struggling with her bulimia. She mentioned her uncle's suicide in the past and how so many memories of this were constantly being triggered. She then mentioned that she was afraid that she would hurt her Mam and she broke down crying. She felt she needed space away from home, yet was confused about this. She felt a tightness in her stomach that was coming and going and was so hard to cope with.

Before guiding her in an exercise I reflected on what she had shared and how I had heard her expressing a number of different strands of emotions, which had many connections with her life story.

I was creating a space for all the strands that had bubbled up, so that she could relate to them as parts internally, rather than having the whole lot of them lumped together all at once.

I invited her to hold all these parts and strands just as they were, letting them be and breathe. Then I guided her in the non-verbal focusing exercise, having art materials to hand that she could use if she so wished.

Initially I guided her to become aware of her external body, its posture, the parts that were touching the chair, the rhythm of her breathing and how it connects the inner and outer world, inviting her to bring her awareness inside, down to the centre of her body, to notice how it was in there. Below is a drawing she did to reflect what she was feeling.

Figure 12.6

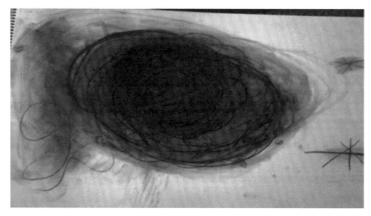

When she was finished I checked with her if it would be okay to share this expression. She was happy to do so.

I always check that it is okay for the young person to share what they have expressed and they need only share what they feel comfortable with.

She said that the lighter dot in the centre is herself. The dark one beside that is all about what was going on inside her right now. This is where it all started and it had grown and grown over the last few days. The black circles around indicate the bulimia she had struggled with and the death of her uncle from suicide a number of years ago.

I reflected back what she said, and invited her to notice how it was now in this moment.

I was inviting her to hold what she expressed with the body sense of how it felt in this moment. This can bring a felt difference in the felt sense. She felt the tightness easing ... *the felt sense had a felt shift/change occur in the body ...* I invited her to allow this easing to fully form in her body.

There were red lines, which were connected to the self harm she feels inside herself; some days the red lines are a lot stronger in colour and visible ... last night it felt so strong.

I took time to reflect this back and she sensed inside how this was for her. She noticed an easing, more and more, in the centre of her body. She took time to give space to this and allow it to be and breathe.

I was providing an inner space for the felt sense to change itself – just a few moments of pausing with 'it' helps that to happen naturally.

She then expressed how another part of the picture was all about her real Dad not wanting to have anything to do with her and the confusion she feels now about all that. She then discussed how she has a half sister six months younger than her in her Dad's current family and how they live together and have a relationship: 'When I was eight years old he told me he didn't want anything to do with me. Since then I have a question in me that it must be me that is the problem.' She feels so hurt by him since that time.

You can see that 'More of her story' is unfolding with her memories, etc., like the iceberg diagram in Figure 12.4 (page 132).

At this point she cried and we just took time to allow the tears to have their space and be released.

I maintained a very gentle and nurturing presence at this point for her as it is really important not to rush past the tears, to allow them to be fully released.

Then I reflected how something around her Dad made her want to cry. After the tears she had a sense of calmness and the tightness had eased, with more space inside. She took time to pause and be with this.

She drew purple lines, which were connected to her uncle's death and how it gets triggered by the least thing in the centre of her body. 'Just like the exchange with my Mam last night caused it to return again.' I asked if the tightness came back after the exchange with her Mam. She nodded, with a strong 'Yes' quality to it.

She drew green lines, which were connected to that part inside that 'is always questioning why he [her uncle] did what he did' and 'I want to know, then part of me realises I will never get the answers I want.'

I reflected back about the two parts, the part that is asking why and the part that realises that she will never get the answers she wants, inviting her to take a moment to acknowledge these two strands just as they are, giving them their own space to be and breathe.

I was allowing all parts have their space – no one part in the process is more important than the other. Both must have the same space and presence to allow the body unfold the next step.

She spoke about the memories of the day her uncle died. He told her that he loved her and said goodbye, she thought it was until she would see him the next day – not that he'd commit suicide. I reflected all of this back and she cried some more. I allowed space for the tears to be released while *again maintaining a gentle and nurturing space.*

There was a period of silence ... then I checked if it was okay to ask her something. *I would never ask anything unless it is okay with the young person; it's their living process.* She said 'Yes.' I reflected back that I noticed her pressing her fingerprints on the page with a lot of pressure while she was drawing. *It is important to reflect the body language and movements as this can allow more of the story to express itself.* She opened up that this represents, 'When people are getting at me they trigger me off inside. The tightness returns and can take hours or days to go.' *I paused and gave space to this, letting it be and breathe in the moment.*

She then said that the heart and the lines in the centre is what her heart has gone through. I encouraged her to acknowledge this and give it space. Some of the lines are 'stuff' she worries about in the future and I reflected this back to her. She paused and spoke about always waiting for something bad to come and happen 'as it always does in my family'. Again, I reflected this back about the part of her that worries about 'stuff' that might happen. She then expressed how underneath all her drawing is connected to her Dad. *The depth of inner knowing – it's all about her real Dad.*

She then experienced a complete easing of the tightness. It went completely in this moment of reflecting. *I invited her to give space to what had changed inside, the felt difference. It's essential to pause and receive this fully in the body.* She then spoke about how she didn't need space from her Mam.

You can see that at the end of the session this girl had a sense of things being more integrated within her. The answer to the question about needing space from her mother came of its own accord. She is somehow more than 'it' all. Sitting with the different parts inside her, during the process, enabled her not to become identified with 'it' all. She is now more than these experiences, even though they were overwhelming at the start.

Case Study 2: Chatting and listening

I called to a foster family to see a teenage girl I was working with. She had regular sessions. When I called we were just chatting generally over a cup of tea about life and how things had been going for her since the last session. She spoke about how she was struggling with the whole issue of trust, that it was bothering her a lot.

I just invited her to pause and to notice if there was something going on for her 'all about trust'.

There was a silence. She then shared how there was a tightness in her tummy, a tightness right in the centre of her tummy. I reflected this back to her and gently encouraged her to give space to this just as it was.

I was allowing space for her felt sense to form fully while holding it with a quality of gentleness. It can help connections to unfold.

There was another silence ... I sat with that silence.

I was accompanying her with my silent presence trusting the process. It is so important to respect the silence.

She then expressed that it was connected to her Mam and Dad, 'I trusted them and they left me.' Tears came ... I encouraged her to allow those tears to have their own space and to hold them gently, while encouraging her to sense the quality of the tears.

I was providing a space for the release of the tears, allowing them to have their space while helping her sense the quality behind them as this can help more of the story express itself.

Silence. I sat in silence, keeping her company. She expressed a sense of sadness and shared how an image of a black ball bubbled up for her. I reflected how there was a part of her that felt sad and how an image of the black ball came. I invited her to hold all of this gently just as it was while noticing how this image fitted in her body.

Here is the emotional feeling behind the tears surfacing, combined with the symbolism of the image that bubbles up. The entry points are present. This can occur when you search for the quality behind the emotion. It allows for the felt sense to emerge more deeply.

She shared how the image fitted inside, even though she still felt tightness in her tummy ... I acknowledged this, and I invited her to give this space and asked her to check if it was okay to sit with this black ball?

Never assume it's okay to be with what emerges – it is important to check.

She said it was okay, and I invited her to sense inside what this image was all about. There was another period of silence ... Something came that she wanted to 'trust her boyfriend but I can't fully let my guard down; How I worry and get paranoid I will never be able to trust anyone in my life. It will haunt me for ever.'

The connections are emerging about aspects of her life that have elements of past, present and future (as in the iceberg diagram in Figure 12.4 on page 132).

SOCIAL CARE

I reflected back how she sensed the different strands around her whole sense of trust. The part where she wanted to trust her boyfriend, and yet knew she couldn't let her guard down. Then how another strand inside gets paranoid (to use her phrase) and she will never be able to trust anyone, and how she worries it will haunt her for ever. I invited her to gently hold all those strands just as they were, in this moment. To notice the body sense of all of this inside.

It is all about ensuring that one part is not more important than the other, giving them all the same space and presence to allow the next steps bubble up.

In doing this she sensed that things fitted as the tightness eased a little and tears came. Again I just provided space for the tears to be released without having to try and figure them out. I encouraged her to give space to this little easing in her body sense.

It is so crucial to give space to the tiny easing in the body. It is where the felt sense is changing in that very moment of interaction inside.

She noticed more images bubbling up of her family life in the past; of her Mam at the kitchen table, her Dad and brother. I reflected back all these images, encouraging her to sense the quality and feel of these internally.

I was creating the sense that there was her and then the different images that bubbled up, so that she would not become identified with anyone; that she would remain open to all of them, while creating a space for more to happen in the process, just as in the iceberg diagram.

She felt they were happy times ... and I invited her to hold all that came with a sense of gentleness ... She paused ... I kept her company ... 'It's like the black ball is going through me.' She let out a sigh *(I am aware it is changing and easing more inside)* and I reflected and mirrored this sigh. There was a pause ... She noticed that the black ball was changing, there were brighter colours coming, the symbol of the black disappeared and all she was left was the bright colour and the pictures.

I reflected all these strands that came and invited to notice how it felt in her body. She noticed that the tightness had eased as the symbols changed. I encouraged her to pause and fully receive this, in this moment.

It is crucial to receive the felt difference in the body, to pause, and not rush past this point. She is beginning to hold this whole issue of trust freshly, in a new way.

In staying with this, she expressed that what was there now was deep calmness right in the centre of her body ... the word 'peace' surfaced within. 'Yet there seems to be something more under this and I don't know what it is.'

I reflected how now the word 'peace' came, and the sense of more, underneath it, was unclear. I checked whether I could make a suggestion.

I always check, I never assume I can make a suggestion; it is her process.

She was okay with it. I invited her to let this place know that she was here to receive whatever 'it' wished to share. If 'it' didn't wish to share at this moment it was okay. There was a long pause. I just kept her company with a gentle presence.

I helped to nurture an open stance, not putting any pressure on anything, or forcing 'it' to happen, allowing whatever might be there to express itself naturally.

She noticed how there was a sense that, 'Yes, there is a lot inside me about needing to look more at trust, yet it wants me to know it will be okay.' I reflected these two strands and invited her to sense how this was in her body. She felt a physical sense of lightness. She took time to soak all this up inside.

I was giving space for the felt change to fully form and be integrated in her body's bodily sense.

As the chat was concluding I encouraged her to take a moment to place a sense of protection around what bubbled up for her and her inner wisdom.

It is helpful to place a protection around what came, as sometimes our inner critical voice can undermine what came in the process.

This girl had more sessions around the whole area of trust and is now an adult happily living with her partner, who was her boyfriend at the time of this session.

You can see from these two sessions that, as Eugene Gendlin says:

What is split off, not felt, remains the same. When it is felt, it changes. Most people don't know this! They think that by not permitting the feeling of their negative ways they make themselves good. On the contrary, that keeps these negatives static, the same from year to year. A few moments of feeling it in your body allows it to change. If there is in you something bad, sick or unsound, let it be and breathe. That's the only way it can evolve and change into the form it needs.

(Gendlin 2007:178)

These case studies show how the felt sense is a living and moving entity in itself, the 'living it', and is the heart of the therapeutic process.

The focusing presence offers a fresh way to attune to children:

To work in this way, you need skills and self awareness. Some of the key aspects are my quality of presence and always attuning with my own felt sense and asking myself:
'Am I where the child is?'
'Am I connected with the child?'
'Is what I'm saying against ... to ... for ... about ... the child?'
'Am I giving the child sufficient distance and space?'

(Kilner 2013)

When I am aware, I can be fully present and know what I have to do:

- Let the child lead and I follow. It's all about accompanying.
- Mirroring their body language, facial expressions, gestures, little sighs and movements.
- Acknowledging the situation they find themselves in, their lived reality.
- Reflecting their words with heart and not adding my own interpretations, and most of all reflecting the quality and tone of how they are expressed.
- Using presence language, for example 'there is something in you', 'they are a part of you', 'you're sensing the queasy sensations', etc. This helps the child not to become identified with and overwhelmed by their issues.
- Attuning to the energy flow in the process and creating a space for when the body's bodily sense changes.
- I always check whether I can ask something and whether I can make a process suggestion in the form of a question – it is their process. When the young person's process is stuck, this can help to unlock the body's wisdom and allow the process move forward.

The benefits of the focusing process for children can best be described as follows:

- Focusing is a process that is all about small steps forward and not about gigantic changes in a listening session. It offers a unique element in that it gives children their own internal reference point, allowing them to develop a capacity to make contact with and listen to their body's bodily senses of any situation.
- It provides them with the opportunity to learn this new life skill that is innate and natural to its core.
- Focusing provides children an inner framework, to regulate their emotional world in a healthy and balanced manner; to enable them to find the right steps and answers that fit for them.
- Focusing can help children gain an awareness of how their own expectations, attitudes and reactions affect their interactions with others.
- The process helps children develop a greater empathy for self and for others, while maintaining healthy boundaries.
- It offers a safe containment in which to process difficult issues and a tangible way to hold the boundaries and limits for each young person.
- It gives children and young people a way of living in the world, in a more responsive rather than a reactive way.

- Carers, parents and professionals can gain greater skills in defusing and dealing with challenging behaviour and providing clarity, when making decisions with young people.

In the Child and Family Agency in the midlands, I and two focusing practitioner colleagues, Ms Phil Kelly and Ms Mary Jennings, recently completed an eighty-hour training programme for staff and foster parents, to offer them this new way of interacting with the young people they care for. We are in the process of completing a research piece into this training process, and we have been invited to run another training programme in the midlands, this time for the staff and the fostering department.

In conclusion, in response to the Ryan Report, my focusing colleagues and I are endeavouring to bring this process out to all those who work with children.

Chapter 13
Waiting: Avoiding the Temptation to Jump In
Des Mooney

> *If only we can wait, the patient arrives at understanding creatively and with immense joy... The principle is that it is the patient and only the patient who has the answers.*
>
> (Winnicott 1969:711)

MY JOURNEY

A large percentage of male social care workers came to this profession after having a previous career. I am one of those. Having done an apprenticeship and worked as a tradesman for a number of years I began to 'stray', as it were, and after a time spent working, travelling and thinking embarked on a new career as a social care worker. I doubt I would have had the ability to cope with some of the emotional effects of this job had I been younger when starting.

I also believe that the life experience I had prior to entering social care has benefited me and shaped the way I work with young people. I have also had the enlightening experience of returning to education, to complete the in-service Social Care degree and later an MA in Education, which was a great contrast to my previous educational experience. Reading about theorists, completing essays, discussing the different aspects of social care and getting used to the rhythm of college life was great fun and great learning.

However, the most important learning has come from the practical work with young people. No two days are the same; every day throws up a multitude of puzzles to which there are a multitude of solutions. And there is no 'one size fits all' solution kit. Three young people might behave in a similar way for three very different reasons and we as social care workers need to be able to shape our understanding and responses accordingly. And it is only through experience, repetition, maturity and positive relationships that we learn how to do this.

DOING OR WAITING

When we first become social care workers very often our first instinct is to 'do', for the young people we work with, when very often 'waiting' is the best thing to do. We can see our young people as slightly incapable of doing for themselves and our job is to fix things for them. So we hustle and bustle around, and very often make life quite pain-free, fixing all their minor problems for them and guarding them from the harsher realities of life, and – if we are honest – sometimes for an 'easy life'. We do this out of a misguided sense of care, as all we are doing is prolonging the agony they are enduring. Very often their reactions to their difficulties is 'the work' and if we help too early we prevent any learning taking place. The 'work' I refer to is the ability to accept that the reality we are living in is just that and no amount of papering over cracks will help in the long term.

After a while we learn to wait ourselves and learn to endure the pain that a young person is going through. Then we learn to encourage the young person to do likewise. And we learn to listen to what the young person is trying to tell us through his or her words and actions.

What often happens in this time of waiting is that the young person figures out whatever it is they need to do as if by themselves. The staff members' acts of waiting, listening and encouraging is a much more democratic and child-centred approach to dealing with a situation and views the young person as an equal partner in the process. It is in contrast to a staff member telling the young person what is troubling them and what they should do about it. For the staff member it can be frustrating when the apparent answer is 'right in front of' the young person, and the young person is engaging in behaviour designed to distract from their reality. The staff member has read the file and discussed with other professionals the minute details of the young person's life up to and including their entry into the care system. They might feel that, given their positive relationship with a certain young person, for example, they could make a significant difference in the young person's welfare by forcing an issue, instead of feeling that they are just standing on the sidelines watching a young person make what appear to be the same mistakes over and over. Demanding to talk about an issue, in the hope of bringing some healing, when the young person has not indicated they are ready will not work. Encouraging talk about any issues when the young person is ready and able just might.

That is not to say that we ignore challenging behaviour. As social care workers we have to manage all types of behaviour that impact on the lives of the young people we work with, our fellow staff members, and indeed the unit itself. And sometimes there is no option but to confront this behaviour, as not responding might be more damaging to everyone involved and potentially feed into the panic the young person is experiencing. Some consequences designed to curb excessive, omnipotent behaviour will have at least short-term success and with them the ability to bring the unit back to some semblance of normality. At this point the causes or reasons for the behaviour can be looked at more closely. However, if the only person who appears to be suffering is the young person themselves, perhaps the best learning will come from within and from the experience. And if we 'rescue' them too early we reduce the possibility of this happening.

But who is in pain here anyway? The staff member, who is waiting and watching as their charges stumble and fall time and again, or the young person, who has honed and practised their distracting behaviour over time? Indeed, this tool has served them well and may even have kept them from further humiliation and anguish throughout their life.

EMPATHY AND SYMPATHY

It is worth noting the difference between empathy and sympathy at this point. Sympathy and empathy are both acts of feeling. With sympathy the feeling is one of pity and sorrow for the young person, with little real understanding of what exactly the young person is feeling. Empathy, on the other hand, is more of a shared experience. Instead of feeling sorry *for* you are sorry *with* the young person, and are connecting with them on an emotional level. Empathy is the ability to understand another's pain. Sympathy is feeling their pain for them and is of little use.

Richard was twelve when he came to our unit after numerous foster placement breakdowns. His father was absent from his life. His mother was incapable of looking after him and showed him little love, and his reaction to this was to become demanding, so demanding that his mother gave in all the time. Nothing was regulated in his life: unrestricted bedtimes, access to food, video games and other toys and a tolerance of demanding and at times threatening behaviour. 'Me Ma let me do what I wanted' was what he said. The result was that Richard was able to substitute material gain for love – a perfectly apt response for a young person attempting to push away the pain and hurt of feeling unloved and unwanted. Over time, Richard's mother's continued inability to care for him and, to some extent, his response to this, got too much and he went into a voluntary foster care placement. Throughout this foster placement Richard's demanding behaviour continued and after a while the placement broke down. This became a pattern. After several foster care breakdowns Richard came to live with us.

It is hard to work with Richard and show a non-judgemental attitude in my responses to situations he was and is in. In the academic arena we learn of Biestek's seven principles of the case work relationship, of which having a non-judgemental attitude is one. However, it is another challenge to the human in us to practise this when you work with a young person closely and have knowledge of their social history, of some of the hurts they have encountered and of the people who perpetrated those hurts. Being respectful and courteous to these people can at times be stressful. Being challenged by these people on your behaviour towards their offspring can bring with it a desire to react and challenge them in turn on their own behaviours, past and present.

This is but one of the day-to-day issues that we as social care workers encounter. In some respects we are not just waiting for the young people to begin the process of enlightenment and change but also for the parents to accept that they have a huge role to play in this process. When I write of Richard I am filled with no little anger at some of the treatment that was meted out to him at an age when he could not mind himself. That I am aware of some of the issues in his mother's life counters this to a degree. So while I write of Richard's mother I try to remember that Biestek also wrote of accepting the client's dignity, worth and needs and that acceptance does not mean approval of the client's behaviour or attitudes. He also reminds us of the need for a controlled and objective emotional involvement in addressing the client's problem. This is not an easy thing to do. However, over time it does get easier.

When I first encountered Richard my heart broke for him. He appeared to me to be among the saddest and most hurt young people I have come across. Not because of any physical beatings or such but because his mother's callous treatment of him – born out of her own troubles I would guess – seemed just as violent. Not only did she deny him love but she actively favoured her other children, and he was so clearly aware of this. She frequently hurt him when explaining that she wasn't able to take him or, in her words, 'wouldn't be able to handle him' on access visits; access visits that he subsequently found out were attended by his siblings.

At times like this Richard would drag himself around the unit, head buried deep into his shoulders, with a somewhat expressionless look on his face. He would remain quiet for some time. He would then approach a staff member and have this urgent need to do 'something', quite often go clothes shopping or buy a video game. Other times he would make unreasonable demands, such as the day he wanted to take the brakes off his bicycle, 'because that's what the professionals do'! The latter incident caused a bit of a to-do, so to speak, as we explained that it would be dangerous and we would not allow him to cycle a bicycle with no brakes; and he explained that he 'could do what I want, 'cause it's my bike'.

We began to recognise that Richard was replaying scenes from his time at home and it became apparent how far he would go to get his way. Shouting and roaring, making particularly nasty comments towards female staff members and attempting to cajole members of staff he suspected of being 'soft' were his forte. Over time we encouraged Richard to wait and to think why he needed to distract himself. For Richard this continues to be a very difficult thing to do. We are in essence encouraging Richard to mull over why he feels unloved by his mother, albeit in an atmosphere of considerable care and, yes, love.

'HOLDING'

Donald Winnicott came to psychoanalysis from paediatrics and his work with children and their mothers led him to construct his most influential concepts, including the 'holding environment' and the 'transitional object'. His writings emphasised empathy, imagination and, in the words of Martha Nussbaum, 'the highly particular transactions that constitute love between two imperfect people' (Nussbaum 2003). Winnicott describes a 'good enough' mother and how healthy foundations are laid down through the ordinary loving care for her baby. Winnicott advocates that a therapist recreate the holding environment where the mother's technique of holding, bathing, feeding and being attuned to the baby's needs add up to the child's first idea of the mother. David Wasdell, in his paper 'The Holding Environment' (1979), notes that anxiety in the early stages of the parent–infant relationship relates to the threat of annihilation, 'the alternative to being is reacting, and reacting interrupts being and annihilates. The holding environment therefore has as its main function the reduction to a minimum of impingements to which the infant must react with resultant annihilation of personal being' (1979:4). Wasdell notes that 'under favourable conditions the infant establishes a continuity of existence' (1979:4). Winnicott describes this as the place where the client can meet neglected ego needs and allow the true self to emerge. Adrian Ward describes these ego needs as 'the capacity to organise and make sense of one's experience' (McMahon & Ward 1998:17). The role of the primary caregiver in this drama is to 'hold' the child. This can be literally holding the child, providing appropriate comfort, food or other nourishment; but it also refers to holding by way of managing or containing the child's emotional experiences and helping them make sense of these emotions.

Our job as caregivers at this point is to learn how to make sense of the child's experiences for them and to 'mirror' them back to them in a way they can understand and so that they will not be threatened or re-stimulated by them.

In a practical sense we can only do this by spending time with the child, by listening and watching, not trying too hard and by being open to the different voices with which the child is communicating.

'ATTUNEMENT'

Richard Erskine, in his article 'Attunement and involvement: therapeutic responses to relational needs' (1998), notes that the need for relationship is a primary motivation of human behaviour. Erskine uses the term 'contact' to describe the means by which this need for relationship is met. '"Contact" refers to the full awareness of sensations, feelings, needs, sensorimotor processes, thoughts and memories that occur within the individual' (Erskine 1998:3). Erskine notes that 'prolonged disruption of the satisfaction of relational needs is evidenced by a sense of emptiness, anxiety, anger, frustration and aggression' (1998:3), all of which could easily be attributed to Richard when he first came to live with us. Erskine writes of attunement being related to both empathy and communication, where a therapist has both the skill to be sensitive to a client's needs and feelings and the ability to communicate that understanding. For a social care worker to be attuned to the needs and feelings of the client is to be in a place where much 'work' can be done. Erskine points out that the process of attunement provides the safety and stability that enables 'the client to begin to remember and endure regressing into childhood experiences. This may bring a fuller awareness of the pain of past traumas, shaming experiences, past failures of relationship(s), and loss of aspects of self' (Erskine 1994, cited in Erskine 1998).

Part of our job with Richard therefore has been to understand the conditions of his earliest care experience. Time and energy is spent noting obvious and some not so obvious care needs. How we approach Richard physically, our tone of voice, what foods he wants to eat, how he explains himself through language and body language, what he is really trying to say through these actions, his way of being himself, his way of settling and sleeping, how he relates to others and his relationship with his family are all part of the process we engage in. In this way we attempt to allow Richard room to think and feel, free from what Winnicott refers to as any 'constricting anxiety'. We do not tell Richard what is wrong. He knows. He has lived it for long enough. We just want to create the conditions where Richard can do this for himself. And he will only do this with people he believes are able to 'mind' him in a way that makes him feel loved and important. So we provide the conditions and we wait.

Over time Richard has begun to identify his need to distract from the sometimes awfulness of reality. The conversations he has now are able to focus on when his needs were not met in the past, his feelings and responses to this and how he can get his needs met more appropriately now. We cannot make promises to Richard that his mother will be available to him; we don't know this anyway. We cannot paper over the cracks in this broken relationship, nor in his attitude to the issue of his absent father, which he has not yet begun to address, or offer soft landings from painful realities. We can, however, empathise with his plight and offer the type of care that includes safety, consistency and the structure and boundaries missing from his early years. And we can remind Richard how important he is.

First, we ask his opinion, because his opinion is important, on even the most trivial matter. We let him know what is happening with issues concerning his family, the social work department and his care. We celebrate with Richard the various achievements and successes in his life and the significant dates in his calendar. We let Richard tell us what he likes and dislikes, things about himself, stories or happenings that might seem unimportant in the general scheme of things. And we remember. We listen to what he says and, equally important, the way he says it. We talk about Richard, who he is, and discuss ways in which we can help him move along: not how we can help him, but how he can help himself. We include Richard in and share with him the different events that happen in *our* community; birthdays, babies, marriages, confirmations, first day in secondary school, last day in school, holidays. Not unlike, dare I say it, the way families do. We surprise Richard by remembering things he said or did, or things he wanted. We praise him for his actions and abilities, but we don't patronise him. We try not to give advice, unless it's asked for, or at least we ask permission before we do. And we tell Richard he is important. Because he is.

SUPPORTING, NOT LEADING

Carl Rogers (1951) writes that a therapist must have three necessary and sufficient qualities: congruence, or genuineness and honesty towards a client; empathy, or the ability to feel what a client feels; and an unconditional regard towards the client and respect for the client's situation. Rogers also noted that it is the client who should say what is wrong and find ways of improving. This client-centred approach should be non-directive; the therapist should not lead the client but rather be there for support. So we offer this approach to Richard while we wait. Richard goes through the painful process of getting to know more about himself and his lot, and we go through the painful learning process of watching it take place.

The hope is that in time this learning experience will enable in Richard some kind of deeper understanding of his journey to now, an acceptance of his previous life situation where blame and forgiveness are equally apportioned, and the ability to begin to love himself more and feel more worthy of love in return. As social care workers we would also hope that this learning experience would enable Richard to have a better understanding of the issues concerning the other young people at the unit and that in turn he will be better able to support them.

The truth is that the majority of young people in care settings will share many of the feelings Richard has. Neglect, abuse, abandonment and rejection are not uncommon reference points for the young people we work with. Different young people will be at different stages of understanding of themselves and their earliest care experiences. So at the unit at any given time you can have a number of 'Richards' experiencing a plethora of emotions and responding in differing ways. Some will be avoidant and may 'hide' in their rooms or at the PlayStation or PC, or on their phones; others will argue and fight with staff or other young people, or self-harm; still others will abscond from the unit; while another group will want the staff members' undivided attention throughout the day and evening. These situations can be quite difficult for a staff member to deal with.

GETTING THE BALANCE RIGHT

The emotional effect of dealing with others' emotions while also dealing with your own can be exhausting. Allied to this is the increasing workload of recent years. Noel Howard (2012) notes a situation where social care staff have less time to care for young people's actual needs. More and more reporting and clarifying situations are required to comply with the high level of regulation and while this is entirely understandable given the number and significance of reports in recent years, it may indeed have the effect of reducing the level of real care the young people are receiving. Added to this, day-to-day household chores and activities including cleaning, driving, phone calls, trips to shops and general maintenance of the house can also reduce considerably the amount of time we spend with the young people.

Staying professional and still approachable can be quite 'the task' at times. It is a real skill to let our young people know we are 'holding' them while also dealing with the nitty gritty of daily life. And time spent 'waiting' or 'reflecting' can be at a premium. Sometimes we just don't have the time to sit and think.

But then neither did the people who loved and minded us. Mistakes are made – we're only human. We just try to make the mistakes small ones. And we talk to each other – 'I'm okay, are you okay?' – and we use the systems put in place by the manager and our colleagues to support each other while on shift.

So what *do* we do while we 'wait'? If it is a skill, how can we improve our capacity to wait? For many of us this time can be fraught with anxiety. However, while we are waiting we are not doing nothing. We are thinking, talking, acting, studying, making sense of, encouraging, reflecting, discussing with colleagues and the young person all the 'what ifs'. Good personal and professional relationships throughout the staff team are vital. The fact that we might be working with our colleagues for anything up to twenty-four hours without much time away from each other demands this. Observing and discussing methods of practice improve overall practice. In addition, the ability to discuss issues related to the care and wellbeing of the young people and their effect on us as social care workers is important, as another person's careful words can be of great succour when times get tough. As well as this, healthy argument makes for good care plans, clear discussion makes for good structure and boundaries and fewer inconsistencies, and good briefing and debriefing help us make sense of situations that at times can be emotionally and physically draining.

Reading articles and any related material that might help us understand the group of young people we are working with is also important. In addition, carefully reading case files, and re-reading when necessary, is essential. While we struggle with Richard's demanding behaviour we also seek to understand the underlying motives for it. Reading theoretical and practice-related material will support our understanding of the deeper issues behind Richard's behaviours and consequently help us in our responses to them. So when Richard tells us that he feels lonely, abandoned and unloved and doesn't know what to do about these feelings except to lash out at whoever is nearest him and do so in a way that blindsides us, we are familiar with this and better able to show empathy, not because he sees us trying to understand him but because we do.

CPD AND SUPERVISION

As discussed in Chapter 3, under the Health and Social Care Professionals Act 2005, a system of registration for all health care workers is being set up 'to protect the public by promoting high standards of professional conduct and professional education, training and competence among registrants of the designated professions' (Government of Ireland 2005). The motive behind this Act is to improve the quality of care and standards of competency, to encourage continuing development and education, and to reassure the general public about the competence of the health and social care professions. Part of this registration process will require registrants to engage in a regular cycle of continuing professional development and, as part of their registration, social care workers will have to list areas in which they have engaged in continuing education and learning. In this way the Act seeks to encourage caring institutions to also become learning institutions, places where knowledge and the evolution of practice and high standards are studied and enacted. This is to be welcomed. It will put the likes of further reading and training and with it the appointment of training officers higher up the agenda of all organisations, which can only be of benefit both to the carers and the recipients of care.

Without doubt one of the best ways to improve practice and gain insight into understanding the task of childcare is through supervision. So while we wait for movement on the part of the young person we can look at areas where we can better support the various relationships that exist. Proper supervision will explore the 'nature' of our relationships with the young people we work with. This way we can look at some of the unconscious elements of our work. Transference is described as the projection of feelings based on a child's previous experience of significant figures, usually parents (McMahon & Ward 1998). Through supervision we can explore this phenomenon, as well as our own feelings about the child. McMahon and Ward describe this as counter-transference. Very often we begin to see why certain young people affect us the way they do and why with some young people we behave or respond to them in a way that in all honesty is about 'our stuff' and not theirs. 'Sometimes our own feelings resonate powerfully with the transference from the child, which may lead us to be extra-sympathetic, or the opposite' (McMahon & Ward 1998:34). McMahon and Ward note that reflecting on feelings of transference and counter-transference 'provides a helpful way of bringing together the inner worlds of child and worker' (1998:35).

Understanding the dynamic of transference and counter-transference demands time and training, but it is crucial if we are to seek opportunities to discover the unconscious or hidden messages that abound, and respond to them in a way that supports not only the young person's but our own understanding of our inner world. The old Greek aphorism, 'Know thyself' seems apt at this point. Plato noted that understanding 'thyself' would better equip us to understand the nature of all human beings. If we are to truly understand and support the young people in our care, it is only fair to them that we have a sense of who we truly are.

REFLECTION

Another way in which we can improve our 'waiting' skills is to keep a personal journal or reflective diary. A reflective diary offers the learner the opportunity to reflect specifically on the various learning experiences, activities, responses and skills they have acquired. It also offers the writer the opportunity to engage in critical reflection and critical self-reflection about incidents that occur. Boud describes these as 'those intellectual and affective activities in which individuals engage to explore their experiences in order to lead to new understandings and appreciations' (1985, cited in McMahon & Ward 1998:218). Over time we can see where we have changed in our approaches to difficult situations. Some might argue that we don't have the time to be doing 'more' writing, and it is hard to disagree with this. However, the time spent engaged in this activity might glean considerably more learning than simply recording an event, the 'who did what and when', and not allowing ourselves time to reflect on it. We can allow ourselves the luxury of seeing how the various happenings in our lives can and do invade our professional life and affect our judgement and responses to issues that arise. A reflective diary will not only help us learn from experience and enhance problem-solving skills but also develop our ability to reflect on our overall practice in the long term and increase our ability to support behaviour change.

> Richard is doing okay. It is likely that he will stay with us until he is eighteen, although this may change. We are on the sidelines, like parents at a football match, mentally kicking every ball and shouting encouragement whenever we can, watching him running and tackling and scoring the odd goal or getting the odd yellow card for fouls and abusive language. And like the parent at that match we can 'do' nothing. He has to do it himself. Run, stumble, fall, get up, try again, laugh, shout, scream, be the hero, make a fool of himself, fail or succeed. The hope for us, the 'parents', is that Richard will accumulate a sense of himself that enables in him the ability to get up from the occasional 'knocks' that living a life visits on us, to value himself and appreciate the value we hold for him.

And we wait for this. We don't do nothing – I hope that is clear – but sometimes it seems like it. When we can't change a situation quickly enough, when the pain and hurt we are witnessing are too much to take, when we have to watch the same situation happen again and again until that hoped-for 'lightbulb' moment occurs – *or* that learning and acceptance – what do we do? We listen, actively. And we read, attend training and develop ourselves personally and professionally. We encourage Richard to think and celebrate his development. We take the opportunities that Richard gives us to be role models, thinkers, confidants, paternal and maternal figures, educators, advisors, advocates, actors in all of life's richness. And we wait.

Chapter 14
Containment : Not Always a Dirty Word
Maria O'Sullivan

> *I am left with a memory of a child coming towards me in a rage, which was totally beyond his control, and the sound of a primordial scream.*

Residential child care is increasingly meeting the needs of children presenting with the most challenging emotional and behavioural problems in our society. This development poses serious difficulties for even the most experienced teams in terms of the raw and powerful emotions that these children present, and the associated behaviours. Utilising a case study approach, this chapter will explore two psychodynamic concepts, 'containment' and 'projective identification', which the author has found useful in understanding and responding to the powerful feelings with which these children present. In addition, it will explore Morrison's (2001) supervision cycle as a framework for helping us to make sense of the children's feelings and behaviours and our own response to them. The second part of the chapter will briefly examine the importance of providing a containing environment for the residential staff team and will explore the role of the manager and the wider organisation in providing this containing environment.

SETTING THE SCENE

The most experienced team, when confronted daily by a severely troubled and troublesome child, can quickly reach the stage where they believe that 'this is not the right placement' for him or her. This statement often follows a situation in which the staff were overwhelmed by the child's behaviour. They experience the child as being outside their control and they fear for both the child's and their own safety. This is a very difficult situation for individual staff members and the team, but it is, in my experience, easier to tolerate if one has a framework for understanding what is happening. When individuals and a staff team can begin to make sense of what is going on they are better positioned to respond appropriately and compassionately to the child, and unhealthy defence mechanisms are kept under control. The following case study, which is presented in two parts, concerns John, a boy who, when we first meet him, has recently been placed in a residential care centre. John is in fact a composite child who is drawn from real practice experiences.

Case Study

John, not unlike many children in residential care, had presented with serious behavioural difficulties from an early age and had been in a number of foster care placements. He had lived briefly in a mainstream residential centre which was also unable to cope with the level of aggression with which he presented. A review of John's file revealed that his parents had had very difficult childhoods themselves and this had impacted seriously on their ability to parent John. John had witnessed domestic violence and alcohol abuse and had experienced serious neglect. John's early years had been particularly difficult ones for his mother, due to the levels of domestic violence in the home, and it was easy to imagine that his needs might have taken a back seat to his mother's own need to survive in an extremely abusive situation.

John was very angry about being placed in the centre and was extremely abusive, both verbally and physically, from the first day of his placement. His behaviour resembled that of many of the children who had lived in the centre, but differed in that it manifested itself as an almost unrelenting stream of abuse. All requests made to John, no matter how simple, were met with refusal and verbal abuse and on many occasions this escalated to serious damage to the residential centre and physical assaults on both children and staff.

In the early days of the placement the social care workers tried hard to respond positively to John: gently explaining the expectations of the centre to him; absorbing the verbal and physical abuse; and trying hard to find activities to engage with him. After a few weeks the staff team were extremely tired, anxious and feeling de-skilled. Given the level of abuse and the ongoing fear of assault it was no surprise that even the more senior and most resilient staff were feeling under pressure.

One cameo from the early part of John's placement gives a sense of how overwhelmed he could become. I was passing the kitchen door and heard his raised voice within. I looked in and John turned his attention to me: I am left with a memory of a child coming towards me in a rage, which was totally beyond his control, and the sound of a primordial scream. At that moment I recall thinking that I had never before witnessed such depth of feeling and I also had a sense that the feelings had their origins in John's early experiences.

APPLYING THEORY TO PRACTICE

One might well ask how does a staff team maintain positive regard and a sense of hope for a child like John: a child who is apt to assault them at any moment; who exhausts them with his whirlwind of activity; and who leaves them feeling they are making no difference despite their best efforts? To maintain positive regard, a team has to have a framework for understanding what is taking place: in other words, a map of the territory. There are many such frameworks available, but the one that helped me to make sense of John's behaviour is one informed by psychodynamic theory and in particular the work of the psychoanalyst Wilfred Bion (1897–1979). I was first introduced to the work of Wilfred Bion in an article by Hamish Canham (1998) and in particular to the whole notion of 'containment'. The term 'containment' resonated with me because of the all-too-frequent despairing rejoinder, 'We are doing nothing for this child – we are only containing him/her.' By contrast, Bion's notion of containment, as explained by Canham, brought with it illumination.

Bion imagines that at birth a child is confronted with a whole world of new sensations, both inside and outside his/her body (Canham 1998:66). 'Bion proposes that it is the mother's job to make sense of these bewildering sensations for the baby: to give them a shape, coherence and meaning which makes them recognisable and tolerable to the baby' (Canham 1998:66). The attuned carer, or, to use Bion's concept, the container, can differentiate between the various states of distress that the baby displays and the container can respond appropriately. For example, a carer will say in response to a baby's cry, 'I think you are hungry, let's get you a little drink.' In this way the baby has the experience of 'feelings being connected up for them in a way which makes sense of them. It has the feeling of being thought about and understood'(Canham 1998:66). Bion called this process 'containment'.

When a child repeatedly has this experience of feelings being connected up for them and made sense of, they will over time begin 'to be able to think about his or her own experience and to tolerate painful emotional states with the hope and expectation of being able to make sense of them' (Canham 1998:66) and so are able to act as their own 'container'. By contrast, many of the children in residential care will not have experienced this containing care and consequently are easily overcome by 'feeling states' that they cannot make sense of.

It was easy to imagine that John's cries, as a little baby, of hunger, pain or discomfort were intolerable for a mother who had herself not experienced containing care and who was living with domestic violence and alcohol abuse. As I experienced scenes such as the one in the kitchen I began to understand that we were witnessing a child who had not had that experience of having his feelings contained and made sense of and what we were now seeing was that infantile rage being expressed by a fourteen-year-old. Our job then as a social care team was, in the first instance, to be able to withstand the rage so as to provide John with the experience that his feelings and behaviours would not overwhelm the staff.

This sometimes meant being able to safely hold John physically and it also meant the team having the emotional strength to bear witness to his pain. In John's case that meant being able to listen and hear those cries of pain and manage his physical outbursts. (For other children the pain can be expressed in running away, self-harming, starving themselves or extreme controlling behaviour).

If we could not safely hold John physically and emotionally, he would then have the terrifying experience of his feelings and behaviours being not only beyond his control but also beyond that of the adults. It is difficult to imagine a more scary experience for a child than being beyond both their own control and that of the adults who are meant to be caring for them: a feeling that Bion refers to as 'nameless dread' (Hughes & Pengelly 1997:177). An understanding of the concept of containment helped to make sense of what was happening and allowed us to provide that emotional containment.

To provide an experience of containment for the child it is essential that a care team retains an ability to think about what is happening for the child. Similar to the mother's task is the task of the care team to 'be open to the bombardment of her infants' inchoate emotions; "of taking them in", processing them and trying to understand them' (Hughes & Pengelly 1997:176). To think about the children in this way is often difficult when one considers the strong emotions and often chaotic behaviours they are presenting us with, and our own feelings of fear, helplessness and anger. This thinking therefore needs to happen in a structured way to ensure that it is constructive and safe for everyone.

To this end I refer to Morrison's supervision cycle (2001), which is adapted from Kolb's experiential learning cycle (1988) and which provides a very useful model for thinking.

The supervision cycle, as illustrated below, has four stages: experience; reflection; analysis; and planning and acting.

In the *experience* part of the cycle, the worker is engaging with the service user and observing what is happening. 'Engaging in the experience is not sufficient on its own. Without reflecting on the experience it may be lost or misunderstood' (Morrison 2001:159). In *reflecting*, the worker is thinking about their own feelings about the situation, for example what made them feel comfortable or uncomfortable. In addition, the worker is thinking about the feelings of the child. The next stage, the *analysis* phase, should result in 'an understanding and contextualising of the situation' (Morrison 2001:160). This phase includes both the meaning of the situation for the child and also how the worker makes sense of the situation. In essence the worker is exploring, 'What bits of research, theory, values, training can help them understand this situation?' (Morrison 2001). In the *action planning* phase the analysis is translated into plans and actions.

Figure 14.1

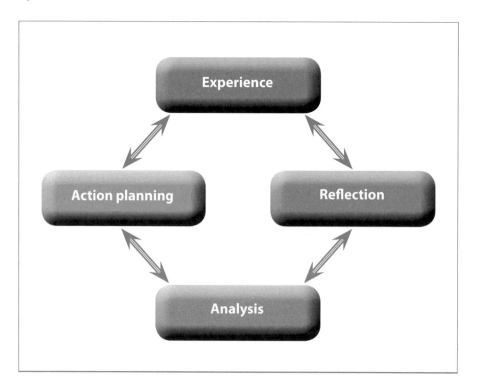

An incident with John serves as a useful way of illustrating the use of Morrison's supervision cycle and introducing the concept of 'projective identification'.

Case Study

Experience

I recall an *experience* where John was very upset about an incident that had happened earlier and as we spoke he jumped up and began kicking the adjoining doors. John moved to the hall and continued to kick the doors, the noise reverberating around us. At this point John was moving in a circular path and kicking each door as he passed it, while stopping to threaten my colleague and me. As John became more and more agitated my colleague and I began to contemplate how we would manage if he should physically assault us. Our deliberations led us to the conclusion that we would need assistance should the situation get worse, and we rang for support. I noticed that my knees were physically shaking with fear. This was not the first time I had felt fear, but on this occasion I had the sense that something bad could really happen and I went to the phone, rang my line manager and asked her to come to the centre. In the meantime I tried to distract John by asking him questions and he gradually began to engage with me. The arrival of another colleague further helped John to calm down.

Reflection

When I *reflected* later that evening, I was struck by the level of terror and panic I had experienced during the incident. It is always useful to examine an unusual and intense response because it can indicate that the 'practitioner is being powerfully "controlled" by feeling from outside' (Hughes & Pengelly 1997:85). In addition, as Shohet (1999) argues, one of the best ways of understanding another is by noticing very carefully the effect the other is having on oneself.

Analysis

As I *analysed* the experience I began to consider the concept 'projective identification'. This psychoanalytic term 'refers to the unconscious process whereby vulnerable, hostile or otherwise difficult feelings may be disowned by an individual and attributed to another who may then (as a result of the interaction) actually experience the feelings as his or her own' (Hughes & Pengelly 1997:80). As I reflected on my own feelings of terror and panic I began to hypothesise that perhaps it was not just anger that John was experiencing, as I had first thought; perhaps it was also terror and panic.

Planning and acting

I *planned* that when John and I completed a life space interview I would be open to this possibility that he was also experiencing feelings of terror and panic; feelings of panic as opposed to anger and aggression. John later described feelings of anger, fear and loneliness. He described himself as slipping into a black hole where he was totally on his own and where nobody else existed. He explained that my random questions had acted as a distracter, which in turn had pulled him back from the brink of despair (the black hole). Observing John's non-verbal behaviour confirmed and emphasised what John was saying verbally. For example, his eyes lit up when he felt I understood what he was telling me and in his enthusiasm to share his feeling he asked for crayons and paper and began to illustrate the black hole. As John and I considered how the team could help him during any future episode, John requested that someone hold his hand so as to keep him with them and help to stop him slipping into the black hole. In this way John was telling us how, and inviting us, to provide him with an experience of containment.

THE IMPORTANCE OF FEELINGS

Having a toolbox of concepts and a model for reflection allowed me to think about John and my own reactions. This in turn created an opportunity for John and me to have what he described as a 'real conversation'. If we can stand with the child in their moments of crisis and do this thinking, the child will have the experience of their powerful feelings being 'survived, "detoxified" and made sense of' (Hughes & Pengelly 1997:176).

Children who have not had the experience of containing care struggle not only with managing their feelings but are also unable to identify these same feelings. The life space interview, originally developed by Fitz Redl and introduced to contemporary social care workers through the therapeutic crisis intervention training developed by Cornell University's College of Human Ecology, provides a model for processing feelings and experiences and assists children to make the connection between feelings and behaviours and to develop more adaptive ways of coping.

PROVIDING A CONTAINING ENVIRONMENT FOR THE CARE TEAM

Given the complex needs of the children in residential care, individual workers can only do so much. These children generally need the combined efforts of a team to meet their need for containment. In order to provide containment for the children, a parallel experience of containment must be provided for the staff by the manager and the agency. As stated earlier, it can be very painful and anxiety-provoking to get in touch with the traumas of another person's life and unless teams themselves have an experience of being contained, the chaos and hopelessness of the children's lives will be mirrored in the team and in their responses.

In addition to the anxieties that the children will inevitably bring with them are the staff responses. Hughes and Pengelly state, 'In turbulent times, professionals' own experience of uncontaining environments frequently serves to escalate their anger or anxiety into almost speechless states of fury or despair – states of mind unlikely to provide containment for feelings of service-users' (1997:177). This can manifest itself in situations where staff become paralysed and disengage from the child and become observers and recorders of the child's chaotic behaviour rather than actively seeking to engage with the child. At the most extreme position, the staff no longer believe they can work with the child and believe that the child should be moved to a new placement. In other situations the more punitive side of our personalities can be released and tougher and tougher sanctions become the order of the day. This section will briefly explore a number of ways in which these parallel experiences of containment can be provided for the care team.

It is to my mind inevitable that troubled children will evoke strong feelings in those who care for them. There needs to be permission given for the difficult feelings to be expressed so that they can be attended to and detoxified. Unfortunately, too often the implicit message given to staff is that the 'good' worker is calm and unencumbered by anxious feelings. Good supervision and team meetings in a trusting environment can provide the safe space for doing this purposeful and honest thinking. The team also needs a model for reflecting and Morrison's supervision cycle, set out in detail in his book *Staff Supervision in Social Care* (2001), provides an excellent one.

In my experience, having a model for reflection is in itself a containing device as it imposes the necessary discipline to separate out and make sense of the various aspects of a situation. For example, if the story of what happened can first be told without reference to the strong feelings that the situation evoked, the scene is set for a deeper understanding of the events. In this way a certain processing occurs, which is not swamped by the strong and overwhelming feelings the situation elicited. And when at the next stage the feelings are explored it is as if they have been put in a container which is strong enough and big enough to hold them and prevent them from spilling out and drowning people. In other words, the feelings become manageable and the necessary psychic space for analysis and planning and acting has been created. The facilitation of this process is the core work of the manager unless they are so involved in the events that they cannot do this with the level of detachment required. In these situations organisations need to be able to provide a competent person who can facilitate the process in a timely manner.

Feelings of fear and hopelessness are extremely contagious. Experienced workers will be familiar with the experience of coming into work in a positive frame of mind only to find that they are drained before they begin their shift having attended an emotional handover in which the outgoing team off-loaded their frustrations from the previous shift. Without doubt, long, difficult shifts create much pent-up emotion, which needs to be attended to, and preferably before people go off shift. Ideally, this process needs to take place in a separate space prior to the handover. When this time is created, the outgoing shift have the benefit of processing their feelings, the incoming team are not unnecessarily burdened and hopefully they can then provide the children with a break from the dynamic of the previous shift.

The wider organisation also needs to provide containing care for its staff and managers. An effective way of providing this care is through an effective system of external oversight. This is necessary, first, to ensure that the abuses of the past are not repeated but it also, which is just as important, provides an opportunity to acknowledge good practice. The day-to-day struggle of dealing with difficult situations can be an isolating experience for a staff team and the organisation needs to have a mechanism for conveying the important message that it supports the staff in the difficult struggle that residential care can sometimes be. And finally, this external oversight can provide staff with the reassurance that they are doing all that can be done for the child. On occasion staff teams can be overcome with feelings of hopelessness that mirror the hopelessness of the child. At such times staff need to be reassured that they are doing the right thing, and this in turn gives them the resilience to hang in with the child while recognising that progress is often slow and incremental. The staff too, as I hope I've outlined, need to be 'contained' if extremely difficult, challenging events, and all the emotional responses these events throw up, are to be met with effective interventions in the lives of those vulnerable people with whom we deal every day.

Chapter 15
Placing Therapeutic Relationships at the Heart of our Work

Laura Behan

> '*A child's life is like a piece of paper, on which every passer by leaves a mark*'
>
> Chinese Proverb

INTRODUCTION

Social care is such a broad and diverse field that when I first began working in residential care with adolescents, I had very little insight into what the work truly involved. The young people we met were often carrying so much hurt and trauma that they were frozen in patterns of self-destructive behaviour. Caring for them and nurturing them to grow in more positive directions was often a daunting task for the staff team. There are many different approaches to this task and this chapter will focus on the use of the therapeutic relationship in my practice.

It is important to note that confusion can often arise from the use of the term 'therapeutic relationship' in relation to residential care. It is most commonly referred to when discussing a psychotherapeutic counselling relationship between 'therapist' and 'client'. In fact, residential centres operating as therapeutic communities are largely informed by the same psychodynamic principles as psychotherapy – these being that all behaviour has meaning and that the relationship should provide a safe space for this to be acted out.

Of course the setting in question is different from that of formal therapy; however, it does allow for cohesion of psychodynamic principles and person-centred work. In a therapeutic setting, relationships are developed within what Winnicott calls the 'holding environment'. In this environment the young people are provided with the 'caring, supportive and integrative holding which every human being needs in order to grow' (Ward *et al.* 2003:9). This chapter offers an account of my experience of using the therapeutic relationship in my work with an adolescent girl named 'Sarah'.

PATH INTO SOCIAL CARE

When I was young I always assumed I would be a teacher. I don't quite know why; I just remember having a sense of wanting to help children. I loved reading and I remember being struck by the complexity of people and their relationships with each other and with the world. I always wondered how some people could overcome adverse circumstances, trauma and disadvantage and go on to live fulfilled lives, while others remained seemingly hopeless for ever. One common thread in the success stories was that someone had helped and supported these people when they needed it the most. Someone had reached out to those who were masking their pain with a smile or the teenager who everyone knew was 'trouble', but no one ever asked 'Why?'. I decided I wanted to find a profession where I could reach out to people in this way and so I found myself studying social care.

THE STORY

Practice setting

The backdrop for Sarah's story is a residential unit for adolescents. 'Residential care' is the term used to describe round-the-clock care provided for young people who have been placed in the care of the state for a period of time. This is usually due to a breakdown in their primary care system, which means it is no longer safe for them to remain at home. These young people often carry with them the scars of emotional, physical and mental trauma and our task as social care workers in this setting is to provide a safe and consistent 'holding' environment within which they can form relationships and learn to trust.

The residential centre I worked in operated as a therapeutic community, which modelled itself on similar communities such as the Mulberry Bush, founded by Barbara Dockar-Drysdale in 1948. One of our main tasks was to help the young people to 're-experience their childhood so that the community could undo some of the damage done by their early childhood experiences' (Stevens & Furnivall 2007:199). I have come to believe that one of the most valuable tools for this work is the therapeutic relationship. If the holding environment is the sea on which healing takes place, the therapeutic relationship is the vessel in which it occurs.

Background to Sarah's story

The reality of trying to form a therapeutic relationship with a young person can be very challenging, especially for those working, as I was, in a short-term unit. We would often receive just a few hours' notice of an emergency placement. I was working an overnight shift when we received news that a fifteen-year-old girl called Sarah was being admitted for the weekend. At this stage we had very little background information about her. We knew that there had been difficulties at home and her behaviour had become unmanageable, resulting in an agreement that she would be placed in care on a voluntary basis. A temporary foster placement had broken down and Sarah had presented at Accident and Emergency in a distressed state. I was allocated as a support for Sarah and was the first person she met on arrival. Our immediate focus was on containing her behaviours and keeping her safe.

Sarah's placement was soon extended, which was not uncommon. There was nowhere else for her to be placed and she said she was happy to stay as she acknowledged that things were difficult at home. The relationship between Sarah and her parents was becoming increasingly fractious and she seemed quite angry with them. Sarah expressed that she felt a connection with me and I was assigned as one of her key workers.

> *One of the central tasks for the key worker is that they become ... someone who holds everything about the child and his needs and concerns in mind, just as a parent would.*
>
> (Worthington 2003:155)

The therapeutic relationship the young person goes on to form may not necessarily be with the key worker, and that is perfectly acceptable. In this case it seemed as though the relationship was developing naturally alongside my role as key worker. Knowing the significance such a relationship can hold, I instantly felt a sense of pressure. Often we are so focused on care plans and challenging behaviours that we want to dive in immediately to 'fix things'. This was certainly the case with Sarah because her behaviours were so unsafe, and I felt an urgency to begin the work. On reflection I realised that building the foundation for the relationship was the immediate work and before this could happen the seeds of trust needed to be sown.

Building the foundations

The first step was for myself and Sarah to meet with the therapeutic consultant, a psychotherapist who could guide our therapeutic relationship, and discuss our expectations. Sarah asked that I would 'just be there' for her and, in turn, I made her a promise that I would be an unconditional presence for her. The cornerstone of this promise was 'unconditional positive regard', a concept championed by Carl Rogers. Rogers believed that:

[T]the quality of the relationship – specifically the therapist's congruence ... unconditional positive regard ... and empathy – were more important factors in therapeutic change than the specific techniques the therapist employed.

(Kirschenbaum & Henderson 1989:62).

Unconditional positive regard is basic acceptance and support of the value of a person, regardless of their actions. We were both clear that while I would not always agree with or be happy about Sarah's actions, the relationship would not be withdrawn as a result and I would continue to believe in the basic good in her. The hope was that within the relationship Sarah could begin to make sense of her experiences and her behaviour and realise that they did not define her. Making such a promise was rather daunting and I remember the questions that filled my mind:

- How am I going to do this in practice?
- How am I going to watch her hurting herself and potentially assaulting my colleagues and remain a constant source of support?
- How can I promise her that if she one day assaults me our therapeutic relationship will not be affected?

I could tell similar questions were filling Sarah's mind. She had to be wondering how in the world a relative stranger could keep such a promise when she had been so hurt by people close to her. I was aware that she would be leaving her guard well and truly in place until I proved I could keep this promise. I resolved to put my worries and doubts aside and proceed with the work.

As Ward *et al.* (2003:149) highlight, attempting to build a relationship with a young person who is carrying the scars of trauma can be very complex and at times can feel like an impossible task. When what is often described by social care workers as 'the honeymoon period' of a placement is over, the behaviour you are met with can be enough to make you want to turn and run in the other direction, never mind sticking around to forge a way through the barriers. We must remember that it is terrifying for the young people to contemplate letting someone chip away at the walls they have built to protect themselves from further hurt. It takes time and patience on our part, as well as the realisation that they may never be able to let us in.

We could easily become overwhelmed and forget that the seemingly unremarkable things are a great place to start. Remembering how many sugars a young person takes in their tea or how they like their toast cut reminds them that someone is holding them in mind and gives them a sense that their needs are valued, an experience that may be foreign to them. I realised quite early on that these things were very important to Sarah and she would be highly indignant if I forgot them. She would express this mostly in jest, but the importance was clear. She was testing me with the smaller things first.

Through a combination of these everyday gestures and Sarah gaining a sense of me being there for her, the relationship quickly developed and she began to let me in.

The turning point

A few weeks into her placement Sarah disclosed that she had been sexually assaulted. She had been struggling to remain in the house earlier that day and had left with other residents.

When they returned later that evening, Sarah was heavily intoxicated and clearly distressed. My colleague and I tried to engage with her, but she was aggressive and hostile, shouting abuse and telling us to leave her alone. I felt that Sarah was testing the relationship and giving me an opportunity to 'be there' as she had asked. She was struggling to stand up on her own, so my colleague and I each took an arm and brought her to her room. She angrily fought against this; however, by the time we placed her safely on her bed Sarah had given up her resistance. Sarah broke down in my arms and told me the story of what had happened the year before in such vivid detail that I was glad she could not see my face. In that moment, I experienced such a conflict of emotions. The human part of me was angry, distressed and appalled at what I was hearing. However, I knew there were important guidelines to be followed in this situation. I was also aware that I must show Sarah that I could hold her pain for her and with her. I mostly listened, offering words of comfort, and reassured Sarah that she was in no way to blame for what had happened. When she finished talking, we sat in silence and I rocked her until she fell asleep. I was exhausted in every sense of the word, but I knew I had to put what I had just heard out of my mind and complete my shift. I shared the information with my colleague, filled out the appropriate reports and the following morning reported the incident to my management and Sarah's social worker. I remember the journey home in the car the following morning. I turned the radio up loudly as I always did after a tough shift and I sobbed.

To engage with a young person on such a personal level you must tap into the human parts of yourself, such as empathy and understanding, while maintaining a professional balance. This can feel like an internal tug of war at times and was a constant challenge for me throughout the process. I learned to acknowledge my human feelings as completely valid. The important thing was that I had to be able put them aside when needed and find an appropriate space to process them later. This is where my supervision was crucial. Good supervision provides a space 'to allow the emotional disturbance to be felt within the safer setting of the supervisory relationship, where it can be survived, reflected upon and learnt from' (Hawkins & Shohet 2012:4).

When I returned to work two days later I was very aware that Sarah would be awaiting my next move. Our last encounter had been a litmus test for what I could handle from her and I knew that how I acted now would be vital in earning further trust. I checked in with her about how she was feeling and suggested we spend the afternoon curled up on the couch watching her favourite movie. Sarah still talks about that day as one of her favourite memories from her placement. She had shared one of her darkest secrets with me and our relationship had not been affected. As Myers (2006) tells us, to confess our worst secrets and still feel accepted brings us a sense of profound relief. I was, however, conscious that having embraced the relationship in this way, young people can feel vulnerable when their significant staff member is unavailable to 'emotionally hold' them, and the reality is that we cannot always be there. I got Sarah a blanket to symbolise the feeling of being held and from then on she kept it wrapped it around her wherever she went. In fact, she laid it across her bed at night, almost like a shield from the world.

The testing

There was a shift in Sarah's behaviour after this incident. Now that I had passed the first major 'test', the real testing of the therapeutic relationship, the team and the holding environment began. Sarah's behaviour over the coming weeks was extremely challenging. She became a chameleon and could go from completely withdrawn to self-destructive in a matter of hours. She appeared almost angry with herself for allowing me into her inner world and did her utmost to push away anyone who tried to care for her. She verbally abused and threatened staff members and damaged property.

One day she assaulted a colleague before I came on shift. It was so difficult to listen to that information without feeling an urge to withdraw, and remaining unconditional that day was a struggle. I was very conscious of remaining accepting of Sarah within the relationship without sending her the message that what she had done was acceptable.

In order to maintain this balance, myself and my colleagues often had to remind ourselves that:

Acceptance has nothing to do with permissiveness ... there may be consequences for behaviours ... but these consequences never include a threat to the relationship or an assessment that there are deficiencies in the self of the child.

(Hughes 2009:79)

From then on, Sarah was often absent without permission, although she would have periods of 'hibernation' when she let us take care of her. She would leave with other residents or go alone to see friends she had made in the locality. She would often engage in alcohol and drug abuse and place herself in sexually inappropriate situations. Sarah had such a low sense of self-worth that when you tried to help her make sense of her actions she could not grasp the damage she was doing to herself. At times it seemed she could not summon the will to even care. During this period I did question the process and wondered what, if any, difference could it all possibly be making? I took comfort in reminding myself that this was the emergence of the 'true self' that Winnicott speaks of and that 'we should feel hopeful when we start to see the challenging aspects of a child's behaviour as it is part of the recovery process' (Barton *et al.* 2011:20).

This comfort was needed to remain positive in what was often a very isolating place to be. When you are invested in being unconditional to a young person who spends a lot of their time in crisis, you can encounter team conflict. Your colleagues may fear that you have lost sight of the line between being unconditional and simply making allowances for unacceptable behaviour. In turn you may not always feel fully supported or understood in what it is you are doing. Supervision, team communication and trust are crucial at these times as 'staff can only provide the necessary caring and "holding" if they themselves are properly cared for and "held"' (Ward *et al.* 2003:15). You will need the objective input of your colleagues to ensure that you remain on task and do not allow yourself to be 'seduced' by the false self. In return you will need your colleagues to trust the process and support you within this.

In the midst of the crisis Sarah very often allowed me to see her vulnerable 'self'. She struggled with night time and would often be at her most challenging then. She would become extremely disruptive, threatening and abusive. She later told me she was trying to avoid lying alone in bed with painful thoughts and memories swishing around her mind. She may have confided her experience, but she was still very much dealing with the residual trauma of this and other hurts from her past.

One night Sarah and her co-resident were being extremely hostile and abusive and refusing to go to bed. I managed to speak to Sarah alone and reminded her that I was here to help her figure out a better way to deal with her fear of going to sleep. She stared at me for a few moments and asked, 'Will you read me a story?' I replied that I would be happy to and she settled into bed.

This became a regular routine and I would sometimes wonder at the sight of this teenage girl, wrapped up like a toddler, gazing at me while I read. Much like a toddler, she would pretend to be asleep to see if I would leave, so I would continue to read until I was sure that she was asleep. When I was struggling with a feeling of being lost, these moments reminded me of what this process was about. These were the healing experiences the relationship was allowing me to provide and no matter how fleeting these moments were, they were worthwhile.

We spent many moments like this on the days that Sarah was able for 'normality', as she called it. We watched movies, had pampering nights and shared many laughs. When I finished a shift I would leave her little notes to say how proud I was of her (all of which she kept and still reads to this day) and I could see her very gradually believing that the 'real' Sarah was loveable. Frustratingly, just as soon as you would see that light go on in her you could turn your back and she would be gone again. I remember a session with the consultant when I was looking for guidance to make sense of how these somewhat scattered experiences could possibly be making an impact. He told me that I needed to see this therapeutic relationship as a flower pot within which Sarah's sense of self could grow. She would hopefully begin to form little roots here with us and would bring them with her to her next 'pot'.

This analogy gave me the clarity I was searching for and the strength to continue the work, while reminding me of the value of reflective practice.

Coming to an end

The final weeks of Sarah's placement were a very challenging time for everyone. It was clear that she had come as far as she was able to at this point in her life and she was putting herself in serious danger almost every day. She was associating with local drug dealers and becoming involved in criminal activity. She was stuck in a spiral of abusing alcohol and drugs to escape the painful memories of past experiences. We continued working hard to help Sarah understand that these were only temporary coping strategies and that her pain would follow her wherever she went. At times this felt futile and almost exhausting but I reminded myself that Sarah was not refusing to understand this out of pure defiance: reality was simply too painful for to face at present. I had to constantly remind myself that the core of unconditional positive regard is meeting the person where they are at and respecting their right to be in crisis.

One night Sarah became very emotional after a phone call from home and was pacing around her bedroom threatening to run away and harm herself. Trying to reason with her was not working and I realised I needed to change my approach. I told her I was going to stay with her in case she needed me and then sat in silence on her bed. She began cleaning out boxes and looking through family photos, tearing each one up as she went. I fought my urge to ask questions and we remained there in silence for the best part of an hour. Sarah gradually calmed down and asked me to go for a walk with her.

That night taught me an important lesson about the value of just 'being' in this work. We want to figure out problems and find solutions for these young people, but sometimes that's not what they need. She did not need me to present her with the reasons why running away wouldn't help or what the consequences would be. She simply needed me to stay alongside her through whatever she was feeling and experiencing.

As the end of her placement drew near, it became clear that Sarah had gained some insight into her behaviour. She would say that although she had come to feel at home with us she could not bear to be around people who cared for her right now and running away felt like a much easier option. It was decided she would move to a foster placement away from the area, where she would have less opportunity to put herself in dangerous situations. The young people we worked with often found endings very painful and saw them as a rejection, so they would sabotage the process by 'rejecting' us first. Sarah's ending was planned as well as possible so that it would feel safe, as she had herself expressed that she would find moving on very difficult. Even though she had not always been able to allow us to look after her, she had come to think of the environment and the relationship as a place of safety and acceptance and it would be frightening for her to leave that behind.

When the time for us to say goodbye was approaching, Sarah bolted from the house. I allowed myself to briefly indulge in feelings of disappointment and then reminded myself that Sarah was dealing with this in the only way she knew how and my feelings had no place in this moment. She did return to say goodbye before I left and told me it was because she didn't want to let me down.

This was a huge step for her as when she had first come to us, she would say she didn't care much about letting anyone down, including herself. Moments such as these, when you can see a glimmer of positive change, are what keep you going in this difficult work. As social care workers we often project our own values and expectations on to the people we work with. However, we must always hold in mind that the seemingly insignificant things are in fact the building blocks for change.

CONCLUSION

If you were to examine Sarah's placement from the outside you could be forgiven for asking, Was her time with us a waste? She came to us struggling to deal with the scars of past experiences and left us with many challenges still to face. You might pose the questions, Did we make any difference? Can we ever make a dent in the armour of these challenging young people? I think these are constant niggles for social care workers, especially in short-term units where we may have a time-limited input. They are certainly questions I have asked myself and my colleagues over the years and on some of the toughest days of this experience I continue to question the value of the therapeutic relationship. These questions usually arise when we feel frustrated that people are not changing as quickly or as much as we feel they are capable of. Perhaps the changes seem almost imperceptible and we wonder if change is occurring at all. As always with this work, if we are prepared to listen, the young people hold the answers to our questions. I spoke to Sarah after she left us and it became clear that her time with us was most definitely not wasted. She told me, 'The experience kept me alive and I feel somewhat like my own person now. I finally found the strength to report what happened to me and the relief of that was huge. You were always there and you always believed in me. I'm gone but the relationship is still there like a background sequence, it's my stepping stone to the future.'

Listening to her I realised these were not the words of the scared and angry girl I had met all those months ago. These were the words of a young woman who had experienced healing, gained a sense of herself and uncovered a hopelessness long buried inside. Sarah attributes these changes to our relationship and so do I.

If you take nothing else from this chapter, please take Sarah's words and keep them with you on those hard days when you are asking, What's the point? The point is that change is a whisper and we may not see it as it often happens after the experience. In some cases people may continue to make poor choices for some time. We can only hope that one day they will recall their experience of a relationship in which they felt safe, accepted and valued and that this will stir them to take a step in the right direction.

Chapter 16
The Therapeutic Alliance in Practice
Helen Buggle

This chapter outlines a particular approach which, in my experience, has proved effective with some children in a residential care setting.

The therapeutic alliance is characterised by three interlinked elements:

1 the contract
2. the aims or therapeutic tasks
3 the relationship.

At any one time a social care worker may be working on one of these elements, but when it comes to using the therapeutic alliance as a healing tool the three elements must be working in conjunction with one another.

When I talk about 'therapeutic' I refer to the psychodynamic perspective of looking at and tending to the child's inner world of emotions, thoughts and experiences, along with the dynamic forces of the ever-changing world around them, being mindful always of where both elements create conflict, hurt, confusion and, of course, possibilities for the child.

THE CONTRACT

To take the 'contract' as a starting point, it has been my experience that at the time of admission, when a young person is feeling unsure, vulnerable, possibly defensive and guarded, they need to be met with a respect and a demonstration of acceptance of where they are at. It is also a natural opportunity for me to demonstrate the values, thinking and practice through which I and, by implication, my agency/service wish to be of help.

In other words, during the admission process we as an organisation and team, and I as an individual social care worker, will lay out our stall, with all that is on offer and available, but with no pressure for the young person to buy in to it. We only request that they at least reflect on it and talk to someone about it. This allows the young person freedom to choose. Once the young person has chosen to come to live with us, all expectations are discussed, argued and agreed on with no hidden agenda. Yet it is understood that as time goes on, the nature of the young person's care and treatment will develop and change depending on their needs and abilities.

The admission of a young person into care is always an emotive time. After reading the referral and talking with all relevant people, including the young person themselves, I am acutely aware of that individual's history and early beginnings, of their hurt, trauma and grief. It is often a time when I am most in touch with their inner world. It is at this time I am reminded of what David Smail said in his book *Taking Care: An Alternative to Therapy*:

> *More often than not people meet the 'truth' of their predicament with relief, what is most painful to deal with is the empty promise of its 'cure' ... Most people are glad ... and enormously relieved if they find someone who will share with them an unflinching view of cruelties and injustices whose marks they will always bear.*

(Smail 1987:90)

Over the years I have returned to this piece for reflection and it helps me to keep in touch with the fact that while young people strive to move forward as best they can, their past is never far away and they have been shaped by it. I feel that while we must build resilience and encourage growth, we must also acknowledge the past. I remember one young person who used to remind me from time to time that, while she was doing great, sitting exams, having a social life and making dreams for her future, she was not 'cured'. It was her way of telling me that she still had a lot of pain and at times it could overwhelm her; I needed to remember that. I always felt this was her way of telling me not to forget about her. I would reassure her that when I saw her giving and receiving joy I was so proud of her, yet I never forgot the sadness she carried with her and the effort it took her to be able to manage it. I used to tell her that when she became overwhelmed with sadness she could give some of it to me to manage until she felt able for it again. We had a signal for these times: she would come to my office, stand there with her head to one side with a certain look in her eyes, saying nothing. I knew then that my job was to take her in my arms and talk softly and lovingly as I stroked her head. She would then know that I knew how she was feeling and I would keep a special eye out for her that day.

THE THERAPEUTIC TASK

The second element of the alliance is the therapeutic task, or the aims of the placement. It is important that the adult enters this stage of the relationship with an attitude of equality. There needs to be a balance and equality between being an expert in your knowledge and abilities and recognising and communicating to the young person that they too are experts in their own history and current problems. Yet they may need help in gaining the skills to help themselves towards healing and reaching their positive potential.

Sensitive and genuine communication about past difficulties and present struggles, along with hopes for the new placement, can be looked at here. Any aims identified at this point must be done by the young person. Clear discussions and agreed views of both the worker and the young person on how the aims should be achieved will lead to better outcomes. As you can imagine, tasks can range from helping the young person to settle in to the routines of the new placement to introducing them to the physical locality, to helping them gain a school placement and maintain it. Added to the practical tasks are the more deeply held emotional needs, such as feeling special to someone, feeling accepted, needing to and being allowed to grieve. The list is endless and must be handled with care and attention. The key worker or significant adult, whoever has been identified as the primary worker, must be able to help the young person to break down the therapeutic aims of the placement and identify the therapeutic tasks that will help achieve the aims. This of course takes time and will continue to be an ever-changing feature of the relationship and the placement.

I am reminded here of the daily struggle care workers have in relation to how the young person's needs are expressed. Many times we are met with anger and hostility, the young person consciously or unconsciously trying to mask deeply felt hurts and their level of frustration and insecurity about trying new things. Believing they will fail can often be the biggest stumbling block to realising therapeutic tasks. The job of the care worker, as Bion proposed, is:

> *To tolerate and understand a child's raw emotional states of distress ... it is the mother's (social care worker's) job to make sense of theses bewildering sensations for the baby (young person) to give them shape, coherence and meaning which makes them tolerable.*

(cited in Canham 1998)

One task I remember having to do a 'hard sell' on was the 'permitted abuse' of a staff member. A young girl was in the throes of projection, using the defence mechanism of putting on to another person one's own undesirable feelings and thoughts so as to 'split them off' from the self so they can be felt as outside oneself. All the pain and hurt she had experienced at the hands of her parents was being projected on to her key worker and this was a safe thing for her to do as there was no fear of a punitive response. If she had presented her raw emotions to her parent/s this may have meant risking losing whatever little relationship she had left. Yet the hurt and fear were all-consuming at times and they needed a space to be expressed. The key worker had been taking the verbal abuse for so long that the relationship was becoming abusive and undermining staff confidence.

I took the decision to sit with the key worker and young person and with their permission I explicitly put forward my hypothesis of what I thought was going on in the relationship. The key worker spoke from a very caring, genuine – yet exhausted – place, saying that she understood what the girl was doing, was sad for her to have so much to deal with and that no one child/young person should have to hold all this hurt on their own. It had, in fact, now become too much for her, even as an adult, to bear on her own, especially when she saw no real decrease in distress or healing happening, and it was time to do something different. I checked with the young person, asking if what had been said made any sense to her and she responded with some degree of relief. She spoke with respect and an acceptance of our interpretation of her behaviour.

While it was decided that the key worker needed a break from being the 'bad object', we understood that the young person still needed to be able to express her inner turmoil, while at the same time she needed to work on finding ways to cope and manage her emotions in a more positive manner.

We decided that she no longer had 'permission to abuse' her key worker. However, if she needed or we observed her needing a place to release hurt emotions, she would have the permission of the staff on duty to take five to ten minutes in a room to shout and scream anything she needed in their direction. No physical violence was allowed and if she used the time as permitted she would be rewarded with praise and acknowledgement. In terms of dealing with her distress, anger, frustration and hurt she would be offered time with staff. The offer of this space and the containment of the process in a quiet room, away from other children, helped to depersonalise the abusive language for staff and they felt that their approach in this controlled way was therapeutic. It was also amazing to see how little the young girl ever used the option. Just offering the space and the attunement with her inner world was often enough to help her self-contain around this issue.

THE RELATIONSHIP

The third element of the therapeutic alliance is of course the relationship itself, the overall 'container' for the work. It is here that the worker may find themselves most challenged and it may be here that they find themselves most vulnerable. Yet it is my experience that it is also here that so many social care workers 'find' themselves, learning and growing and possibly being most satisfied with their practice.

The individual worker may also be the focus at this point in terms of what they are willing to do for the young person and how far they are willing to go to help. And, of course, no therapeutic contract or goals will be reached if not within a safe and containing relationship.

In 1972, when Newson and her associates carried out inspections on children's homes in the UK, they remarked that the best community care could offer was impartiality, to be fair to every child. However, she went on to say that a developing child needed more. What was vital was that a child needed to know that they were special to someone, that they would be placed above others and that someone would go not just to ordinary lengths but to extraordinary lengths for them.

It is my hope that we have moved beyond the impartiality that Newson spoke about, but I do fear that we are still stuck somewhat on the fairness issue. Fairness does not mean treating everyone the same, but treating each person according to their needs. It's funny how simple this concept is, and how easily it can be explained to children when they first perceive themselves not getting what another has. What is important to remember and to safeguard is that each child does in fact get what they need and that each child has at least one adult on the team who has a special interest in them. As Newson said, it is 'vital' (which, according to the Oxford English Dictionary, means 'essential to the existence of life'). Bronfenbrenner put it in very simple terms when he said, 'Every kid needs at least one adult who's crazy about him or her.'

I have two stories I would like to share with you at this point to show just how simple acts of love and understanding can make a difference. One involves a young child who had had many moves before she came to live with us in residential care. She had a very attentive key worker who worked very much in the public sphere and with all the children in the group. However, at bedtime, whenever the key worker was on shift she would make it known that she would be the one to settle her key child to bed. They developed a routine whereby the key worker would tuck the child in to bed and sing her a certain song every night; she would then kiss her on her forehead and leave the bedroom door ajar, always promising to return to have a last check in and close the door when she herself was on her way to bed. This was individualised by the fact that the child did not have to ask her key worker to settle her at night; she knew the key worker wanted to spend time with her; the song that the key worker sang was for her alone. However, the key worker was also aware that the child woke up during the night and was often frightened and propelled back to early times when she had often woken in the middle of the night and no one was there for her. So along with giving the child full permission to wake the staff up at night for reassurance (she never wanted to disturb us), she asked the child if there was anything we could do to demonstrate that we had checked in on her and that we were there for her if she needed us. The child took a few days to get back to her key worker and when she did she asked for a flower to be placed beside her bed each night. As manager it is my duty to make sure any requests such as this are given due consideration. After discussion with the young person it was agreed that each sleepover staff member would place a small flower beside the child's bed at night and during the winter the staff would draw a flower and do likewise.

This was introduced to the team by the key worker explaining the need it was fulfilling. The response was so great that in two years no one ever forgot to place or draw a flower and the drawings were often accompanied by a phrase or sentence such as, 'Sweet dreams', 'We are so proud of you' or 'Thanks for that lovely cup of tea today', etc.

I would from time to time check in with the child to ascertain if the flower was still needed and if we were still getting it right. Then one day she told her key worker she no longer needed the flower. This was a cause for excitement and celebration as it signified that a sense of security and trust had been reached and she now felt safe enough in our care to know that we would not abandon her during the night. This simple act of acceptance by her key worker and the staff team's intuition and professional commitment enabled this child to transfer her trust in her key worker and the team in this one area of her life to many other areas. (Every one of the flowers had been stored safely and she took them with her when she left our care some years later.)

My second story involves a young girl, nearly a young woman by the time she came to live with us. Her story was one of the worst I had encountered for many years and she carried with her the scars of many years of abuse and fear. This young woman found the transition from day to night difficult and she would wake many times during the night. At one of our weekly team meetings one of the male workers, who had recently become a father for the first time, noted that this young person was waking up at what seemed like regular intervals and that maybe this was indicative of a very primitive need to be tended to – just like his own child at home. The short silence in the staff room was broken by the team discussing how or what they could do to tend to the inner child and how long it might take for the young girl to consciously or unconsciously feel that her need been met in an unconditional way. From that night on, every time she woke up (about every four hours), a staff member would go to her side and offer reassurance, a tuck in, a head rub or a kiss goodnight. Sometimes a glass of milk or water, or some food was brought to the bedside. Tone of voice was important, and the loving expression with which we looked at the girl was also seen as part of the whole message that we were trying to convey.

Within a month she was settling better. She also came to me to discuss how she was feeling and without any staff member talking explicitly with her about the inner need being addressed she started to piece things together and talk about what she had missed out on and how she was beginning to feel she could have some of her needs addressed with us. It is an amazing moment in a social care worker's career when they witness the ordinary acts they do become extraordinary events in a young person's life. I remember the pride I had in my team and in their unconditional commitment to this young girl and my only regret was that she came to us so late and we had so little time with her.

DEVELOPING A THERAPEUTIC ALLIANCE

So what does the care worker need in order to do this type of work, to develop a therapeutic alliance? Winnicott stated that:

> *The identification with the child does not have to be as deep as that of the mother with her new-born, except of course when the child under consideration is ill, emotionally immature ... When the child is ill then there is a crisis and the therapy that is needed involves the therapist (care worker) personally, and the work cannot be done on any other basis.*
>
> (Winnicott 1965:71)

John Bowlby compared the therapeutic relationship to one between mother and child. He believed that 'What is believed to be essential for mental health is that the infant and the young child should experience a warm, intimate and continuous relationship with his mother (or permanent mother-substitute) in which both find satisfaction and enjoyment' (Bowlby 1951, cited in Bowlby 1973:xi).

Well, my own belief is that any social care worker wishing to enter into a therapeutic alliance needs to have some very specific personal qualities, or at least the disposition to acquire them, which will form the basis of their engagement and connection with the young person. They should have a good working knowledge of attachment theory; understand the different attachment styles and the symptoms each may present. They should know how to respond from a psychodynamic and humanistic point of view to the young person's communications and unmet needs. They need to have a working knowledge of trauma and its debilitating effects on the child's development from a physical (both brain and body) and psychological point of view.

I also feel that it is imperative that social care workers working in this type of relationship should have good supporting structures to aid and monitor the relationship and its effects on the worker. Such supports include regular team meetings where the worker is able to share with colleagues their practice and ask for help and where they can give and receive objective feedback on observable behaviour. Also essential is good supervision from line management with an emphasis on self-awareness, professional development and case review from a psychotherapeutic viewpoint. External consultation, in which group and individual practice is clinically reviewed, also forms part of the supporting scaffolding and is strongly recommended.

ATTACHMENT

While this chapter is not an academic piece on attachment theory it is important to note that some elementary aspects of attachment apply to the theory that children who end up in residential care, as the examples above have shown.

The primary biological function of attachment behaviour is survival. Its psychological function is security. At its most basic the baby will die if it has no one to care for it and meet its needs. Attachment theory usually explains the child's behaviours from their point of origin rather than the display of symptoms in later years. However, it is important that the behaviours we as social care workers encounter in older children are seen and thought of as symptoms of their primary caregiving experiences.

No matter what attachment pattern a child presents with you can be almost sure that this pattern developed in direct response to the parenting style encountered when they were most vulnerable and when attaching to someone meant survival – even if that someone was the source of confusion, pain or trauma.

Attachment can be defined as:

*A deep and enduring connection established between a child and caregiver
... it profoundly influences every component of the human condition*

– mind, body, emotions, relationships, and values. Attachment is not something that parents do to their children: rather it is something that children and parents create together.

(Levy & Orlans 1998:1)

The attachment behaviours young people present to us are normative and make perfect sense to the young person. However, when removed from the dysfunctional or deprived caregiving situation and placed in an emotionally containing and appropriately responsive environment, the behaviours no longer seem normative and often present as very antisocial and outwardly do not serve the child well.

I find that many social care workers are often afraid of the whole concept of attachment. They feel that they will be negatively judged by peers and superiors for getting over-involved with a child and losing their objectivity. They may be accused of private practice and exclusivity; they may also be accused of having their own needs met by the child. Of course, all of these things may indeed happen and that is where good supervision and professional training come into play.

So let's just say that the social care worker is not doing any of these very unethical and unprofessional things but instead has a real understanding of the needs of children and knows that making themselves emotionally available and allowing a child to become attached to them and creating a dependency (secure base) in the relationship is how the child will have their needs met. It is exactly what is needed to aid the healing process. Then, surely, our professionalism and our duty to care mean that we should be striving towards creating the right environment where this therapeutic alliance can be developed?

I know when I was an infant I needed my mother to depend on for all my needs and I was attached to her for many years of my life. This attachment, this 'secure base' she created, allowed me to go out and explore my world. Why, then, would it be any different for the child in care?

Ah yes, of course they come to us, not as infants but often as older children or, indeed, as big, strapping teenagers. However, if we are to take a psychodynamic approach and look for the inner child, the one who is hurting and afraid, we often find a much younger child than the one who is presenting to us chronologically.

So is it the size that frightens us? Are we afraid that if we offer this relationship, this therapeutic alliance, this secure base, the fifteen-year-old will never want to leave? That has never been my experience. Yes, in the beginning when the young person is basking in the feeling of security and affection, when they maybe feel for the first time real unconditional positive regard or even love, when someone thinks they are special, wonderful and worth going to extraordinary lengths for, then they may not want to be very far away from the primary caregiver. (Of course, for staff, such intensity may mean exhaustion by the end of their shift!)

So we plan for that. Shift endings, handovers, holidays and leave all have to be managed sensitively. With a little thought and creativity these times can add to the therapeutic alliance rather than rupture it. The simple exchange of a personal item, to be held and minded by the worker and child, is one way of bridging the time away. One child in my care used to have her pillow sprayed with her key worker's perfume before she went home. Another key worker kept in touch while she was on maternity leave by letters, phone calls, gifts and the odd visit to the unit to see her key child. The other staff kept the relationship alive and the person looking after the child was in contact with the key worker throughout the leave period. The young person knew this and understood that she was being kept in mind. Another child and her key worker exchanged small teddy bears while they were apart.

However, once a key worker and team make a decision to meet the unmet primary need, nothing is left to chance. The care around meeting the need is planned and discussed and understood by all. The practice is supervised and monitored at all times and everyone is kept safe. A teenager, even one with primary needs, is for a great part of their day still a teenager; they have the same dreams, wants and urges to go out and live their lives. Staff need have no fear that the teenager will stay dependent for too long. If the need is met the change can happen very quickly and on we move to the next need, which could be something completely different, until such time as the teenager becomes a young adult and the staff member continues to respond appropriately to the inner child while continuing to build resilience and help the individual to move forward.

The creation of a secure base is not a regressive step. For young people who have continued in emotional confusion and frustration and a state of immaturity, growing physically and socially yet struggling emotionally, it is in fact a liberating and progressive development towards the healing and integration of a fragile personality.

> I am reminded of a time some years ago when one of my staff was key worker for a young girl, a dependency within the therapeutic alliance had developed and the young girl was beginning to experience unconditional regard for the first time in many years. One day the staff member was cleaning the young girl's bedroom with her and was met with the question, 'Do you love me?' The staff member was stunned into silence. It was the first time she had been asked this in her professional career. She was unsure of how to respond and managed to talk her way out of the question, but was acutely aware that she had not given the child a proper answer and that the question would be asked again in the future.

In supervision the staff member was upset about the situation and upset at herself for not responding differently. We explored her feelings for the child and discussed the different types and degrees of love one might have for various people in our lives. She agreed that the young girl was very lovable and that she did have loving feelings towards the girl. The next time the young girl asked if her key worker loved her, the worker was able to say with confidence that of course she loved her, that she was indeed a very lovable person and that many people thought lovingly of her. Saying these words did not create a regression in the young girl. The relationship continued to develop with the young girl growing into a young woman and moving on with her life. However, one of the experiences she did have while living with us was being able to say she loved someone directly to them and to have it said back to her (not only by her key worker but also by a small number of staff on the team). An experience many of us take for granted as children in a normal family setting?

> Another time I was supervising a male worker who told me that his key child asked him why he spent so much time with him, and why he cared so much. The worker gave some response that was only half thought-out and he knew by the way the boy had asked the question that was looking for more and had taken a huge risk in the asking. On reflection, the worker knew the boy was looking for a loving response that would let him know how special he was to this male worker. He was looking for reassurance that he was worthy of such positive regard and attention. By the end of the supervision both the worker and I were hoping that the young boy would take the risk of asking the question again.

When the opportunity did come about the key worker was well prepared for it and he gave a full explanation of why he thought so much of the young boy and how he liked him so much and liked spending time with him. He also told him that he should know how worthy of love he was and that he hoped one day he would find it easier to give and receive love. This relationship is still developing and a therapeutic alliance is being well maintained.

Social care workers have plenty of theory available to them as reference points. The principle of matching theory and practice is so well documented that workers should be able to back up their practice with recognised theory and evidence that it works. I find this a comfort in this age where accountability and professionalism is vital if we are to provide a quality service to children in care.

CONCLUSION

Attachment in all our lives and the need for social care workers to be brave and allow themselves to become the available adult for a child's attachment is ever more necessary.

The topic of the therapeutic alliance deserves reflection and deep consideration by all who are dealing with vulnerable children. The 'relationship' can be all-consuming, demanding and frightening, yet exhilarating, and the messiest of all human experiences, creating and eliciting a myriad of sensations, emotions and thoughts. Yet where would we be without it? Just cold and clinical, perhaps? I will end by sharing one of my favourite quotes from Schön, which gives me inspiration and hope when I most need it.

> A high hard ground overlooking a swamp. On the high ground manageable problems lend themselves to solution through the application of research-based theory and technique. However in the swampy lowlands, messy confusing problems defy technical solution ... And in the swamp lie the problems of greatest human concern.
>
> (Cited in Johns 2013:4)

I wish you many messy but fruitful times on your journey.

Chapter 17
A House for One: Single-occupancy Residential Units

Further Isolation or a Progressive Response?

Niall Reynolds

INTRODUCTION

This chapter focuses on my experiences of working as a social care worker in a single-occupancy residential unit. The unit was set up to provide a therapeutic intervention for a young person who presented with serious challenging behaviours.

There were many competing narratives that dominated the discussions about how best to manage the presenting behaviours and the safety and welfare of the young person. One such narrative focused on questioning whether the Irish care system could provide a placement with the capacity to intervene meaningfully in changing the direction of the young person's life. The adversarial discourses that prevailed narrowed to two options: sourcing a placement outside the state; or creating a single-occupancy residential unit tailored to the needs of the young person. Following deliberations and submissions to the High Court, it was decided that the young person would remain in Ireland and be placed in a single-occupancy unit. This decision was crucial in supporting the young person to remain in the country with a continuing hope and investment in his ability to change the direction of his life.

The ethos, purpose and function of the unit were all created with the unique and subjective challenges experienced by the young person in mind. The team at the unit worked using a multidisciplinary approach. The disciplines of social care, social work, forensic psychology and clinical psychology were utilised, supported by a number of ancillary services. The external oversight of the project was managed by the social worker and was closely monitored by the Integrated Service Area (ISA) manager and the Health Service Executive (HSE) monitoring officer.

A number of unique interventions and behavioural management techniques were deployed in managing the young person's behaviour, mainly through the multidisciplinary approach. The core values espoused by the team included a collaborative systems approach, which focused on equalising the power relations between the team and the young person. There was a shift away from a position dominated by 'risk anxiety' to a more therapeutic intervention, when the narrative of the case moved from the possible negative outcomes that can often be feared by professionals to a focus informed primarily by the young person and supported by the multidisciplinary team.

While it may be difficult to provide a comparative analysis of the success of this unit, I hope that sharing my experience of it will enrich the discourse of finding alternatives to sending children out of the state for their care.

PATH INTO SOCIAL CARE

My career as a social care worker began more as the result of a fortuitous meeting than as a well-thought-out career move. While working as a credit controller in a large multinational company, I was discussing with colleagues my desire for a change in career direction and a move away from work practices in which all contact with other people was through either a telephone or a computer. I had always been involved in local sports clubs in Dublin's north inner city and had enjoyed the interaction and guidance from local youth leaders. During the discussion on changing career, one of my colleagues suggested contacting an agency that she had done some work with in the area of providing social care for children.

Although I had no formal experience or qualification in this area, I wondered about the feasibility of gaining a position in a social care facility. I made contact with the agency and it quickly set up an interview. Following the interview I got a call that same evening enquiring as to when I could start. I was nervous and excited all at the same time.

I was given my first assignment later that week and instructed to report to Ballydowd Special Care Unit. Although I did not know it at the time, this was the country's largest special care unit. I worked two jobs for a number of weeks before the managers at Ballydowd offered me regular shifts and subsequently a permanent contract. I remained working at that facility for seven years, gaining invaluable professional and personal experience and having the opportunity to play a part in the lives of some of the most deserving young people in society.

During my time working for the HSE I have had the opportunity to expand my experience; and this included working at the single-occupancy residential unit that is the subject of this chapter. Currently I am working as a social care worker in a social work team in Dublin's south inner city. I completed my formal qualification in Social Care Practice at Dublin Institute of Technology and am currently undertaking a master's degree in Systemic Family Psychotherapy at University College Dublin.

THE BACKGROUND

It is important to provide at the outset some background information on the model of care that is provided in the Irish context. This will highlight how unusual it was to respond to this particular case through the development of a single-occupancy residential unit. It could be said that the Irish care system operates a mixed economy of social care provision: provision delivery comes from organisations in both the public and private sectors as well as from voluntary and charitable services. Within this model the overarching statutory obligations towards children in care are the responsibility of the HSE (and, since January 2014, Tusla, the Child and Family Agency).

The delivery of services to children in care, as offered through the current mixed economy model, may be described as limited in their variability. Since its inception and move away from large institutional-type care, the modern Irish care system has delivered social care provision mainly through the two central pillars of foster and residential care. Following the publication of the Kennedy Report (DoH 1970) and subsequent recommendations, these two forms of alternative care have dominated provision in the Irish system. At different times each form of care has been given preferential bias, guided by changing ideological forces and driven by social transformation. O'Sullivan (2009) highlights the trends of the provision of care over a period from 1970 to 2006, during which period both residential and foster care shared a bidirectional fluidity and at different times each intervention dominated the provision of care.

Currently the overwhelming majority of young people in care are placed within foster families and enjoy successful and stable placements.

Typically, residential care homes cater for between four and seven children and are located in ordinary neighbourhoods around the country (Crimmens 1998; Gilligan 2009).

In contrast to these preferred types of care provision, single-occupancy residential units are reserved for the most challenging cases. Gilligan (2009) describes the development of these units as a response to the inadequacies apparent in the current facilities and a failure of capacity to deal with the needs of the most challenging young people in care. As with many different realms of society, it is often the most challenging circumstances that create precedent and sometimes controversy. By their nature, using single-occupancy residential units as a response to managing critical challenging behaviour may seem like creating an insular and isolating environment in which to contain the 'problem child'. It was my experience that this was not the case; it was rather an opportunity to do things differently. With this opportunity we could challenge the practices of standardisation and create a shared space in which meaningful and subjective interventions could be attuned to the individualised needs of the young person.

THE STORY

As a prelude to the story of everyday practices in the unit it is important to demonstrate how rarely these units are authorised. Outside the remit of general residential care, children whose cases present as more complex and challenging are often placed in high-support and special care units. The purpose and function of a special care unit is to provide a secure and stable placement through which a 'young person's liberty is restricted' as a means of ensuring that their 'safety and welfare needs' are met (HIQA 2012).These cases are heard in the High Court and are generally escalated when a young person is continuously posing a serious risk to themselves or others. Overall, special care placements represent a minute proportion of care provision within the Irish system. In 2012 twenty-three children, out of a total of 6,332 children in care, were detained in special care units, representing just 0.4% of care placements for that year (HSE 2013a).

While our special care units are representative of an envisaged specialised intervention for the most challenging cases, there are still some cases where a special care placement has been deemed not suitable. It is in these cases that consideration is given to more unconventional arrangements.

In the case that I am detailing, the young person had been in the care of the HSE since the age of nine months. He had experienced multiple placement moves throughout his care history and had spent time in each option available on the care spectrum. This included numerous foster, residential and high-support placements before he was eventually detained at a special care unit. He then transitioned to a placement at an open residential unit. During this time his behaviour deteriorated significantly, including not coming out of his room for a number of months. It may be said that both the clinical and social profile of this young person was very complex, posing a serious question of how best to intervene. At this point he was seventeen years old and the care system in all its facets had been his primary care giver all this time. In this instance it was decided that the best option would be to set up a single-occupancy residential unit and tailor its operation to his particular set of needs.

In these rare but significant cases it is incumbent on professionals involved in the case to systematically consider all options available. In 2012 a total of only six single-occupancy residential units were authorised in the state (HSE 2013a). While the figures provided do not set out details of the circumstances leading to each scenario, it can be said with some degree of certainty that they were a last option solution where current capacity in the existing services had been deemed unsuitable and there was resistance to a placement outside the state.

THE UNIT

The unit in question was based in a north Dublin suburb with many local amenities nearby. The detached house, set on a small piece of land, had four bedrooms. The staff team consisted of a manager, deputy manager, two co-ordinators and, on average, ten social care workers working at different times during the week. During weekly staff meetings, the forensic psychologist involved in the case would give direction and suggestions on the presenting behaviours. The social worker did not attend the weekly meetings but visited the young person frequently and was accessible to the core staff team. The clinical psychologist visited at times and would assist with the different aspects of managing the environment safely in response to different incidents and the profile of the young person at the unit.

The importance of the two-pronged approach to collaboration that existed in the multidisciplinary approach to this case cannot be understated. The central tenet of the collaboration focused on the idea of creating strong and versatile relationships between all the stakeholders involved. There was a very significant drive to create a narrative that placed the young person at the centre of all decisions and for the staff team to embrace him as the most serious stakeholder in the system.

Stepney and Callwood (2006) refer to the concept of collaboration in describing different professionals with varying levels of academic attainment working together for the common aim of an improved service. This was really evident at the unit and was one of the central components in responding differently to this young person's needs.

It is impossible to give a complete description of the clinical profile of the young person, but it is possible to describe some of the major features of his behaviour that were at times difficult to manage. There was a hugely controlling and manipulative orientation about his behaviour that was supported by an attitude of implied violence that was apparent almost daily in the initial stages of the unit's operation. These types of behaviour can be very intimidating, even for a team of very experienced social care workers.

Most of the practices that developed at the unit were in response to some of the different behaviours presented. The team developed an ethos of constantly reflecting and modernising their work practices in response to the needs of the young person. This ethos was an indulgence in many ways and a refreshing change from the constraints of standardised practices of care that are often implanted in general residential care settings catering for a larger number of residents. For example, there was more flexibility around the daily planning for the young person, which often changed regularly throughout the day depending on his mood and interests. Often in larger residential units it was my experience that this would not be possible as the structure of the daily plan was central to maintaining control and order with a larger number of residents.

INCLUSIVITY

One of the first practices that developed at the centre was that the young person attended the multidisciplinary meetings whenever he chose. This practice began following a number of incidents in which he became aggressive and occasionally violent, knowing that these meetings were happening on the unit. Initially these meetings were for the staff team to discuss different elements of the young person's care and, as is customary in many other care settings, only the team attended.

Often the young person would hover around the entrance door to the meeting room and would be loud and obnoxious. Through a reflective process it became apparent that the meetings were serving to make the young person more suspicious and were creating an 'us and him' situation. We decided to invite him to attend these meetings whenever he chose. We also explained the importance of these meetings to him and that there might be issues discussed when he would be free to leave. He attended many of these meetings. The agenda would remain unchanged whether or not he attended. This was my first experience of a staff team openly discussing any element of a young person's care while they were present. While they were certainly not the first meetings I had attended in the company of a young person, they were different in that sometimes sensitive information was discussed. At all times the young person was encouraged to participate and give his view on the issues being discussed. While not all the staff team agreed with this approach and some had reservations, the overall approach of engaging in a more collaborative practice was trialled.

Initially, the young person would at times use his invitation to the meetings as a way of 'hijacking' them or ensuring that not all the issues on the agenda could be addressed. The very nature of some of the points on the agenda was, at times, adversarial and this provided an opportunity for him to try to control decision-making. Over time these attempts to control the meetings gradually changed to trying to influence rather than control. With the staff team operating from a position of honesty, openness and inclusiveness, the young person's anger about the particular issue of staff meetings faded to a minimum. Allowing him to be at the meetings was a simple way of serving an underlying need for him. It also reduced the amount of time and opportunity that the staff team had to discuss his care and life while he was not privy to the content. This was a huge issue for the young person, who later explained that these situations had been used in other care settings and he perceived them to be a means of bullying him and reinforcing an element of control the staff team had over him.

AN UNCONVENTIONAL APPROACH

Another issue that was addressed through a collaborative approach was the emergence of difficulties within what might be termed the normal, everyday communications process at the unit. Through the use of aggression and, at times, violence the young person was extremely controlling and attentive to any aspect of communication, either between staff members while they were on shift or in and out of the unit. For lengthy periods of time he would take all the phone connections from the walls and keep the phone handsets. While both staff on shift would carry mobile phones, at times their use was compromised depending on the intensity of the young person's will to control the house communications. The staff had at times to compromise their own safety as a way of demonstrating to the young person that we were very serious in listening to his concerns. For example, when he hijacked the phones and controlled all the house communications, the staff would sit it out and address the question of why he needed to control the house comms instead of aggravating the situation further by leaving and calling in external assistance.

Following a number of incidents of property damage it was decided to extend and accentuate our ethos of inclusiveness. Again, through our multidisciplinary approach we decided to take down any physical barriers that would impede the young person's ability to have access to any communications at the house that were relevant to him. As most of the communications generally took place via the staff office, the door was removed and full access granted to the young person at all times. This allowed him to attend the handover meetings, which he generally did, and he also had full access to any daily notes or reports written by the staff relevant to him. (Reports written by other professionals were kept in a separate storage area outside the staff office.) This was not the first time a young person had asked to see their written notes, but this was different in that the young person did not need to ask permission; he had full access to the staff office. The staff team had different views about the office space being opened up, and not everyone agreed with the decision.

Following this intervention the young person spent much of his time in the staff office, which quickly became a more communal area. The idea of 'mutualising' the power between the staff team and the young person was clearly demonstrated by the practice of transparency regarding communications. It is also important to highlight that there were occasions when the young person observed decisions being made that he did not agree with; and occasionally he would become excited or agitated. However, overall there was a significant decrease in incidents of general aggression once the staff office was made accessible to him.

Sharing the office space and relinquishing control of what is often the bastion of the staff team in a residential unit was highly unusual: some of the staff team, including myself, had never experienced it before, and some raised a number of concerns about it. It was, however, a commitment to collaborative practice that made this idea a different experience for both the staff and the young person. Indeed, it was this very experience of a different response from usual that enhanced the relationship between the staff team and the young person.

Initially, the kitchen was closed during the night, as is the practice in many residential centres. Following a number of incidents where the young person had physically kicked the door into the kitchen after hours, this practice was reviewed. At one weekly staff meeting a social care worker said that only the night before she had woken up hungry during the night and that she had gone to get something to eat from her own kitchen. The general consensus that evolved from this was that the practices of locking the staff office and kitchen were driven by us trying to redress the way the young person was attempting to control movements on the unit. It was decided with the young person and the team that the kitchen door would also be removed. While maintaining the house rules in relation to use of the kitchen and eating times, these instead became suggested ideas as opposed to being physically enforced through locking the young person out of a kitchen that was shared by all in the house. The young person rarely entered the kitchen after hours following this intervention.

PROGRESS

It is important to say that most of 'what worked' with this young person were ideas generated in response to his challenging behaviours. It should also be emphasised that over time he began to engage more freely and meaningfully with the staff team once issues about power and risk were genuinely addressed by the team. Smith (2010) discusses some concepts of risk as a means of legitimising and influencing power relations, which can at times disenfranchise vulnerable people. Aspects of this theoretical position are often overlooked in residential settings and at times are taken for granted.

Another intervention that appeared to work at the unit revolved around responding to a couple of serious incidents when staff members were effectively held captive. During these incidents, the young person was verbally and physically intimidating and displayed extremely controlling behaviours, including instructing staff members as to which rooms they could sit in and attempting to control communication between the staff. It is important to point out that the young person was physically bigger and stronger than many of the staff and often exerted this physical superiority as a means of intimidation. At one point we did consider getting panic alarms, but considered this to be a retrograde intervention that would create a power imbalance, which could be negative for the young person.

There was a delicate decision to debate about whether the safety and welfare of the staff should be of equal measure to the welfare of the young person. It often transpired that in managing such incidents the staff would have to call the Gardaí to come to the house and assist them. This often led to a greater level of seriousness being attributed to the incidents as the arrival of the Gardaí would only serve to exacerbate the situation for the young person. However, often there was simply no other choice.

Following a number of lengthy meetings involving all the professionals and sometimes the young person, it was decided that the safest response to these incidents would be for the staff to leave the unit for a period of time and leave the young person there on their own. This intervention carried other risks, but it was decided that it should be included in the individual behaviour management plan and was authorised by all involved. The behaviour management plan set out the different specific actions to be taken in response to certain behaviours and was agreed by consensus in our multidisciplinary meetings. The rationale for the decision was based on creating a 'double bind': by leaving the house the staff were taking control of these situations and ensuring their safety; but leaving the young person there by himself allowed him control of the house for a period of time. Once the staff had left the unit and after an initial period of time they would try contacting the young person on the unit phone. The young person would sometimes speak on the phone; at other times he would not. The purpose of the phone call was to decide when would be a good time to re-enter the house. Staff would also keep at a distance from the house, but with a full view of access points.

While it may seem that leaving the house at times of crisis could possibly have reinforced the young person's intention to control, the opposite was the outcome. After a number of incidents when staff members left the house and did not call the Gardaí the frequency of these particular incidents was reduced significantly. The practice demonstrated to the young person that we could remain safe and were at times happy for him to have control. As the months passed, we spoke personally to the young person about the significant drop in the number of these incidents, and he openly reflected on his behaviour. The central motivation for his behaviour, as he described it, was to test whether the staff team was truly collaborative in not involving the Gardaí on every occasion when he wanted control. He also spoke about testing the nature of the relationships that were continuing to evolve with the staff team at the unit. Given that, based on his own past care experience, this approach from the staff was different, he therefore needed to scrutinise it to see whether it was authentic.

As a social care worker, hearing and reading information about a young person's profile can often be significantly at odds with my own conclusions following meetings and on building a relationship with that same person. In the case of this young person this was an important factor that needed to be addressed. The story or narrative that accompanies a young person, if it is allowed to, can often define or stereotype a person's character and personality. This is a very significant demonstration of a power imbalance that immediately influences the origins of a relationship between a social care worker and a young person.

The young person had gained notoriety among social care professionals. This was not surprising, given the number of different care placements he had experienced from the age of nine months. Therefore, in practice his case was often referred to as 'high profile' by social care professionals and undue focus was placed on the risk elements in his behaviour and presentation. This was an issue that was addressed through the multidisciplinary approach at the unit. Rather than compounding and confirming further the negative narrative surrounding the young person, we decided to make a conscious effort to readdress this when discussing aspects of his case, both internally on the unit and with external professionals. The use of more constructive narratives can be a central aspect of change in trying to re-author a person's story into a more positive space (Morgan *et al.* 2011; White 2007).

Importantly, as mentioned above, the young person was exposed to most of the communications both in and out of the unit and also within the unit. Over time and with practice, the team began to accentuate the positives regarding the case as their default position. At all times we provided balanced assessments of the behaviours and significant events from a position of unconditional positive regard for the young person. Over the course of his placement the staff team had trained themselves, with assistance from the other professionals, to create new narratives about the young person. This encouraged others to look through a different lens when interacting with him or when communicating to others when not in his presence. Again, over time the young person began to reflect this practice when speaking about himself and his life and a noteworthy shift was observed. On reflection, this focusing on the impact of narratives was probably the most important intervention that was made by the team at the unit as it provided and promoted hope for the future for this particular young person and his story.

CONCLUSION

A lot of positive initiatives were created through this single-occupancy unit. It provided an opportunity for a young person to remain within the structures and culture that he had known throughout his life. While he had very limited involvement with his family, the decision not to send him out of state for his care accommodated this limited contact. More important, it accommodated the young person's wishes that things could improve between him and his family. The logistics involved in sending him to another country might well have threatened his contact with his family, however limited it was, and we simply don't know what the implications of this might have been. It also inspired some degree of confidence that our system of care can adapt and be innovative in creating tailor-made interventions.

While there are a number of factors to consider, not least the cost of running such units, there are some grounds for optimism that we can look after our most vulnerable and challenging young people ourselves. It was also possible to make a more detailed examination of the importance of relationships and systems within residential care settings.

My own experience of working in this field has taught me many lessons. One of these is the importance of engaging in a process of continuous self-reflection and development. When we feel that there is nothing else to learn or know is the point where we become stagnant as social care workers. Self-reflection dictates a constant curiosity about why we approach things in the ways that we do as social care workers. Throughout this chapter I have spoken about the concepts of power and collaboration in relationships. It is a given that, as social care workers, we possess a privilege and power while engaging with the clients we work with. The process of self-refection has challenged me to influence my practice in my own relationship to clients where power is an issue. The sharing and dilution of my own power within relationships with clients has made my job a whole lot easier. Having an understanding that young people in care are the real experts on their own lives has enlightened my relationships with most of the young people I have worked with as we attempt to meet each other as equals. It is my hope that I can continue to promote the concept of real collaboration with young people in care as a means of creating meaningful interventions that can enable a positive change in their lives.

Chapter 18
Supporting those Who Self-Injure in Social Care Settings
David Williams

> *Just because we can put a name to it doesn't mean we understand it.*
>
> (Smith 1998:2)

INTRODUCTION

This quotation from Mike Smith aptly describes the challenge for social care workers who come across self-injury in their daily work. This chapter explores the complex issue of deliberate self-harm in social care settings and offers guidance for workers in responding to self-injurious behaviour. Through my own experiences of managing this issue, the topic of self-injury is explored in relation to myths often associated with this behaviour, functions of the behaviour and lessons I have learned in attempting to respond to this complex issue.

I feel it is important to state that I do not claim to be an expert on the topic of self-injury. This chapter captures my journey from a social care worker with very little knowledge of this issue to one who increased their awareness of it in the hope of being able to support and respond to clients in a more empathetic, constructive and holistic manner.

A note on terminology

The phrase 'individuals who engage in self-injurious behaviour' is used in this chapter because I believe it is unhelpful to use terms such as 'self-harmers', which labels people purely by the behaviour they may be engaging in at a particularly difficult stage in their lives. This viewpoint is supported by the findings of a long-term study of almost two thousand adolescents in Australia, 8% of whom had engaged in deliberate self-harm. However, in the follow-up to that study, it was found that 90% of those engaged in self-injury had ceased by early adulthood (Moran *et al.* 2011).

The terms 'self-injury' and 'deliberate self-harm' are used interchangeably throughout this chapter.

MY JOURNEY TO SOCIAL CARE

Writing this chapter has afforded me the opportunity to reflect on my time in the social care field and I cannot believe it is almost twenty years since I began working in the sector. It would be untrue to state that I had always wanted to work in this area as it only seems like yesterday that I was sitting down to complete my CAO form for the second time, as I prepared to repeat my Leaving Cert exams. I was supposed to be a year older and a year wiser, but I still wasn't sure what career path I wished to pursue. However, I had taken an interest in a Certificate in Applied Social Studies course being offered by the Dublin Institute of Technology, as the CAO handbook recommended the course for students who would like to work with people. Looking back, with nearly twenty years' experience of social care practice, management and education under my belt, little did I know then that choosing that course would lead me to some of the happiest, most humbling, scariest, proudest, most special and challenging moments of my life. It was one of these challenging incidents that led to my deep interest in the topic of this chapter, self-injury.

THE INCIDENT

When I first encountered self-injurious behaviour I was already a reasonably experienced worker, having been in social care for almost ten years. I viewed myself as a confident and competent worker, having worked with clients in a range of areas such as residential child care, elder care, disabilities and youth work. I also had experience of managing a range of different behaviours in these social care settings, such as aggression, violence and sexualised behaviours. However, it was when I went to work in a mainstream children's home one Tuesday afternoon that I was faced with an incident that caused me to re-evaluate how I viewed myself as a social care worker.

A young teenage girl, Ciara, had just moved to our service. (The name of the young person and some details of the incident have been changed for the purposes of confidentiality and anonymity.) She was finding it difficult to settle into this new placement and was reluctant to build relationships with most staff in the unit. She had moved from a successful placement in another residential home, where she had built strong attachments with some of the staff, but had had to move on. Ciara had expressed her unhappiness in the new placement and wanted to return to her old placement. However, this was not possible.

When I came on shift on that Tuesday afternoon, staff informed me that Ciara seemed quite down and was saying that she didn't want to live here. She had begun to disengage and refused to speak to staff. After the handover, my colleague and I decided we would try to engage with Ciara and try to speak to her about how she felt. My colleague went to Ciara's bedroom while I waited outside on the landing, as we didn't want to crowd her. Almost immediately my colleague returned from the room to inform me the situation had escalated to a different level. Ciara had cut herself on her wrist using both a broken CD and the blade from a pencil sharpener.

> I can still remember very vividly my feelings around this situation. Despite being a social care worker with years of experience, I felt totally helpless. Frankly, I felt scared, anxious and completely out of my depth in how to respond to this young person in crisis. I wanted to feign sickness and go home, such was my discomfort in having to manage this situation. I had been verbally abused, physically assaulted and threatened in my work, but this incident was the one which made me feel totally inadequate – I didn't know how to react or respond. I was afraid of saying or doing the wrong thing in case I might exacerbate the situation or, worse still, escalate the situation to where Ciara could possibly take her own life.

Fortunately, the colleague I worked with that day was really supportive. She had worked with this issue in a different setting, and so we developed a plan to support Ciara. I followed her lead and we managed to engage with Ciara and access the support she needed that day. Her self-injurious behaviour did not stop overnight and she continued to self-injure on and off in the coming months, particularly in times of crisis when she felt she couldn't cope with certain feelings or incidents.

This incident had a huge impact on how I viewed myself as a social care worker. I had never felt as vulnerable and ineffectual. I had never come across this behaviour before and self-injury was not an issue we had addressed in college or in any in-service training. I later vowed to learn as much as I could about self-injury, so I would be better able to support the clients with whom I work and become a more knowledgeable worker in the process. So my interest in self-injury began, and over the last number of years of reading, researching, training and meeting other professionals who have addressed this topic, I feel more comfortable as a worker and educator in addressing this issue and more confident in dealing with it.

From early feelings of helplessness in working with self-injury, there were two key areas that were essential in helping me become more competent in dealing with the behaviour: understanding the causes of the behaviour; and expanding my knowledge of how to respond to clients engaging in self-injury. The remainder of this chapter will take these two areas as its focus in further detailing my experience of managing self-injury and, in turn, assisting readers to explore and reflect upon the topic of self-injury in relation to their own social care practice.

SHE'S JUST LOOKING FOR ATTENTION, ISN'T SHE?

After the incident with Ciara I soon learned that I was not the only worker on the team who felt unprepared in managing this issue. At our next team meeting the presentation of this behaviour dominated the discussion. Apart from one colleague, who had a little experience in dealing with this matter, the rest of us were honest enough to openly express our anxiety, lack of knowledge and lack of confidence in dealing with deliberate self-harm. We struggled to understand the behaviour and through ignorance we started to repeat myths about the topic that we had heard over the years, for example that Ciara was only exhibiting this behaviour for attention. This led us to making some early mistakes in supporting Ciara. We became so absorbed in focusing on trying to stop the behaviour that we failed to try and look at the reasons.

Arnold reiterates the importance of carers both responding to the behaviour and also responding to the reasons for the behaviour:

> *Many women say that no-one ever asks them why they self-injure (although professionals often seem to tell them why they think they do so, and why they should stop). Women want to be asked why, and to be helped to find their own way towards the answers, by someone who hears them and acknowledges them as the expert on their own experience.*
>
> (Arnold 1995:23)

Through reflecting on my learning from responding to this case I realised how easy it is, but also how unhelpful it can be, to resort to myths often associated with behaviours that we struggle to understand. Walker (2012:34–5) provides a valuable overview of some of the myths that we, as professionals, often resort to when discussing the topic of self-injury, and invites us to consider more fact-based assumptions that can help us in our practice approaches.

Myths about self-injury

Myths	Fact
Self-injury does not hurt	Cutting and other acts of self-injury are painful, although the pain threshold for some who self-injure may be dulled by the intense emotional turmoil they are experiencing. For some, self-injury may be used as a way of trying to feel something as they may be numbed through surviving a range of traumatic experiences.
Only teenage girls engage in self-injury	This myth is being continually challenged by updated research findings and statistics. For example, most recent Irish figures identify that the rate of male self-harm increased by 20% from 2007 to 2012 (Griffin *et al*. 2013).
The person is only attention seeking	First, it is important to recognise that a person engaging in self-injury has needs which require the support of professionals. Second, many individuals who display self-harming behaviour tend to conceal it due to the associated stigma. They often self-injure in private, thus avoiding attention.
The person is suicidal and wants to die	Most people who self-injure do not want to die; moreover, they use self-harming behaviour as a way of coping and surviving. However, it is important to acknowledge that there can be a connection between self-harm and suicide. Between September 2008 and March 2011 the Suicide Support and Information System revealed that in Cork 45% of 190 cases of suicide had a history of self-harm (HSE 2013b).
Some use self-injury as a way to manipulate others	Some individuals may use their injuries to control the actions of others, although this is not the case for most. For those supporting people who engage in self-injury, it is important to focus on identifying the functions of the behaviour and trying to support the individual through supportive lines of communication.

The gravity of the problem is related to the severity of the self-injurious behaviour	It is important not to judge the problems of an individual by the behaviour being displayed. A person displaying fairly superficial self-cutting wounds may be struggling just as much as a person engaging in more severe forms of self-harm. For example, I worked with a young woman who displayed furious, repetitive hand washing as a form of self harm. Naturally, this left her skin very raw but she did not require hospitalisation. However, after working with her through this issue, it transpired that she had suffered long-term sexual abuse over a long period of her childhood.

One of the main concerns of our staff team was that Ciara was suicidal and we feared that she might take her own life. We were ultimately afraid that if we did or said the wrong thing it would upset Ciara further and hence make the situation worse. I have since learned that this concern is not uncommon among professionals who come across this behaviour in their work. Inckle (2007) identifies the complications in attempting to define self-injury, due to the often interlinked motivations and intentions of the behaviour being exhibited and its close relationship with other social issues, such as body modification and para-suicide. However, it has become clear to me in working with and researching deliberate self-harm that it is vitally important for workers to identify the differences between these behaviours in order to holistically support the person in crisis.

Para-suicide, which is often confused with self-injury, describes repeated, unsuccessful attempts to commit suicide (Babiker & Arnold 1997). Self-harm, on the other hand, might be seen as the opposite of suicide, as it is often a way of coping with life rather than giving up on it (HSE 2013c). Much of the confusion exists in relation to self-injury, as we are often not clear about the intentions or motivations for the individual engaging in self-harming behaviour. Fitzpatrick (2012) reminds us that, while some people engaging in self-injurious behaviour may be motivated by a wish to die, more often individuals engage in self-harm for other reasons, often using it as a tool to manage stress and pain in their lives.

Although the primary focus of this chapter is on non-suicidal self-injury, it is important for us, as social care workers with a duty of care towards vulnerable clients, to be mindful of the fact that often individuals place themselves at great risk by engaging in some self-harming behaviours, even if they do not intend to kill themselves.

THE ORIGINS OF SELF-INJURY

In exploring the complex issue of self-injury it is essential to recognise that its origins may be multi-faceted. Furthermore, the individual may not be able to communicate why they self-injure, or may struggle to understand themselves why they behave in this manner. This was clearly the case for Ciara, who began to use self-injurious behaviour as way of dealing with the difficult emotions and feelings that arose for her following another placement move and separation experience in her life. Pieta House, a non-profit organisation that provides specialist intervention for people who engage in deliberate self-harm, suggests that injuries and scars give a person something physical to show for all their emotional pain. Wounds are tangible, external and treatable, whereas emotional pain is confusing and hidden. People who self-harm may do so to ground themselves or bring themselves back to reality.

It also became clear to me that Ciara's behaviour became a way for her to regain some control over her life, which she believed was being taken from her by various professionals who were making decisions with regard to her life situation.

Hawton and Rodham (2006) suggest that when a person inflicts pain on themselves, the body produces endorphins, a natural pain reliever that gives temporary pain relief. This, for some, can lead to self-injury becoming addictive, as physical pain becomes more manageable and bearable than emotional pain, as outlined in the diagram, which shows the addictive cycle of self-injury and deliberate self-harm (diagram adapted from Hawton & Rodham 2006:206).

Figure 18.1

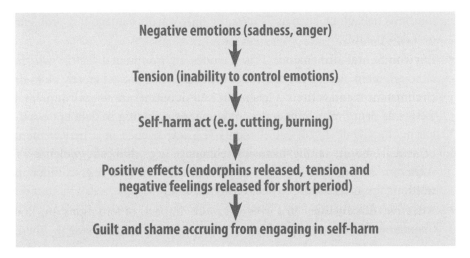

Negative emotions (sadness, anger)

↓

Tension (inability to control emotions)

↓

Self-harm act (e.g. cutting, burning)

↓

Positive effects (endorphins released, tension and negative feelings released for short period)

↓

Guilt and shame accruing from engaging in self-harm

A range of theories exist to explain the causes of self-injury. Considering my early struggles in attempting to understand deliberate self-harm, I believe Walsh's (2012) biopsychosocial model is of most use to social care workers, as it most thoroughly examines the complex factors influencing self-injurious behaviour and therefore provides an insight into the causes of self-harm for many clients in social care services. For example, the behaviour of clients in care is often influenced by a range of criteria such as environment, emotions, family circumstances and attachment issues. Walsh (2012) suggests that self-injury can be best understood through examining the interplay between the following dimensions.

- **Biological dimension:** Studies of biology and self-injury offer some insight into the causes of the behaviour. Most biological studies link self-harm to factors such as lower levels of serotonin (a hormone that plays an important part in regulating learning, mood and sleep) in those who engage in self-harming behaviours (Osuch & Payne 2009), and higher pain thresholds in those who self-injure (Sher & Stanley 2009).
- **Cognitive dimension:** Walsh (2012:67) explains that this dimension in understanding self-injury is focused on two key factors. First, the cognitive interpretation of environmental events – how a person views a situation in their life – impacts on how they cope with the associated thoughts and feelings. For example, a young woman I worked with, who had been sexually abused, held some irrational thoughts about the experience; blaming herself for the abuse and believing that perhaps, at some level, she wanted it to happen. Second, self-generated cognitions may also relate to self-harm as individuals generate a range of cognitions that ignite their self-injurious behaviour, such as 'This is the only way to manage this problem' or 'I deserve this'.
- **Environmental dimension:** This includes environmental factors which, although often outside the control of the individual, impact greatly on their circumstances and actions. Walsh (2012:60) identifies three environmental factors as being most influential for someone engaging in deliberate self-harm: the client's historical elements (e.g. experience of a bereavement or sexual abuse); family historical elements (e.g. domestic violence or substance abuse); and current environmental elements (e.g. conflict in relationships or exposure to peers who self-injure).
- **Affective dimension:** This refers to the impact of emotions on the frequency and types of self-harm engaged in by an individual. These negative emotions, such as sadness, tension, anxiety and anger, exist prior

to self-injury. Thus, it is important that these are understood by carers in order to help support individuals attempting to manage or/desist from self-injury (Walsh 2012:69). For example, I have worked with a client, John (not his real name), an adult with intellectual disabilities who is non-verbal. He becomes agitated and frustrated when staff members struggle to understand what he is trying to communicate. This often leads him to punch himself or bang his head off walls to manage this frustration.

- **Behavioural dimension:** The actions of individuals before, during and following their self-injurious act. These might include choosing a location to self-harm or an item with which to self-harm. An analysis of these factors may provide important insight into understanding why the behaviour is repeated.

IF I KNEW THEN WHAT I KNOW NOW

In reflecting on my early experience of working with self-injury with Ciara, I often think of some of the errors my colleagues and I made in attempting to respond to her. This was mainly due to our lack of knowledge about this behaviour. As mentioned previously, as a team we became too focused on trying to stop the behaviour, not realising that by not looking at the underlying causes we were misdirecting our energies. We tried to encourage Ciara to sign contracts to promise she would not harm herself and used more traditional behaviour modification approaches in an attempt to stop the self-injurious behaviour. This not only proved ineffective in managing the behaviour but also seemed to impact negatively on our ability to build and maintain meaningful relationships with her. We soon came to the conclusion that we needed to further improve our knowledge of this issue if we were really going to help Ciara through this difficult period in her life.

We began by proactively researching the topic of deliberate self-harm and visited organisations such as Pieta House in order to receive guidance on working with clients engaging in self-injury. This began a more proactive and child-centred approach in helping Ciara manage her behaviour. We began to use the staff who had a stronger relationship with Ciara to help her explore the reasons for engaging in self-injury. They also supported her to consider other ways of coping with difficult emotions or events.

Managing deliberate self-harm places great pressure on social care workers and can result in a 'fight or flight' response for the worker as they veer between wanting to avoid this situation and doubting their ability to respond appropriately to the needs of the client. Many social care workers wish to gather greater knowledge of how to respond to clients in their care who harm themselves in order to support clients better. Greater knowledge can also help workers cope with the strong emotions that can arise in dealing with this complex matter.

Williams and Gilligan (2011) found that social care workers felt that specific training on deliberate self-harm would greatly improve their ability to care for clients engaging in self-injury. In this desire they are not alone. Research exploring the perspectives of people who self-injure has shown that they also voice the importance of carers having an understanding of self-harming behaviour and being able to listen in a non-judgemental manner (Levenkron 1999; Piggott *et al.* 2004; Heslop & MacCauley 2009).

In my research examining the experiences of social care workers who had managed incidents of self-injury, I found that some workers believed that the personal issues that the behaviour elicited in the workers themselves affected how they responded to the behaviour (Williams 2008). For example, one worker spoke of her fear of blood, which affected her response in caring for a young teenage girl in her care who used to cut herself. In another example, a worker, who was a mother, was challenged by the fact she could not take the blade from the young person in her care (due to agency policy), even though she might have done so if it was her own child.

As pointed out by Fitzpatrick (2012), carers often feel powerless when addressing the issue of self-injury. This is further intensified, I believe, in social care practice, where workers often feel that they have to be able to deal with these very difficult circumstances, without recognising the toll it takes on them personally. They can feel that their colleagues and managers will perceive them as weak.

Personally, from undertaking training and improving my knowledge of the topic of self-injury, one of the most important lessons I have learned is that we cannot always stop the clients in our care from self-harming. However, what we can do is support them, listen to their concerns, help them understand their reasons for self-harming and assist them to explore more proactive ways to manage their feelings and concerns. Although there is no one definitive way to respond to self-injurious behaviour, as people who self-injure all have their own individual story, our increased knowledge and research on the matter suggests some guidelines (Walker 2012:95) that may help social care workers in supporting people exhibiting self-injurious behaviour.

Supporting people who self-injure: dos and don'ts

Do ...

... open up channels of communication.

... give the person time to talk to you if they want.

... ask them what, if anything, led to the incident of self-injury.

Don't ...

... force the person to talk.

... make them feel that the behaviour is something that is wrong to talk about or that it should be kept secret

... assume that every episode of self-injury is for the same reason.

In addition to these suggestions, there are a number of other practice guidelines which can help inform the response of social care workers in supporting clients:

- When injury occurs, involve the person in tending to their injuries, for example helping to clean wounds or care for injuries. This shows the person that their body is worth caring for and, following an episode of self-injury, may give the opportunity for the social care worker and the client to explore some of the reasons they engaged in the behaviour. In the example of Ciara, the team learned to say to her, 'Let me help you clean your arm and put a plaster on it.' This further helped to develop the relationship with her and was aimed at helping her to feel in control of the situation. Staff were helping her, while she took the lead in caring for her body after the event.

- Don't just focus on the self-injurious behaviour; look at feelings behind it. It is important that we do not become overly focused on the behaviour. It is identifying and addressing the cause of the behaviour which will lead to its reduction and possible cessation.

- Emphasise the non-harming aspects of the person's life. It is important that the client does not become labelled by their self-injuring behaviour. It is vital for social care teams to focus on other elements of the client's life. This can also be useful for the social care team, who may become frustrated if the client goes through periods of cessation and relapses in their self-harming behaviour.

- Encourage the person to draw on their own strengths and healing resources. Nearly all the clients we work with in social care services have encountered trauma and challenges in their lives. Social care staff can help clients focus on the strengths and resilience that have helped them overcome some of these challenges, in order to manage their self-injury.

- It is important that we do not try to force the person to stop the behaviour; this may drive the person to conceal the behaviour or, worse still, consider more risky means of managing their difficult emotions or thoughts.

- If the person decides they do not want to stop self-harming, it is worth encouraging them to consider other avenues, such as using harm reduction methods that can reduce the risk and harm to their bodies. Harm reduction methods might include using clean blades to cut, submerging their hands in a basin of cold water/ice or drawing on their arms with red marker to replicate the self-injurious behaviour. It is important to recognise that this should not be a long-term approach, as the person should be continually encouraged to explore the reasons behind the behaviour and also to use other therapeutic interventions.

- Try to listen in a non-judgemental and non-critical manner. One might use questions such as: 'How do you feel when you self-harm?'; 'How does self-harm help you with difficult times?'; or 'Is there something difficult happening for you now that I can help with?' This can be challenging for us, particularly when we have close relationships with clients or when they relapse into episodes of self-harm following a period of abstinence.

- Selekman (2006) suggests that, following slips, carers should explore with the person how the slip happened and how it might be avoided in the future. This approach is quite similar to the life space intervention approach, which will be familiar to social care workers who have completed therapeutic crisis intervention (TCI) training: staff assist the client to explore more positive ways of coping with difficult situations or emotions. (Life space intervention is a therapeutic verbal strategy for intervening with young people to help them learn new coping skills through engagement in everyday life events; TCI is a behaviour management therapy framework that helps children and young people develop new coping skills to deal with difficult emotions or situations in their lives.)

- Try to respond to episodes of self-injury with a low-energy approach. It is important that, although we may be shocked or alarmed by the behaviour, we stay calm and in control in order to be able to support the client and keep them safe. This is an important element of attempting to prevent copy-cat behaviour from other clients who might otherwise think that harming themselves is a quick way to access a social care worker's time and attention. For example, when I worked with a man who displayed head banging as a form of self-harm, staff initially reacted quite strongly to this, and a number of us would gather around him trying to prevent him seriously damaging his head. This drew a lot of attention from other clients and only succeeded in escalating the behaviour. Very soon we learned a new approach, which was for one staff member only to place a cushion between his head and the wall to prevent further damage and show that they were there for him, until the client felt able to disengage from the behaviour. Walsh (2012:87) advises that the initial response of carers should be one of respectful curiosity with a low-key, dispassionate demeanour. Over-emotional responses may 'inadvertently provide a secondary reinforcement'.

I believe these practice guidelines provide a strong foundation for workers who come across deliberate self-harm in their work and I am certain that, if I had had this knowledge when supporting Ciara in my first experience of self-injury, I would have been a more confident and able worker in helping to support this young person in crisis. Although I believe knowledge, training and education are essential to making us more confident social care workers in handling difficult issues such as self-injury, we should never feel truly comfortable in dealing with the complex issue of deliberate self-harm. It is through constant reflection, self-awareness and debriefing that we ensure we are able to best meet the needs of our clients, while also ensuring that we care for ourselves as social care workers and teams.

CONCLUSION

This chapter has mapped my journey through my earliest experience of self-injury and explained how this experience ignited a desire to become more knowledgeable, aware and capable when responding to this most complicated area of social care practice. The incident and subsequent events will always remain a key experience for me as a social care worker. They helped me become a more knowledgeable, reflective and humble worker.

The situation taught me that, in the complex area of social care work, there are often more grey areas than clear-cut black and white answers. We will not always have all the answers. However, by dealing with the challenges, frustrations and fears aroused by managing this incident, I have learned that it is important to be open to learning and developing new knowledge in order to help clients in crisis. I hope that by documenting my experiences of self-injury this chapter will act as a useful foundation that other social care workers can use to reflect on this complicated topic and, furthermore, come to a more informed position from which to support clients in their care in a holistic and meaningful way.

Chapter 19
An A, B, C Approach to Challenging Behaviour

A Reflective Tool for Service Users and Social Care Workers

Marguerita Walsh

INTRODUCTION

Foster care, substance misuse, domestic abuse, special physical/intellectual needs, childcare, youth work, elder care and mental health – these are all very different services, but they have two things in common. These are services where social care workers often find themselves in employment and, of course, services in which one may experience challenging behaviour. Challenging behaviour can be exhibited in many forms (outlined later in this chapter) and so is not restricted to the disability sector. With such a high likelihood that social care workers will come into contact with challenging behaviour, it is surprising that very few third-level institutions offer modules on challenging behaviour as part of social care education. Many social care workers therefore leave their studies unprepared for incidents of challenging behaviour, only learning from practice how to approach or manage such incidents. Many organisations no longer have sufficient funding for training and this can create further difficulties.

It is important that social care workers are able to define challenging behaviours in order to identify the best possible management strategy; a number of examples will be used in this chapter to illustrate different strategies. The chapter will also look at the various forms of challenging behaviour, and some possible causes for it. Challenging behaviour presents as a client who is stressed, upset or volatile for a particular reason. When faced with such situations, staff too may experience similar, heightened emotions, and self-awareness, therefore, is vital in assisting a client through an incident.

A number of different methods of dealing with challenging behaviour have been adopted in different settings in Ireland. These include therapeutic crisis intervention (TCI), crisis prevention intervention (CPI) and multi-element behaviour support (MEBS). My concentration will be on the A, B, C approach, while adverting to aspects of TCI. The A, B, C approach is quite often used to examine a client's challenging behaviour following an incident. From experience I feel that this approach is not only beneficial in developing interventions for client behaviour, but also a useful reflective tool for staff practice.

PATH INTO SOCIAL CARE

In all honesty, I stumbled into social care. I thought I wanted to become a counsellor, work with people and help them. The school guidance counsellor advised that I study social care and complete an add-on course in counselling. Social care was not well known as a profession, and I had the common misconception, which many people still have today, that social care is the same as social work. For me, it was simply a stepping stone to becoming a counsellor. However, once I began my college placement I realised that social care allowed me to work directly with people and help them – the reasons I had wanted to become a counsellor; and the fact that social care was a very broad area also appealed to me.

During my studies I completed three placements, the first of which was in a special needs school for children with severe to profound intellectual disability (ID). Here, I developed my understanding of autism and ID, learned how to communicate using Lámh and PECS (picture exchange communication system: a method of communication using pictures), assisted with classroom activities such as 'table top' and language, helped service users with personal care, and had my first experience of challenging behaviour. I can remember the initial shock and fear that came over me at the time of the incident; and the initial panic, as I didn't know what to do.

I then shadowed a youth worker working with individuals with physical disabilities of various levels. This involved assistance with personal care/needs, accompanying clients on activities and liaising with families. Finally, I completed a placement in a refuge for women and children experiencing domestic abuse. I was involved in assisting refuge workers; answering helpline calls; assisting clients to secure accommodation; liaising with social workers, Gardaí and legal representatives; conducting support and information sessions with clients; accompanying clients to court; and visiting local schools to deliver a positive relationships programme.

My professional experience includes working with children with mild to profound IDs in a respite setting. This involved a lot of interaction with client families, teachers and special needs assistants (SNAs), and some involvement with GPs and social work departments. As well as managing challenging behaviour, key tasks involved in this role included assisting clients with personal care; helping them to develop interpersonal skills and independence skills; integration within the community; implementing behavioural plans; and completing relevant paperwork (daily reports, risk assessments, monitoring forms, etc.).

Currently I work in an assisted living service for clients with acquired brain injuries. My role involves supporting clients in the activities of daily living to enable or re-enable them to live as independently as possible following their brain injury. This support includes assistance with household duties, maintaining and developing positive relationships with family and friends, and participating in community/recreational activities. Supporting clients to achieve the goals outlined in their rehabilitation plan may include liaising with medical and government agencies, community organisations and clubs, and accompanying clients to appointments if necessary. Dealing with challenging behaviour is also a regular feature; so let's look at it in more detail.

WHAT IS CHALLENGING BEHAVIOUR?

The term 'challenging behaviour' became the umbrella term used in place of terms such as 'abnormal, aberrant, disordered, disturbed, dysfunctional, maladaptive, and problem behaviours' (Emerson & Einfeld 2011:3). Challenging behaviour is most commonly defined as 'behaviour of such intensity, frequency or duration that the physical safety of the person or others is likely to be placed in serious jeopardy, or behaviour which is likely to seriously limit or delay access to and use of ordinary community facilities' (Emerson 2001). Examples of such behaviour will later be outlined under the headings of 'aggressive' and 'non-aggressive' challenging behaviour.

Behaviour is seen as a 'social construction'. Defining a behaviour as challenging depends on the context in which it is experienced (Emerson & Einfeld 2011). For example, a client who shouts and screams in church is seen to exhibit challenging behaviour. However, if a client exhibited this kind of behaviour in a night club or at a rock concert it would not be viewed in the same manner. So views of behaviour vary according to social views, beliefs and values. Again, take church services as an example. Some services encourage individuals to participate in the service, interact with each other and sing; others tend to promote more discreet, tranquil behaviour. By the same token, what one staff member in a care setting considers challenging may not be viewed the same way by other staff (Farrell *et al.* 2010). Indeed, I have often

noticed that the reactions and responses of individual staff members vary widely, and they can, at times, disagree strongly.

In order to avoid inconsistency with clients it is important that staff members are clear as to what exactly constitutes challenging behaviour. For instance, one staff member may feel that a client shouting profanities is merely giving out; another staff member may view it as being verbally abusive, and therefore challenging. I think this can depend on a social care worker's previous experience and the types of behaviour they have encountered; and behaviour that becomes 'the norm' in a setting are often no longer viewed as challenging.

The following table (taken from James 2011:14) lists aggressive and non-aggressive forms of challenging behaviour that social care workers may encounter.

Aggressive	Non-aggressive
Hitting	Apathy
Kicking	Depression
Grabbing	Repetitive noise/questions
Pushing	Making strange noises
Nipping	Constant requests for help
Scratching	Eating/drinking excessively
Biting	Over-activity
Spitting	Pacing
Choking	General agitation
Hair pulling	Following others/trailing
Tripping someone	Inappropriate exposure of parts of the body
Throwing objects	
Stabbing	Masturbating in public areas
Sneering	Urinating in inappropriate places
Screaming	Smearing
Shouting	Handling things inappropriately
Physical sexual assault	Dismantling objects
Verbal sexual advances	Hoarding things
Acts of self-harm	Hiding items
	Falling intentionally
	Eating inappropriate substances
	Non-compliance

REASONS FOR CHALLENGING BEHAVIOUR

Client communication difficulties or difficulties in expressing emotions may make it difficult for social care workers to understand the reasons behind an incident of challenging behaviour. Some general causes can include one or more of the following:

- **Environmental factors:** Overcrowding (too many people in one's personal space); temperature; over-/under-stimulation – too much information for one's cognitive abilities (e.g. clients with learning disabilities) – or not being challenged enough (e.g. clients with ADHD); isolation from family/ friends/activities; relationships with particular staff members (clients may have better rapport with certain staff members).
- **Communication:** Difficulties in expressing themselves, e.g. a client with a speech impediment following a stroke may get frustrated when they cannot be understood; a child with autism who is signing Lámh is frustrated when staff do not understand.
- **Learned behaviour:** A client may get a desired reaction from a social care worker if they begin to self-injure and so they engage in this behaviour in future in order to get this level of social interaction. (See Chapter 18 for advice on how to support a client who self-injures.)
- **Physical and mental health:** Clients with communication difficulties may exhibit challenging behaviour in order to express physical pain or discomfort; mental health issues such as schizophrenia may also influence a client's behaviour.
- **Neurobiological factors:** Certain abnormalities in brain function may have implications for client behaviour, e.g. self-injurious behaviour, and for the development of dementia.
- **Stressful life events:** Clients who have been exposed to severe abuse, trauma or loss may feel that they cannot trust others and so may act out when a social care worker attempts to work with them. (South Eastern Health Board 2004)

Staff turnover and staff shortages may be other contributory factors. For instance, relief staff may not be familiar with a client and therefore not be able to assess when a client is becoming anxious or going through various stages of crisis behaviour in comparison to their usual temperament. This is referred to as one's 'baseline' when assessing challenging behaviour on the stress model of crisis, as outlined in Figure 19.1.

Figure 19.1 The stress model of crisis (TCI approach)

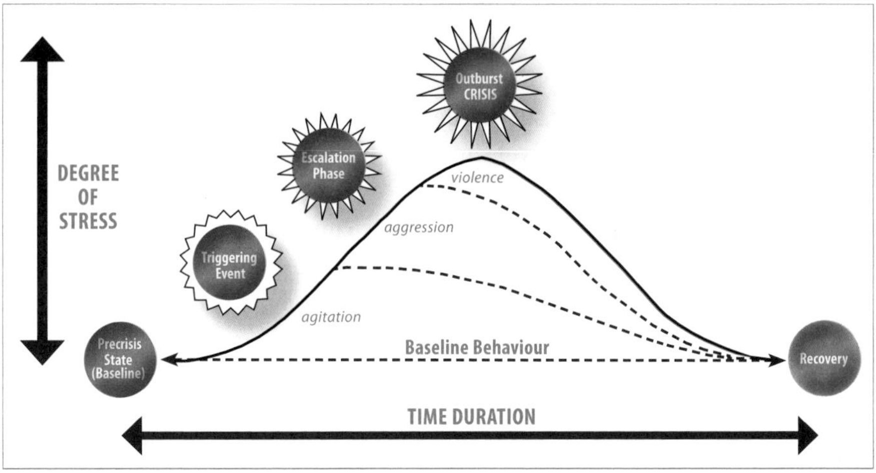

(*Source:* Holden 2009:13)

Ginott (1972) highlighted how teachers can influence a pupil. The same can be said for social care workers' interactions with clients.

> *It is my personal approach that creates the climate ... In all situations it is my response that decides whether a crisis will be escalated or de-escalated.*
> (Ginott 1972, cited in Holden 2009:vii)

HOW TO ADDRESS AN INCIDENT OF CHALLENGING BEHAVIOUR

It must first be highlighted that there is no 'one size fits all' approach to addressing incidents of challenging behaviour: each situation and client is different. The 'human element' is also a factor: witnessing challenging behaviour can be distressing or raise personal issues for staff and this can mean that staff might not address an incident exactly the same way on different occasions. The human factors can include: the working environment (e.g. staff on sleepover may be sleep-deprived because they have been woken by clients; staff members have had a disagreement); the rapport staff have with the clients to whom they are assigned on a particular shift; the staff member's personal or health issues.

As much as it is highlighted that social care workers should separate themselves from their own emotions and not take challenging behaviour personally – which can impact on their practice – the reality is that we are all human and therefore we will be affected emotionally by challenging behaviour. Having a client lash out verbally or physically at you, spit in your face, scream for hours at a time or engage in self-injurious behaviour – one or all of these types of behaviour are bound to impact on a social care worker emotionally in some way. Personally, I can admit that I've encountered a whole range of emotions in response to a client's challenging behaviour; from disgust to anger, fear, sadness and self-doubt. If not dealt with effectively with support from colleagues and management, over time social care workers can find themselves on the road to burnout.

There are however, some general approaches that can help de-escalate incidents. The most effective interventions that I have used in my practice are based on the principles of operant conditioning (Devlin *et al.* 2011). Operant conditioning is a 'learned response as a result of either positive or negative reinforcement; for example, working hard because of praise for doing so in the past, or bullying others because in the past it has stopped them annoying you' (Carr 2006:104).

First you must know the client. The more knowledge social care workers have about clients, the greater chance they will have of understanding their needs and assisting them to come back to their baseline. It is also vital that a social care worker has a level of self-awareness. All forms of training around dealing with challenging behaviour refer to self-awareness; we ignore it at our peril. For example, the TCI approach advises that, before intervening, staff ask themselves four questions:

1. What am I feeling now?
2. What does the child (or client) feel, need or want?
3. How is the environment affecting the child?
4. How do I best respond?

The first question relates to staff members' awareness of their own feelings in the moment. This can be applied across the board when determining the most appropriate approach to challenging behaviour. Social care workers must bear in mind that their body language and tone of voice (which can often be influenced by personal issues), as well as the approach they adopt, can influence the outcome of an incident. Therefore they should first assess their own feelings so that they can think clearly about the remaining three questions – including a risk assessment of injury and possible harm to all parties involved. Sometimes, of course, incidents occur out of the blue and do not allow for risk assessments. Disregard for and a lack of understanding of a social care worker's own feelings can lead to a hasty and perhaps inappropriate response to an incident, which may lead to physical and/or emotional harm to all involved.

The stage at which the social care worker intervenes is of utmost importance. The earlier one intervenes and attempts to de-escalate the situation, the greater the likelihood that the client will not reach the outburst phase. However, it is not always possible to intervene before the outburst/crisis phase. If a client reaches this phase, protocol should be followed as per the client's individual crisis management plan. This outlines elements such as potential triggers, the types of challenging behaviour the client may exhibit, intervention strategies to use at each phase of the crisis and any emergency contact details.

If a social care worker knows that a certain trigger presents as a possible concern, it may be possible to manage the environment and divert or distract the client from engaging in the triggering phase. Instead of distracting a client entirely from a possible incident of challenging behaviour, or if it is not possible to distract, the social care worker might prompt the client that a specific trigger is about to present itself, so that they are prepared; this can help them deal with the situation themselves in the future. Prompting can also involve literally prompting the client as to the 'appropriate' or 'desired' behaviour that one expects of them, expressed in a positive tone and manner, for example 'I know you can do it, you managed very well the last time you were in a similar situation.' This can be done verbally or non-verbally (Holden 2009).

Diversion and distraction can be very useful for managing challenging behaviour even when a client is moving from the triggering phase to the escalation phase. Diversion can take the simple form of moving a client from a stressful or over-stimulating environment to a more calming environment. For example, moving someone away from an escalating argument in the sitting room by asking for help with dinner in the kitchen can sometimes help. Similarly, showing a child with autism an object of reference or PECS/ picture of the sensory room where they get their sensory needs met to distract from the stressful environment can also help. The key is to transfer the client to a more positive environment in a physical sense (asking them to help with a task in another room) or an emotional sense (suggesting that they listen to their favourite music or watch their favourite television programme).

Approaches such as proximity (closeness/nearness to the client) and touch (a reassuring hand on the shoulder) should be used very cautiously. Should a social care worker have a close relationship with a client, these approaches can help de-escalate a situation: for example, being in close proximity to a child can reassure the child that support is close should they need it; and placing a hand on a client's shoulder may offer comfort. However, these can also upset a client and escalate a situation further. From my own experience I feel that a social care worker's intuition and knowledge of the client are vital in assessing which approach is best.

Sometimes the social care worker needs to communicate with a client through directive statements (Holden 2009), indicating exactly what they would like them to do in a calm, assertive but respectful manner. For instance, a client with an acquired brain injury to the frontal lobe may have difficulty focusing on a task; in order for them to complete the task the social care worker must break down the task into steps and clearly relay to the client the exact steps they would like them to take.

Taking time away from a situation to reflect on behaviour is also a useful technique. For instance, if an argument occurs between two clients it may be useful for each person involved to take time away in a neutral area, away from the space where the argument occurred, to calm themselves before returning to the group, where the social care worker will help them try to resolve their issues. However, this may not work for children with intellectual disabilities. They may need time away from the area in which the trigger occurred, but being entirely alone may escalate their behaviour and so they may need supervision and specific items to give them the stimulation or feedback needed in order to self-regulate.

The client's needs and safety concerns are what should drive a social care worker to adopt a particular approach in managing challenging behaviour. As clients' behaviour can change over time, these approaches may need to be changed or altered slightly. In order to discover the most suitable approach for each individual, some level of trial and error may be involved. I have found, however, that documenting incidents of challenging behaviour on an A, B, C form can be a useful resource in identifying the types of management strategies that benefit the client in different situations. This particular approach, as a reflective tool for workers, can also be of particular benefit.

THE A, B, C APPROACH

The A (antecedent), B (behaviour), C (consequence) approach is a framework commonly used to analyse an incident of challenging behaviour. It identifies three stages relating to the behaviour:

1. **Antecedent:** What occurred before the onset of the behaviour, i.e. the apparent trigger.
2. **Behaviour:** The forms of behaviour the client exhibited, e.g. aggressive or non-aggressive challenging behaviour.

3. **Consequence:** The consequences of the behaviour for the client and others. (INTO 2004:9)

The following case study highlights each section of the A, B, C model and relates to an incident of challenging behaviour I experienced while working with children with IDs; one from which I gained great professional and personal learning.

Case Study

Antecedent

I and another staff member were returning to the unit by car with two service users ('Tom' and 'David'). We stopped at the supermarket to purchase items needed for dinner. I was driving and parked in the car park across the road from the supermarket. The other staff member (relief staff) was asked to get a short list of items. However, she said she would prefer to remain in the car – I knew what was needed, so I would be faster. I asked if she was sure about this as she was new to both service users in the car. She insisted she was. While I was in the supermarket, David opened his seat belt and would not close it. When I came out of the supermarket I observed the other staff member get out of the car and open the rear door beside David.

Behaviour

As the door opened, David pushed past the staff member and attempted to run into the car park. I caught David by the sleeve of his jumper to stop him running in front of a moving car. He then stopped in that spot and attempted to pinch me, seeming quite anxious (repetitive talk, covering his ears, clenching his teeth together). He then dropped to the ground and began rolling back and forth on his stomach, banged his fists, repeated words and sounds, and clenched his teeth. I stepped back a little from David and bent down to his level. I tried to reassure him by speaking to him in a quiet tone, using short simple sentences ('David, it's okay. Car, then respite, then dinner'). His behaviour continued so I then used objects of reference (car keys) and PECS, along with verbal communication, to help David absorb the information.

I continued this for approximately twenty minutes. David then appeared to relax. He began to get to his feet but then ran again, towards oncoming traffic. I and the other staff member therefore decided to guide David towards the car for his own safety and the safety of others. In the car, David put his seatbelt on but continued to clench his teeth and engage in repetitive speech and cry intermittently. We played music quietly in the car as we returned to the unit and David was offered a sensory toy to try to help him self-regulate.

On our return to the unit, David had ceased some of his behaviours but still appeared anxious (jittery, clenched teeth). The front gate was locked and as staff opened it David's anxiety seemed to increase and he shouted and lunged toward Tom, who had behaved very well in all of this. I guided Tom away from David, but David then pushed me and I hit my back against the gate.

Consequences

David was given space to self-regulate and given supports such as music and sensory items to assist him, while monitored by staff from a distance.

Following the incident, my back pain persisted and so I was prescribed medication by my GP. However, the medication did not ease the pain and after talking with a colleague I went to a holistic therapist in an attempt to alleviate the pain. It transpired that I had been holding on to anger from the incident, of which I was not aware. On speaking about the incident I realised that I was angry as a result of being injured, but also as I felt that my particular approach had led to the incident in the first place.

I chose this case study as it highlights some important points. First, on viewing the antecedent in relation to my own practice, the incident could have been avoided completely if I had insisted on remaining in the car, as I was the staff member most familiar with David and Tom. I was more experienced and would not have opened the back door to fix David's seat belt but rather assisted him from the front seat. I do believe that from a practice point of view, the behaviour and consequences were dealt with in the best possible way as the behaviour seemed to stem from anxiety, and so David needed to self-regulate in order to de-escalate back to baseline. Second, this incident indicates the personal impact of challenging behaviour for staff emotionally and the importance of self-awareness in order to deal with situations on a personal level and avoid the possibility of concurrent physical effects and possible burnout.

On a practical point it is important to remember when completing an A, B, C form to write only the facts of the incident and avoid any personal opinions. For example, 'Mary threw the plate and it hit the wall to the right of me' (fact) versus 'Mary threw the plate, aiming it right at me' (personal opinion). Mary may not have been aiming at the staff member, but sometimes personal feelings and opinion can influence the tone of a report. Also, when naming a type of challenging behaviour it is useful to follow this with what you have observed, e.g. 'Client X appeared angry (X shouted profanities at staff and attempted to hit staff in the face)', to ensure that there is no room for misinterpretation and misunderstanding. While the social care worker completing the form may know exactly what happened, someone who was not present at the incident could have another interpretation for the word 'angry', hence the importance of further defining a behaviour. This can assist new staff to learn what types of behaviour are linked to certain client emotions/needs. Furthermore, this helps staff identify behaviours that coincide with different stages of the stress model of crisis.

CONCLUSION

In conclusion, it is of paramount importance that social care workers have a level of self-awareness, as Ginott (1972, cited in Holden 2009) indicated; they are the medium through which an incident can escalate or de-escalate. Social care workers are a vital resource to an organisation and its clients, as they assist clients to manage individual incidents of challenging behaviour. It is therefore crucial that social care workers are aware that they must put their wellbeing first. Hence the first question Holden (2009) advises we ask: 'What am I feeling now?' It is also important that social care workers realise that it is perfectly natural to experience negative emotions as a result of an incident of challenging behaviour, as highlighted earlier in this chapter. It is the realisation of, and ability to name and deal with such emotions (perhaps in supervision or team meetings) that enable social care workers to learn from experience, whether good or bad, to better work with clients that exhibit challenging behaviour, thus making burnout less likely.

Furthermore, it is vital that social care workers realise that they are not expected to 'fix' clients who exhibit challenging behaviour. They simply intervene in the best possible way to assist clients manage incidents of challenging behaviour and learn from it. As stated earlier, there is also no 'one size fits all' approach. Each incident is different and therefore social care workers must assess situations in the moment. As each client is individual, it is important to be as familiar as possible with a client's triggers, behaviours and subsequent understanding and response to incidents.

Finally, it is imperative that social care workers understand that they will not always use the correct approach/language/body language to de-escalate an incident. This is where the use of an A, B, C approach is beneficial. The process of reflection involved in the completion of an A, B, C form highlights areas of improvement and growth for clients and workers alike. Therefore, one continues to learn from practice.

Chapter 20
Learning to Practise: The Role of Practice Placement in Social Care
Lillian Byrne-Lancaster

INTRODUCTION

I come from a place that is a little unique in Irish social care education: my academic qualifications and practice experience are all in social care. Placement on my course was three days per week every week of the academic year and twelve weeks of 'block' placement that was broken into three two-week blocks and one six-week block over the duration of a three-year National Diploma in Child Care. As a student, I found placement an active, dynamic, real-time learning environment. It provided me with an unquantifiable opportunity for learning practice and understanding theory. I have been the placement supervisor of social care students in practice and now I am both a lecturer and placement tutor on a Social Care course at IT Carlow. The position of placement tutor allows me to stay connected with the mixed emotions students have about placement and with the rewards and responsibilities associated with being a student supervisor.

I hope this chapter will clarify where placement 'fits' into social care education. I hope that students and supervisors find my suggestions about choosing and securing placement helpful and that they will gain an insight into placement-based learning. I want to acknowledge the vital role student supervisors play in helping students learn about social care practice.

Unfortunately, there is limited research and few publications about social care placement (Byrne 2000; Doyle & Lalor 2009, 2013; Hanlon *et al.* 2006; IASCE 2013). For this reason, much of the content of this chapter will draw on research findings from Byrne (2000); a focus group with ten students who had completed 800 placement hours; and the naturally occurring conversations with student supervisors about the rewards and challenges they experience as social care student supervisors.

EDUCATIONAL ROUTE TO SOCIAL CARE WORK

To become a professional social care worker you must successfully complete an NFQ Level 7 Social Care course that provides 800 hours of professional practice placement (HETAC 2010) at one of the fourteen Irish higher education providers that offer social care education. (All formal education in Ireland is defined by the National Qualifications Framework (NFQ); the Level 7 award is also known as a BA award (QQI website).)

Although not required for employment or future registration with the Health and Social Care Professions Council (CORU), many students complete the NFQ Level 8 BA (Hons) award (Courtney 2012). The general aim of social care education is to prepare students for employment in a broad-based social care field (Lalor & Share 2013). Achieving this aim happens in four ways:

1. Through the provision of discipline focused theory, identified in the Social Care Awards Standards (HETAC 2010).

2. Using active learning techniques, continuous assessment and examinations that require the application of theory to social care situations (Doel *et al.* 2002; Shardlow & Doel 2009; McSweeney 2012).

3. Completing 800 hours of professional practice placement. The Social Care Awards Standards (HETAC 2010) set the minimum duration of exposure to professional practice at 800 hours, which must be completed during the NFQ Level 7 award or in the first three years of the NFQ Level 8 award.

4. Although not yet required for social care, many social care course providers will be mindful of CORU's Standards of Proficiency when monitoring students' academic, professional and interpersonal development. (These standards are: professional autonomy and accountability; interpersonal and professional relationships; effective communication; personal and professional development; provision of quality services; knowledge, understanding and skills (CORU 2012a).)

Social care students enter a profession that provides services to people who, through life circumstance, life choices or health difficulties, require professional assistance to create or maintain the best possible quality of life. This means that social care operates within people's life space; and working in people's 'life space' is the distinctive feature of social care as a profession (Williams & Lalor 2001; Smith 2005; Share & Lalor 2009; Lalor & Share 2013; Grunwald & Thiersch 2009). For Sanderson and Lewis (2012), these life spaces belong to the person or people using the service and it is the workers' responsibility to facilitate the service users' needs and interests within a professionally accountable environment. The three accepted definitions of social care (JCSCP 2001; IASCE 2000; CORU 2012b) reinforce this point. Underpinning skilled social care practice are theory and professional ethics. Further to this, complying with national legislation and policy keeps social care practice within legal parameters. While memorising theory, law and policies allows students to know about social care, time spent in a practice environment is necessary to establish links between such propositional knowledge and professional actions and responsibilities.

PLACEMENT: A STRUCTURE IN SOCIAL CARE EDUCATION

The importance of placement in social care education is emphasised by the mandatory nature of 800 placement hours (HETAC 2010). On most social care programmes students go on placement in years two and three of study (Courtney 2012). All students are required to be Garda vetted under Section 12(d) of the National Vetting Bureau (Children and Vulnerable Persons) Act Ireland 2012. This section of the Act prevents programme providers arranging for the placement of unvetted students in services for children or vulnerable adults. No college, institute of technology or social care agency may allow any student begin placement without satisfactory Garda vetting.

Doyle and Lalor (2013) identify three placement stakeholders: the student; the placement-based student supervisor; and the college-based placement tutor. While placement is an opportunity for students to learn how to 'do' social care practice, it happens within the context of service users' life, education or training, and it is essential for college tutors and students to keep this point in mind when organising and completing placement. Student supervisors are renowned for considering the impact of a student placement on service users and do (in my experience) decline requests for placement if it occurs at a time that is unfavourable for service users or agency development.

As with other modules on the social care programme, the placement module must be passed to gain academic credits. Passing the placement module on a social care programme is a little complex. While conditions vary slightly between colleges and institutes, the following combine to achieve a 'pass status' in the placement module.

1. Attain Garda vetting.
2. Complete placement preparation workshops.

3. Attend meetings with the placement tutor.

4. Visit the placement agency and meet with the student supervisor prior to beginning placement.

5. Complete the required number of professional practice hours to an acceptable professional standard.

6. Articulate practice and learning achieved during the placement at the end of placement meeting.

7. The Student Supervisor Report Form acts as evidence that practice is acceptable for the year of study.

8. Complete and attain at least 40% on a Portfolio of Professional Practice Learning.

The Portfolio of Professional Practice Learning is a student-compiled repository for evidence of learning that stems from practice or reflection on practice. Also included in the portfolio are connections between social care theory, ethics, law, policy and social care practice (IASCE 2013).

Getting organised for placement

Pre-placement workshops and meetings with placement tutors prepare students for placement, but they may not alleviate all placement concerns and anxieties (Gilmore 2012; Waterman 2013). The main sources of anxiety for students are: their suitability for social care as a profession (Byrne-Lancaster 2013b); acceptance by staff and service users; maintaining professional boundaries; and having a good relationship with the student supervisor. Securing a placement early in the placement preparation process can help reduce anxiety about placement (Byrne 2000). Knowing the placement venue allows students make better use of placement preparation workshops, as they will have context in which to apply the content of placement workshops. This in turn will help increase confidence about going on placement.

Three tasks will help any social care student identify and source a placement.

1. Identify the field you are interested in.
2. Secure a placement.
3. Do the administration.

1. Identify a social care field in which you would like to gain experience.
Module content and in-class examples of social care practice can help identify a field of practice in which you might like to complete placement.

The second and third editions of *Applied Social Care: An Introductory Text for Irish Social Care Students* (Share & Lalor 2009; Lalor & Share 2013) provide a good outline of the fields of social care practice. Discuss with your placement tutor your desired 'field of practice'. What needs do these service users have? What knowledge, skills and competencies are useful when working in this area of practice? What organisations provide services in this field of practice? Remember that completing placement with a particular social care agency implies agreement to practise under the guidance of an employee of that agency and behave in a way that supports the agency's policies (IACSE 2013); so it is important to know the agency's mission statement and what the agency is trying to achieve with or on behalf of their service users.

2. **Secure a placement.** The guidance and support of the placement co-ordinator or tutor is essential at this stage. Do transport, family or sporting commitments, financial costs, part-time work or college policy restrict the geographical area where placement can be completed? Some colleges will secure a placement for the student; others expect students to secure their own placement, but these colleges usually share with current students their list of agencies where previous students completed placements. It is imperative at this stage of placement organisation that students stay in close communication with the placement tutor, both for administrative purposes and also because the placement tutor can support the student through the process of organising placement.

3. **Do the administration.** Complete any placement forms required by your college or institute. Go to your placement preparation workshops. Update your CV, write a cover letter and visit the agency. It is advisable that all students ring their intended placement to arrange a meeting with the manager before the start of placement; or, preferably, the student supervisor should ring on their behalf. This visit will allow the relationship between the placement-based student supervisor and the student to begin. For the student, it is an opportunity to get 'a sense of' the agency. For the agency, it allows them to get 'a sense of' you. Are you organised, informed about the agency and its work? Bring your updated CV and a cover letter. Use work, hobbies and activities to identify skills and qualities (e.g. organisational skills, leadership, teamwork and punctuality) that are useful in social care work. Do not neglect the hobbies and interests section of the CV (Waterman 2013). This section can show your ability to maintain work–life balance, and also your long-term commitment to an organisation or issue. The cover letter needs to include information such as: the college you are attending; the dates and number of placement hours to be completed; the name and contact details of your placement tutor. Draw

attention in the cover letter to any experience or skills that could be useful to the work of the agency. Do not forget to include your contact details, your mobile phone number, your student number and your college email address. If you have any placement documentation, such as a supervisor's handbook or placement forms, bring these with you too. Dress smartly and treat the meeting as an informal interview. Some agencies will want to know if you have received hepatitis B vaccinations, and all placements will be concerned about Garda vetting. Be open and transparent in these matters.

STUDENTS' EXPERIENCES OF PLACEMENT

As outlined in the student narratives in Doyle and Lalor (2009 and 2013), students' anxieties tend to reduce when they have been on placement for a couple of days. This allows placement-based learning to begin.

Placement-based learning was the main point discussed in a focus group held with ten students who had completed 800 hours of placement. Participants emphasised placement as being the 'best' part of the course. It was the place where they 'got to know how to "do" social care' practice and 'where theory and ideas from books became real'. All participants agreed that they felt more confident in using social care skills as an area of learning. When one participant spoke about their increased awareness of professional boundaries, self-care and emotional reaction to clients' life circumstances, others joined in and began an energetic conversation. The ability to establish professional distance was an area of concern for all participants prior to going on placement. However, one student reported being able to monitor the depth of relationship with clients in a way they did not expect.

Time management seems to be a skill that helps students 'survive' the time demands that placement brings to their lives: as one participant said, 'during placement, life needed to be more organised'. Being on placement is probably busier than being in college. As well as the work completed during placement hours, the academic work required by college has to be done. Naturally, family, work or sporting commitments continue to exist. Even though a few participants mentioned the difficulty of maintaining hobbies and interests during placement, others said this helped deal with the emotional impact of providing human services and the stress of an increase in workload. This is an important aspect of practice to consider, as self-care can help avoid burnout (Smullens 2013).

STUDENT SUPERVISORS' EXPERIENCE OF PLACEMENT

Agreeing to provide placement to a social care student is a commitment by the social care agency. It carries an assurance to provide opportunities to engage in meaningful social care practice that reflects the students' level of expertise. In addition, one member of staff acts as the student supervisor and this may mean an increased workload for the staff. Presently, there are three routes to becoming a student supervisor (Byrne 2000): by request from a senior staff member; a responsibility of the role held; or by volunteering for the role out of a sense of professional commitment. In the future, supervising students will be a professional responsibility for registered social care workers (CORU 2012b, 2013).

The main remit of the student supervisor is to support the student to learn ethical, client-centred social care practice (IASCE 2013) and to provide formative feedback to the student so that they can build on strengths and reduce weaknesses in their practice (HETAC 2010). Direct practice, conversations with members of the social care team and weekly supervision that focus on the student's practice learning and professional development are all structures that support student learning on placement. Student supervisors constantly strike a delicate balance between mentorship, collegial support and acting as a gatekeeper to the profession.

Watching students develop, seeing their confidence grow and being re-energised by students' enthusiasm are among the rewards of being a student supervisor. Student supervisors who participated in Byrne's (2000) research also said they enjoyed the way in which discussions with students about practice and the work of the agency reinvigorated their contact with social care theory and the use of reflective practice. The least preferred aspects of student supervision revolved around motivating learners to act on suggestions to improve practice and bringing any reluctance in this area to the attention of the college. Ensuring time for supervision was essential for Byrne's (2000) participants. From speaking with student supervisors, protecting time for student supervision is still a controversial issue today.

Student supervisors are the people who see the students' practice and they are in the ideal position to gather evidence about the quality of that practice. Social care workers are skilled at using practice and real-time events (Eraut 1997, 2000; Sheppard et al. 2000; Osmond 2005; Trevithick 2008). Student supervisors use this skill to bring insights to student supervision meetings and the end of placement triadic meeting, and to complete the Placement Report Form.

Participants in my placement learning focus group spoke very highly of the positive influence their student supervisors had on their learning: 'My supervisor never gave out to me, even when I made a mistake. They talk to me about what I did wrong and how the service user was affected by my actions';

'My supervisor told me things I did right, but asked me explain why it was right.'

Student supervisors take an interest in college assignments. All focus group participants spoke of their supervisor being interested in and helping to plan activities with service users that were part of assignments. However, supervisors themselves say that at times they feel 'distant' from social care theory (Byrne 2000). This concern may be misplaced. It is likely that, rather than forgetting theory altogether, student supervisors integrate theory into their practice and 'forget' the labels attached to this theory (Thompson 2008; Trevithick 2008; Payne 2013). Helping students link theory to practice and plan college-required activities reminds supervisors about the theory labels associated with their practice. Current supervisors say that this is one way to keep their practice informed by theory and research.

Student supervisors meet students at a pivotal point in their career path. They help learners realise their suitability to the profession, help develop practice skills and a service user-centred perspective, pass on practice wisdom and create a collegial network. Often, student supervisors make excellent mentors to new graduates. While holding the qualifications and baseline competencies and skills for employment, new graduates are transitioning to the world of work and professional accountability. Some graduates may need support in this transition. While social care workers receive professional supervision that focuses on accountability and case management, graduate mentorship could be a parallel structure that focuses on the transition from student to worker.

THE PLACEMENT TUTOR'S PERSPECTIVE

The placement tutor co-ordinates the logistics of placement and makes the final assessment decisions. Having acted as placement co-ordinator and tutor since 1998, I tend to consider placement a dynamic and energetic time, tinged with its own stresses and concerns. The word 'placement' has a number of meanings for me. At a logistical level, placement means that a certain number of students must be on placement and be supported by student supervisors. At a practical level, placement means preparing students for the experiences they may have during that placement. This requires meeting students individually and in small groups to attune to their interests and anticipations and, where possible, to allay their concerns. Contacting, supporting and providing workshops or training for student supervisors as needed is part of the practical aspects of placement co-ordination. To meet the training needs of student supervisors, IASCE's placement subcommittee (2006) developed a Student Supervisors' Course, which is currently offered by providers of social care education.

Student supervisors who completed the course have described it as invaluable to their understanding of professional practice learning (Gilmore 2012).

At an educational level, placement means assessing the 'placement readiness' of a student, reminding students of the knowledge and skills they can use on placement and evaluating placement learning through the evidence presented by both the student and the student supervisor. Administratively, placement means files, folder and reports. At an emotional level, placement means a constant hope that placement will be a positive experience for all parties involved. If this hope does not materialise, students or their supervisor contact me with the aim of resolving difficulties that have emerged. This means taking time to clarify what the difficulty is and developing a solution with the student and supervisor.

Overriding all these meanings of placement is the professional desire to guide a new generation of social care workers towards ethical, client-centred practice. After all, social care is a profession aimed at helping people who need additional support to live the best life they can and to advocate for and with them when budgets, social policy and political ideologies may hinder this basic human right (Byrne-Lancaster 2013a).

CONCLUSION

Placement can be an exciting time for students, student supervisors and college-based tutors. It offers the opportunity to simultaneously learn and teach how to 'do' social care practice and make links between social care theory and practice. Strong relationships between the student, student supervisor and placement tutor allow decisions appropriate for service users, agencies, students and the profession of social care to be made, thereby allowing the regeneration of the social care community of practice.

Chapter 21
Supporting a Team to Direct and Lead Change in Social Care
Claire Leonard

MY ROUTE INTO SOCIAL CARE

After leaving school I undertook a FÁS course in home support for people with disabilities. This service challenged the status quo, in that people with disabilities directed their own service, rather than being passive recipients of care. This was good training for a service user-led approach to care. After two years of this work I decided to return to education. I started by doing a VEC course and from there transferred into Applied Social Studies at Dublin Institute of Technology. I subsequently completed a master's in Applied Social Studies at the National University of Ireland, Maynooth. While undertaking this academic work I continued to work supporting individuals with disabilities, first as a service co-ordinator and then as a service manager in Home Care Services. To assist me with the management aspect of this role, I completed a two-year part-time Management course at the National College of Ireland, in the International Financial Services Centre. I am currently the manager of a day service for seventy adults who have an intellectual disability. People using this service all have a mild to moderate intellectual disability, and some have additional support needs (for example physical disability, dementia, challenging behaviour or psychiatric support needs). In this role I am line manager of a large team and additional auxiliary staff.

I often now, fifteen years on, think back to and reflect on my work placements. They provided me with a frame of reference for the goals I aspire to – and those practices I wish to avoid! I hope that sharing my experience with you will help inform your work and that you can learn from our challenges and successes.

Our centre is not unique in what we do. However, our journey through change is an interesting story and something I hope you will find informative.

My role as manager of the centre has been to co-ordinate and strategically plan the implementation of change, based on the views of stakeholders. As leader of a team I am one component of the team and I feel this is an important perspective to have. This chapter is an account of my personal journey through these phases of change, and core to this process is enabling the staff team to direct the change, rather than change being imposed upon them.

INTRODUCING CHANGE

Over the last nine years, during which time I have been manager of a day service, the service has undergone significant change. The most significant change has been that from a workshop to a training and activation centre. When I joined the centre I currently work in, change featured as the first priority of my role. I received clear direction from my line manager and senior management that this change should be led by the service users' needs and involve all the stakeholders. This was the framework in which I was to work. I feel that having this clear goal and direction was a huge advantage and influenced my practice – both then and now. The approach to supporting the team through change was an organisation-wide one. The stakeholders were the service users, their families, residential support staff, clinical expertise (psychologist, psychiatrist, social worker, physiotherapist), management and senior management. Other departments were also utilised at various stages during the process, such as the human resources department and the training department, which provided standards and targeted training. From my experience I feel that using all the resources available gave great support to the team during the change process.

The 'workshop' environment was a factory environment. The centre was filled with pallets and machinery (e.g. production belts, heat sealing machines, etc.). The manager was the 'boss' and support staff were the 'supervisors' of the service users' work. This was an entrenched hierarchy. Although some staff had social care backgrounds, historically some staff had been recruited based on prior experience in production. The majority of these centres are now over thirty years old: in their time they were progressive, providing people with 'like work' experiences and activities that they might not otherwise have had. In addition to the workshop service there was also a smaller service for people who were 'ageing' and required a different type of service. When I joined the workshop it was at a time of change nationally for these types of service. Internal factors influencing change included less availability of work and service users having individual plans that looked at them as individuals rather as than part of a group. External factors influencing change included the National Disability Authority's report on sheltered occupational services (NDA 2009) and the changing role of people with disabilities in society.

As a result of the change process the service changed to a training and activation service. The role of staff changed fundamentally, from the supervision of work in a workshop to providing service user-specific training and activation (e.g. social activities). Service users' needs were assessed and their opinions and preferences taken into account. Slowly staff moved from their traditional roles to support the emerging preferences of service users. Staff skills and strengths were assessed and a timetable drawn up of classes/activities that service users could engage in. The traditional work continued to be available, but as service users sampled and experienced new things there was a movement towards the new activities. Over approximately two years we moved from a workshop to a training and day activation service offering a timetable of options from which service users could choose. During the following years we continued to work on this timetable and as our confidence and skills grew we enhanced the service we provided.

Prior to my recruitment, the senior management team had 'set the scene' for change, by demonstrating that time would be spent working with the team to develop the service. They began the process of involving the team to lead change by undertaking a SWOT (strengths, weaknesses, opportunities and threats) analysis. This occurred before my arrival, which was useful in helping people see that it wasn't the new manager who had decided to initiate change, but that change was an organisational priority. Second, the staff team (as one of the stakeholders) was, from the outset, directing and influencing the change.

I was very lucky that my line manager was a very progressive thinker who gave me some wonderful nuggets of advice. Before I stepped through the door of the day centre she told me that my work would be about the service users' needs and advised that I should spend each morning working directly with service users to get to know them, rather than being drawn into the administrative needs of the unit straight away. The initial stages of developing change within a centre can be challenging, and having an established knowledge of the service users was hugely beneficial when I had difficult decisions to make.

TEAMWORK AND TRAINING

Training was an important element in developing skills in our team. Sometimes the very process of attending training together can build team relations. For staff who work in a busy centre, being outside the usual environment, sharing lunch together and even having the opportunity to chat informally are all valuable outcomes. In addition, the skills development area was something that required work and we all needed to be upskilled to help us make the transition. Training was delivered in communication, managing conflict, challenging behaviour, dignity at work, and training delivery to service users. Staff were funded to attend training in individual areas of interest. In my experience, training was a very useful resource for dealing with skills deficits in a neutral manner. For example, I had observed that while the team members worked alongside each other they had very different methods of managing challenging behaviour. Some of the issues were a residue from the hierarchical nature of the workshop environment. We were very lucky to have a psychologist who was extremely highly skilled and also saw the link between effective teamwork and effective service delivery. Our psychologist designed a training day, a proactive move that enabled people to link their practice to organisational policies and procedures, before any crisis management situation could arise. Although people's deeply held beliefs probably didn't change immediately, this training, like all training, gave them an opportunity to think about things differently. On this particular day, staff gained an insight into the difficulties they all experienced. At the end of the day an off-the-cuff remark by one staff member opened a forum for a really honest conversation. This staff member said that they struggled to support a particular service user. Other people talked about situations they found challenging and offered each other their support. This was an important stage in developing a more cohesive team. On reflection, I think that providing opportunities where people could find common ground was an important point of reference that as a manager I could refer to again when people had conflicting views. As our psychologist was a stakeholder in the change process, she was fully au fait with the changing needs of the unit and was a huge support to me and all the staff.

CHANGING STRUCTURES

One area that required development was the way the team worked with each other. The staff spent all day together, but worked *alongside* each other, rather than *with* each other as a team. The 'workshop' environment lent itself to people having sole responsibility for specific pieces of work; people would meet in the morning for a cup of tea and then all go their separate ways to do their separate tasks. Building a more cohesive team was a priority if people were going to work together to lead change. I was of the opinion that for people to work most effectively, they have to be able to work together. Systems and structures were put in place to give the opportunity for people to have a formalised and timely discussion on issues. Staff meetings were changed from monthly to weekly, which allowed issues to be addressed as they arose, and also set a pattern of discussing issues as a team rather than solving problems in small groups or as individuals. Other systems that were put in place included a communication diary and a daily planning meeting. These were simple structures, but effective.

Originally there had been no system that allowed staff to know what other members of the team were doing every day. This led to grievances between staff due to a lack of understanding about the pressures others were under. Conflict could arise when a task had to be done and no one would offer to undertake this task. Gradually we started talking about what needed to be done each day, at the start of the day, and over time this discussion was formalised. Initially some people received this with a degree of resentment as they felt the manager was trying to monitor their work. Changes like this were very difficult for some people, especially those who for many years had not had to answer to anyone (manager or colleagues) about what they did with their time. While it was a difficult stumbling block, it helped to be clear about the rationale for the discussion (meeting the needs of the service users in the most efficient way) and, in truth, to be persistent.

In order to be fair to all team members it was suggested that the morning planning meeting should have a rotating chair – this would not just be the manager's/deputy manager's responsibility. Again, this was difficult for some people. However, having a greater understanding about what needs to be done day to day encourages people to see the running of the centre as the team's – not just the manager's – responsibility. It also gives the team the opportunity to determine the priorities for the day, week or year. Now our morning planning meeting is a very formalised structure which we cannot imagine being without.

Following suggestions by staff, there is now also an afternoon meeting. This gives an opportunity to review the day's progress, to identify whether a planned activity didn't occur and to problem solve around this. The learning from this influences future planning and enables the staff team to determine the changes that need to occur. After all, the degree of complexity required to support seventy service users requires staff to be able to work together in a cohesive way.

We also have a communication diary. In the past there was no formal mechanism for sharing day-to-day information, which often resulted in some people knowing what was happening and others being excluded. We introduced the communication diary to avoid communication pitfalls; it enabled all staff to be up to date and empowered us to be as effective as possible.

Maintaining accurate records is also important. It is in the very nature of human services that the needs of service users are constantly changing. In the past, decisions were often made based on anecdotal evidence rather than solid fact (e.g. 'Mary's challenging behaviour is increasing ...'), so we developed one recording system for all accidents and incidents. The team is committed to keeping these records and we will remind each other if there are lapses. This has been a very useful means of ensuring that decisions are based on solid evidence (e.g. 'In 2013 Mary had two incidents of throwing chairs in January, three in March and one in June').

All of these systems (communication diary, morning planning meetings, afternoon meetings and weekly staff meetings) maximise the opportunities for staff to be as involved as possible in the running of the unit. These systems were useful for staff to see the 'bigger picture'; from seeing themselves as individuals, people began to see themselves as part of the wider team.

Individual support/supervision meetings were established. This enabled reflection on work and also enabled me as manager to support people individually as issues arose. Previously the manager's office was somewhere people went when there was a problem. If I asked service users into my office, their first reaction was 'Am I in trouble?' Staff probably held similar views. Implementing supervision was a step towards working *with* staff, though initially some staff members went out of their way to avoid attending these meetings. Much of my work at this point was working with staff to see the way forward. There had been a period without management in place and we were in a state of change. Unresolved issues among team members had become part of the way business was conducted. The one-to-one support meetings were an ideal opportunity to deal with these issues in a more appropriate forum, while for some people informal meetings were a more valuable starting point. Now supervision is the norm.

As the agenda for change was driven by the views of service users and stakeholders, the process of involvement was important. Through the consultation process everyone was involved in decision-making and the steps undertaken were based on the knowledge gained after each step. Change was incremental. Someone recently told me that 'big changes may deliver big results, but these are often short-lived. Small changes get big results in the long run.' I feel that this reflects what happened for us as a team. Our change was successful, and maybe that was due to a 'drip, drip' effect rather than a raging river flooding the centre.

The numerous steps included: staff meetings; regular clinical input; brainstorming sessions; service users' interviews; service users' visits to other centres; recording service users' preferences on a database; questionnaires for families; and an open day. All of these processes helped develop a culture of staff involvement in determining the future changes for the service. On reflection I feel that the brainstorming sessions were probably the most beneficial for the staff team as they allowed people to consider various opinions, as a team. This was a new way of working and had to be managed carefully in the beginning (to ensure that the quieter members spoke up, etc.). Taking the above steps builds a culture of staff involvement and staff-directed change. If staff are not used to working in this manner, it can take a period to adjust. Being clear about structures and expectations helped progress run more smoothly.

STAFF AND CHANGE

We talk about 'the fear of change' and this can be a real concern for people. In my experience, facilitating staff to discuss potential changes, think about them and adjust to them gives them time to see how they will 'fit' in a changed environment. Ultimately, when there are changes, we all wonder if we will be able for this new way of working. Will someone see that we are less competent than others? Will we fail to 'hit the mark'?

Giving staff time to consider what their role will be in the new environment reduces the fear element. For example, the change from a workshop model of service to providing activities and classes was a huge change for staff. Many people had been recruited because of their skills in production work (e.g. managing contracts or maintaining machinery), so there was going to be a huge change in roles. However, we had the best possible starting point – staff themselves had identified the need to change. Over the course of many discussions, staff brought forward ideas about things they could do that service users would enjoy. For example, one staff member, who was interested in sports and exercise, organised sports and exercise activities; other people had skills in personal development and ran courses in this area. Recognising and encouraging staff strengths is an element of supporting them to see how they can contribute effectively in the new environment. Once staff could see that they could undertake these tasks, they felt comfortable; then they were more open to running activities in other areas. Their confidence had grown. They were also the people leading the change and determining the priorities.

Developing skills and confidence is something that we worked on as a team. For example, we knew that the need to provide FETAC-accredited training for service users was on the horizon. We met to discuss how this would be implemented and to give people an opportunity to express their genuine concerns and worries. We set a goal for 2010 that each staff member would design a training programme for service users. After attending training, the team drew up the lesson plans for use in the centre. Staff worked on areas where they had experience or confidence and shared their training programmes at staff meetings. By the end of the year everyone had drawn up a training programme and had read or seen a number of other programmes. At the beginning of 2014 we are planning to provide FETAC-accredited training to service users, and each staff member has had the opportunity to grow in confidence in this area and so the task is less daunting. Introducing the concept of change early and slowly allows people time to grow in confidence and skill.

Figure 21.1

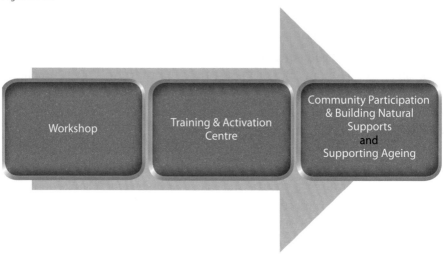

CHANGE IS ONGOING

I have outlined the main aspects of the work we undertook which enabled the staff team to lead and direct change; but we are now in the midst of another change. The training and activation service will remain in place, but our service will need to change again, and there are two strands to the next set of changes. First, in line with best practice, we will be working towards more community participation for service users (supported by the community and natural supports). For people who don't have these 'natural supports' in place we will be working to build these supports (through working with families in a different way and also through recruiting volunteers). The second strand of this change is the support of people's ageing-related needs. For our centre this includes medical support and dementia support.

Figure 21.2

Other changes that that will affect our service are the provision of FETAC-accredited training in 2014 and a move from traditional residential placements to more progressive home support packages.

Staff have already transitioned from supervisors in the workshop environment to trainers and activities co-ordinators in the day activation and training centre. Now they have to change again. Their new role will comprise their existing responsibilities and the additional duties of:

1. Supervising volunteers (both in the unit and out-of-hours supports for service users).
2. Engaging and working with extended families in a more inclusive way (advocating for service users' needs).
3. Taking a leadership role (e.g. supporting the increased number of casual staff we rely on to provide basic care).
4. Co-ordinating and supervising teachers to provide training as staff resources are reallocated to shifting unit priorities.

The lessons we have learned about shared decision-making will be key in helping us manage these latest changes. The first step is to acknowledge that things will be different. Other important elements are ensuring that we have management and clinical support; that we receive training; and that we have structures and systems in place to monitor and evaluate the new ways of working. For example, we set about, as a team, to recruit volunteers. Two staff members volunteered to undertake this work and as it was a goal determined by the team, they received the full support of the team. The team planned how this would be structured into the timetable and have been kept briefed at staff meetings. The team was kept up to date on the investment of time versus the outcomes (i.e. numbers of volunteers recruited). The 'matching' of volunteers to service users is agreed with the team, so each success we have when we match a volunteer with a service user isn't the success of an individual but a team success, of which everyone feels proud. This ensures commitment to the process and increases motivation.

REFLECTION

On reflection there are many things I would do differently. The balance between autocratic and democratic management styles is always a challenge. So too is the challenge of always seeing the bigger picture and not getting drawn into micromanagement. These are the supports that were helpful to me as a manager in the change process:

- peer support from others
- learning from key skilled staff
- having a supportive line manager who sees quality as the highest service priority
- learning from existing services, seeing the 'pockets' of quality that exist and bringing those ideas back to the team
- staff training
- being around positive and progressive thinkers
- building good professional relationships with clinicians and listening to their advice
- role modelling: I have learned so much from individuals on the staff team as well as people senior to me.

In many careers, the job you start with is usually more or less the same job you leave. Social care is quite unique in that it is totally determined by the needs of the service users. If service users' needs change, so too does our job or role. As social care workers we do more than just experience change; we are active participants in the change process. I would expect that the service we have in five years will be dramatically different from the one we have today. I would hope that things continue to change and move forward.

Chapter 22
Supervision: A Reflective Guide
Fiona Doyle

PATH TO SOCIAL CARE

I have worked in the area of social care for thirteen years. After completing my Leaving Certificate, I took a course in Health and Community Care, and at the same time I was also working part-time/weekend relief in an residential and day service for adults with intellectual and physical disabilities and challenging behaviour. After working here for some time, I applied for a full-time position in another service working with children with intellectual and physical disabilities, challenging behaviour and autism, where I still work. I have since qualified as a social care worker with a BA (Hons) degree in Social Care (Disability) and currently work as a social care house manager. After completing my degree, I was able to further my knowledge by taking other courses that were also of relevance and of interest to the area that I work in, and one such course was neuro-linguistics.

INTRODUCTION

In social care, the main area that needs to be developed and professionalised is supervision of staff. No supervision leads to increased stress and burnout, especially when working with service users who exhibit challenging behaviour. Staff need to know that they are being supported. Professionalising supervision would lead to better service delivery and a higher standard of quality of care for individuals. Professionalised supervision is the core of service delivery and part of the process is that 'between someone called a supervisor and another referred to as the supervisee' (Ferguson 2005, cited in Davys & Beddoe 2010:10). Supervision is usually aimed at enhancing the helping effectiveness of the person supervised. Social care workers who avail of supervision are then able to reflect on their own working performance and communicate more effectively during challenging times. Supervision can also be used as a time for staff to learn about their strengths and weaknesses; it can be a teaching tool to guide staff who are new to the area; and it can be used when communicating with staff so that people do not take what is said as criticism but view it as a learning curve. Professionalised supervision will lead to highly qualified professional staff who will be able to deliver a high-standard service.

Regular supervision allows staff to reflect on their own practices and not always see things from a negative viewpoint. It also enables staff who have been trained to work in the medical model to adapt to working in the social care model, which benefits the service user's quality of life. Not having supervision in place can, for many different reasons, lead to negative attitudes and a resistance to change.

Due to the current economic downturn there are increased financial restrictions in the disability sectors, and service users rely on staff to overcome these difficulties and to ensure that a high level of quality care is still provided. Social care workers have to be more innovative in their approaches to service delivery. This alone has added extra pressures to staff teams. Supervision would be of huge benefit to staff who have been affected by financial cuts and consequent restrictions to service delivery.

ASPECTS OF SUPERVISION

> *Supervision is a process by which one worker is given responsibility by the organisation to work with another worker(s) in order to meet certain organisational, professional and personal objectives which together promote the best outcomes for service users.*
>
> (Morrison et al. 2005:32)

The purpose of supervision is to provide a framework for giving support and helping the supervisee to focus on issues relating to their practice; to clarify, challenge, discuss, check feedback and facilitate. The framework is important as it needs to be adjustable to meet the needs of the supervisee. According to Kadushin (1976), there are four key elements to supervision: education, support, accountability and mediation.

According to Sunbeam House Services (2013):

> *The aim of supervision is to provide a formal process of support and learning which enables the person (supervisee) to develop knowledge and competence, assume responsibility for their own practice and enhance the quality of service to service users and staff. Supervision does not interfere with appraisal within the organisation.*

Supervision is clearly linked to learning and to continuing professional development (CPD). It should be a continuous process, no matter how senior the member of staff or how close they are to retirement. In CPD, personal support is important. Supervision should not be used or viewed as a venue for counselling or marriage guidance.

The purposes of supervision are:

1. To ensure that the worker is clear about their roles and responsibilities.
2. To ensure that the worker meets the agency's objectives.
3. To ensure quality of service to clients.
4. To develop a suitable climate for practice.
5. To assist professional development.
6. To reduce stress.
7. To ensure that the worker is given the resources to do their job.

Supervision, which is important for every staff member at all levels of the organisation, is a space for the staff and/or supervisee to talk about positive or negative work-related issues that they have experienced; it is not intended as a place for staff and/or supervisees to express harsh criticism of other staff/colleagues. The supervisor will give constructive feedback to the supervisee on strengths and areas for development. Supervision can be used as a tool to discuss overall performance in line with the centre's standards and expectations, including the implementation of the service user's person-centred plans (PCPs). Supervision is also for the staff member to understand its educative function as a means of enabling team members to measure their own level of skill and competence and to develop these as appropriate. Supervision can also be used as a space to discuss issues that may arise and as a tool for reflecting on one's overall work performance.

The role of the supervisor should involve some, if not all, of the following: documenting the session with the supervisee to prove that the sessions have taken place; taking minutes of the topics and outcomes and areas for improvement; and arranging the next date to meet with them. Ideally, supervision should take place weekly or fortnightly, and each meeting should last no less than one hour and no more than two hours. Each organisation will have their own policies and procedures on supervision and some organisations will provide it more frequently than others. In my workplace I received supervision weekly or fortnightly. Supervision may need to be made available sooner if pressing issues arise.

If supervision is not in place, it can lead to staff having to manage as best they can by themselves. The staff on the ground floor may end up supervising each other, which is not an ideal or safe situation for staff to be left in.

During supervision sessions, it is important for both the supervisor and the staff/supervisee to set boundaries of what is appropriate and what is not appropriate to discuss. Confidentiality is vital to enable trust to be developed and maintained. A time for the meeting should be planned and allocated in advance. Each session should have few or no interruptions. Supervisor and supervisee should bring a list of items to be discussed and agree on an agenda.

In my professional opinion, supervision should be universally used in all social care disciplines. All service providers should facilitate supervision as part of good practice policies in their facilities. This will lead to good practice among all staff and in turn service users will receive adequate support and care; and their needs will all be met.

STUDENT PLACEMENT SUPERVISION

Supervision should not necessarily be limited to staff in the working environment. It should begin to be implemented when students are in college and are taking part in work placements. Work placements can be a daunting enough experience for students, especially if it is their first experience of working in social care or even with a particular client group. Supervision for students during work placement allows the student to identify their strengths and weaknesses. It allows them to realise that it is acceptable to seek help or guidance when they need it. It opens a path for them to realise that they will not be judged or penalised when asking for help. Accessing and taking part in supervision will also help students understand the theory behind supervision and why it is considered to be good practice. And if they understand the theory, it will help them to develop professionally and have a solid grounding when they qualify and enter the social care work environment. This will hopefully lead to supervision becoming a natural process for all social care workers. It will become part of the job.

EXAMPLES OF SUPERVISION

Supervision is part of a complex, professional and ongoing relationship. It is much more than a session, a method or an event. Supervision in my practice is a vital element of my overall performance. It is still relatively new in my working environment, but I have already begun to reap the benefits. It allows me to reflect on difficulties that arise, and discussing these difficulties helps me to reach solutions that will be of benefit to all. It also helps me to move on from issues and leave them there. I do not feel that I have to carry extra burdens that could cause undue distress and in turn lead to high levels of stress and eventually to burnout for me.

Let's look at two case studies. In the first situation there was no supervision, and the second describes a positive experience of supervision.

Case Study 1

I was taking part in a community activity with a service user and another staff member. We were bringing the service user to the coffee shop. The service user wanted to sit in one particular area of the coffee shop, but we were unable to sit there so tried prompting the service user to sit in another area. The service user began to display challenging behaviour, knocking over tables and chairs and spilling other customers' drinks.

We had to remove the service user: first, for safety reasons – there were hot drinks around, which could have caused serious injury to the service user, staff or general public; second, because of our duty of care to the general public; and third, because the situation could have escalated to the point where the Gardaí were called, which might have led to a Garda investigation and/or a member of the public taking a claim against the company. There is also a duty of care to the service user to protect their dignity; and removing them would have de-escalated the situation.

One staff member stayed with the service user while the other staff member ran to get the people carrier. One staff member had to drive the people carrier up onto the kerb and the other prompted the service user to get into the people carrier.

The other staff member and I talked through the situation that had arisen with each other. We talked about how we had handled the situation and if there was anything we could have done differently. It was a tricky situation that we had been in, but we did not receive any response from management level to see if we were all right or if we needed to talk about what had happened. This was a situation where supervision would have been very effective and worthwhile, but it was not offered. Our position as staff members highlights what was mentioned earlier about staff having to supervise each other. We both felt isolated and unsupported. At the time we dealt with the situation but after talking about it we looked at the different variables that could have arisen from this incident that could have put us – the staff team, the service user and the general public – in danger.

This example highlights a case where supervision would have been of great benefit had it been in place. There was a lack of professionalised support in place for the staff team when they needed it most and were at their most vulnerable.

Case Study 2

In my current place of employment I was assigned a supervisor whom I met on a weekly basis. We set out a time and place to meet and my supervisor would talk to me about how I was getting on and areas that I felt I might need to develop on. We talked about incidents that occurred and after discussing them we were able to move on.

I found this to be of enormous benefit and it helped to reflect on work issues. I was able to move on and was not left with feelings of having over-analysed situations. The topics in supervision would vary according to what had occurred since the last supervision session. One topic we discussed was staffing issues, which had reached crisis point: due to staff shortages I was unable to complete rosters and the shifts would not be filled. I talked to my supervisor about my concerns and what course of action I could take. I needed a new perspective on the situation. My supervisor reassured me and listened to my concerns. After our session, I was more focused and was able to reach a solution. The supervision had helped me to regain a rational approach and a new way of thinking, and as a result I found I could re-focus my mind on finding the solution.

Supervision allows for the process of learning, which in turn leads to reflection. The employee becomes a more effective worker and a better team worker, and levels of burnout and absenteeism are reduced.

Needing supervision is not a sign of weakness but a positive force in an individual's ongoing professional development. Supervision is used to strengthen an employee's overall performance level, helping them to understand their strengths and weaknesses and areas that might need to be developed on. When they are aware of this they can use CPD in a focused way, which will in turn make them a more effective member of staff; and the service user will receive better support to meet their needs and wants. Supervision is about developing as a person and growing within, both professionally and personally. Supervision should be recognised more professionally, and it should be used as a form of accountability for all staff.

Supervision is not just a means of reflecting, it is also a way of educating oneself about one's abilities and skills. I hope that after reading this chapter you will agree.

Chapter 23
The Significance of the Small Things

Teaching Independent Living Skills to Young People in Residential Care

Kathy D'Arcy

INTRODUCTION

Many studies, and the experiences of care workers, often highlight a lack of basic independent living skills in young people in care. Studies like Focus Ireland's *Left Out on their Own* (Kelleher *et al.* 2000) and my own *Working Backwards* (D'Arcy 2003) highlight how much maturity, resourcefulness and ability is expected of young people leaving care, and how little they are, and feel they are, prepared for this. Inability to manage basic life skills such as budgeting, nutrition and hygiene can easily precipitate a breakdown in independent and semi-independent placements and bring young people into the vicious cycle of adult homelessness. Of all the various factors contributing to such breakdowns, independent living skills are possibly the easiest and least expensive to work with. Staff in a residential unit for teenage boys where I work piloted an independent living skills programme with their clients, and this chapter gives a simple breakdown of how the scheme was designed and implemented, and what the outcomes were.

MY PATH INTO SOCIAL CARE

My path into social care was complicated; I initially trained and practised as a doctor, but found the system I was working in restrictive and not entirely helpful to many of my clients. I had an interest in young people's mental health and had done some paediatric research into social care (D'Arcy 2003), and decided to move in this direction to see if it would be a more fulfilling career. It was and is. I worked initially in special care, and moved from there to emergency care, taking in the spectrum in between. I now have about ten years' experience as a social care leader, and also work freelance as a youth arts facilitator and creative writing teacher for young people. I am currently working on a piece of research into the benefits of creativity for mental wellbeing in marginalised young people.

BACKGROUND TO THE STORY

The clients in the centre where the scheme was piloted are older teenagers, and many transition into supported lodgings or other semi-independent living situations, or simply 'age out' of the service. These young people may find themselves in a range of semi-independent and fully independent living arrangements, all of which will require a certain amount of independent living skills to maintain. After care services are not engaged with by many of these young people for various reasons, and other supports are often not readily available to them.

PROJECT DESIGN AND IMPLEMENTATION

Staff designed a basic independent living skills (ILS) programme around the needs these young people will face during their first experiences of living independently. A schedule was designed around a typical week, and this was used to create a system of 'tasks' which staff would facilitate the clients to engage with and grow proficient in. To maximise the usefulness of the programme, each client was given food storage facilities in their own room.

Every Friday, each young person would check their food store and, with the support of staff, fill out a 'what I have, what I need' worksheet. This would be done in conjunction with a 'meal plan' worksheet, with which staff would support the young clients to make healthy, economical and practical choices for their shopping. These worksheets made compiling workable shopping lists easily achievable for the young people, and as proficiency grew the majority of clients became independent of staff support for these tasks.

Every Sunday was shopping day, and staff members would bring the young people together to a local budget supermarket, where each boy would take a trolley and have responsibility (with staff supervision and guidance as required) to fill his shopping list within his allotted budget. Each boy's abilities, developing skills and meal plans were taken into consideration in setting this budget, and the boys used their mobile phone calculators to check their total expenditure – this proved easy and enjoyable for them. As their skills grew and they became used to shopping for themselves, the boys generally did not need to use calculators any more and were able to estimate overall totals with accuracy and confidence. Boys taught and helped each other out when new clients were learning the system, and shopping trips became positive outings where staff and young people worked together. As well as adhering to the meal plans, clients had some freedom to choose treats too, within their budgets – just like in real life! The boys packed their shopping into bags, interacted with supermarket staff, and unpacked their shopping appropriately (again with staff guidance as needed) once back in the centre.

Every evening during the week, each boy made his own meals with individualised supervision, teaching and guidance. Every Wednesday, staff members helped the clients to tidy their fridges and food storage areas, and all through the week staff would remind the boys to check if anything was out of date, to take frozen meat out to defrost for dinner tomorrow, and so on. At weekends staff prepared proper Sunday dinners and so on, which everyone ate together, and the boys would be taken out for the day to do some activity chosen by them and generally including some exercise. Weekend 'chores' involved changing bedding, laundry and cleaning bedrooms. As skills developed, the level of staff involvement was sensitively reduced with the aim of each boy attaining self-sufficiency in each task.

SOME OUTCOMES

Skill-building

The boys appeared to acquire the skills outlined above with relative ease, and would generally demonstrate increased proficiency from week to week: many became confident about shopping, preparing meals and taking care of their food and living space during their often short stays, which is impressive when considered alongside the often quite limited independent living skills many would have presented with, as well as the difficulty many would experience retaining and integrating other learning.

Togetherness and co-operation

Although objections could have been raised initially that the individual preparation of meals would prevent the centre group from eating together, thus leading to a loss of socialisation and the possibility of feelings of isolation, what actually occurred when the project was really working was that the boys spent the evenings helping each other out, sharing food and co-operating together in the kitchen, while staff kept an eye and lent a hand where necessary. The fact that the boys often learned new skills from each other in this way was seen as a definite advantage of the programme, and mealtimes were generally very positive.

CONCLUSION

It often seems that with young people in care and in crisis, so many other factors demand attention that teaching and modelling life skills can take a back seat. But research like *Left Out on Their Own* (Kelleher *et al.* 2000) and *Working Backwards* (D'Arcy 2003) show how vulnerable young people ageing out of care are, and how even seemingly insignificant things like being able to change and wash a duvet cover, and knowing when this should be done, could make the difference between managing an independent placement and not. I think that a project like this could easily be remodelled to suit almost any care setting, and that the inclusion of more caring support with the acquisition of independent living skills can be an extremely positive element in a young person's experience of care and leaving care.

Chapter 24
Thoughts on the Good Enough Worker
Paddy Ormond

When I was working in a very special community-based residential unit that provided a specific service for the immediate local community, a nine-year-old boy once knocked on our hall door. He proceeded to explain to staff that his father had died the previous year and his mother was now seriously ill (both drugs-related situations) and he was very soon going to need a place to live and be minded. Basically he was now demanding to be considered for a placement since he lived in the locality and, as he said himself, 'This house is for kids like me.'

I remember quite clearly when I first became involved in residential care, all of thirty-five years ago now. Initially it involved a very powerful stirring of emotions – a surge of empathy and sensitivity towards the young people and their circumstances. My underlying motivation was a desire to help, to console, to make things better. This was fuelled by my curiosity and fascination as I learned more about them as individuals and as I acquired more information about their life experiences and backgrounds.

I discovered quite quickly that I really liked the young people, enjoyed working with them, being in their company and getting to know their families. I was captivated by their natural enthusiasm and vitality, despite having had so much adversity in their lives – they were like physical and emotional dynamos, burning lights with a spirited longing for life. I got to know many diamonds in the rough with their sparkling personalities. Their uninhibited acceptance of me came as a marvellous surprise and I soon realised how deeply privileged a position it is when young people allow you into their lives. I found their resilience and courage in the face of adversity very moving – actually, in many cases an absolute triumph – and their capacity for endurance and perseverance inspirational.

Humour played a leading role in much of the interaction, in the guise of a main character who surprisingly and regularly would appear on the set and with a deft and light-hearted performance catch us all off-guard and steal the scene.

Of course there were times when the lights were dimmed. Thus began my own journey to understanding a deeper, darker side of our existence of which I was barely aware or conscious. The adversity for some of the young people was staggering – even attempting to imagine the unthinkable horrors they had gone through was a deeply shuddering experience. I have witnessed children falling apart in a place beyond terror, primal emotions coming up from the depths of despair, profoundly disturbing discharges of raw anger and distress. The levels of deprivation, brutality, insensitivity and depravity of some of the abuses never ceases to remind me of how truly heroic some of them were.

The child I mentioned at the beginning was, through the appropriate process, placed with us a short while later. His mother sadly passed away soon afterwards. I will eternally stand in awe at such individual endeavour and resilience in a small child.

THE WEEK BEGINS WITH 'ME'

During the initial phases of becoming familiar with residential care I was feeling something akin to having an innate affinity, a natural closeness to the work. I had a genuine and wholehearted interest in the young people's welfare. My own feelings featured prominently – caring, affectionate, loving even, a longing to make a difference, a deepening sense of solidarity with those I was working with, their families and the personal challenges with which they were grappling. However, I gradually became aware of something else moving beneath the surface. This was not just about the young people and their needs; it was also very much to do with me, my own needs and understanding of myself. To be effective in my work, to be a good enough worker, to begin to make a difference was dependent on how much I understood myself.

I am reminded of a number of conferences I attended, some years ago, at which Pat Brennan was a speaker. Pat was the director of one of the first childcare courses in Ireland. He had a deeply humanitarian insight into the underlying dynamics of residential care and was, in my view, a man of immense emotional wisdom. He explored the interpersonal nature of the work: the critical importance of relationships at the centre of it all; the fundamental necessity of getting to know each other and, especially, getting to know ourselves – where our own reactions and responses come from.

At some level we are hoping to facilitate some positive and constructive change for the vulnerable people with whom we work. It's only when you try to change anything about yourself that you begin to realise how seriously demanding a task this can be. This commitment to self-reflection and exploration has always rung true for me and I feel it redounds with enormous effect to the young people. They are far from stupid: it has been my experience that they invariably and instinctively identify and locate insincerity, falseness and pretentiousness. Being particularly sensitive to inequalities of opportunity, they can rapidly close down the shutters in a manner that can have some very sharp edges to it.

Our own personal life experiences are obviously hugely influential and remain an active and constant force in our work. The kind of authority we experienced in our own upbringing, our experience of affection versus aggression, to what extent we were accepted or rejected, our understanding of dependence in relation to independence – all of these truly dynamic forces are swirling around our everyday working lives. Staying in touch with our own emotional reality is essential if we are to be alert to the possibilities of our own bias and prejudices and how they affect others. Pat Brennan talked about how he felt that there is at least the possibility that we are all individually a terrific source of inhibitions and repressions. Yet that does not mean that we have to bare our souls to those around us to ensure that this does not adversely affect our work.

In the context of a team of professional workers charged with the responsibility of caring for a very specific group, we need to be more mindful of all the forces at play and particularly those within ourselves. We need to be attentive to the emotional demands imposed by the work and proactively nurture and develop our own emotional competence.

If that is not worked on we will seldom be ambitious enough to attempt to elevate the truth above the often muddied and murky circumstances that characterise many of the lives of those with whom we work. We will fail to provide clarity in the midst of some very messy situations, especially when the 'gloss' element of the work has faded and the grim realities are even more evident.

WHAT CONSTITUTES THE GOOD ENOUGH WORKER?

The different facets of what constitutes the good enough worker and what it is that we have to measure it against has always fascinated me. The concept of the 'good enough worker' is a take on the 'good enough parent' introduced by the late Donald Winnicott (1988). He argued, significantly, that when a child reacts negatively to its mother she does not overreact but sees the child's negativity as an expression of its inability to cope with the external world. Winnicott believed that it is very hard for any carer to be 'good enough' unless they themselves are held and supported. There are many useful offshoots to this concept and it's in that context that the following is written.

With regard to Irish society it is interesting to take a look at what's been happening and to consider the broad historical background. There have been quite dramatic and rapid changes in Irish society in recent years, and there is hardly a major institution that has not been deconstructed/dismantled and turned upside down and inside out.

All of these developments have occurred against the backdrop of a deepening expansionist, multi-corporational globalisation of the political landscape, in tandem with highly complex social structures that are making it increasingly difficult and problematic for the ordinary person to feel that they fit into this picture, that they have a role to play, a voice to be listened to, and that they have sufficient power to safeguard the very circumstances of their own lives. It is not amiss to wonder at this point about the external and highly influential forces operating out there that are simply beyond the grasp of the ordinary individual. The good enough worker, conscious of all this, knows that the standards demanded are now far higher – and rightly so. However, the good enough worker must not sacrifice the essence of what the work demands to really help vulnerable people turn their lives around.

For me, the prevailing atmosphere engenders feelings of alienation, isolation and disempowerment. Our society is afflicted with very worrying and serious difficulties for some of our young people. Social insularity and homelessness is on the increase. Suicide rates among our young people are tragically some of the highest in Europe. I have heard a number of clinicians state that anxiety disorders are endemic. Eating disorders and self-harming feature prominently in vulnerable people of all ages as they struggle with their own inner demons of self-doubt and insecurity. I suspect that were we to scratch the surface, we would find feelings of self-loathing not too far beneath.

For me this scenario evokes considerable professional pain, which I offer up in solidarity with the immense suffering associated with the situations outlined above. In my own view, we as a society have barely stopped to catch our breath, to reflect on the scope of the significant changes that have occurred all around us in recent times and how these have impacted upon us. With hardly a backward glance we seem to misfire, malfunction and splutter along unthinkingly. The good enough worker cannot allow this lack of reflection and strange complacency to creep into their attitudes and value systems.

I was once over in the Four Courts, outside the library, with an eight-year-old child and his solicitor. We were there to meet with the child's father, a man who was notoriously involved in the criminal underworld, so that the solicitor could explain how the child's situation was being processed through the courts. While this discussion was going on, we were approached by another individual, coincidentally an acquaintance of the father, whom I recognised – we had both grown up at the same time in the same neighbourhood. I reminisced with this man for a few minutes, then the two men huddled in a corner and had their own private conference for a short while.

Within about six weeks of this encounter, both of these men were dead, one picked out by an assassin and shot dead as he sat drinking at the bar in a renowned public house. The other died following an unsuccessful bank robbery and a frenetic but fatal attempt to escape from the pursuing Gardaí. Thinking about this child and all we learned subsequently, we effectively knew very little about him and the case history was flimsy and sparse from the outset. The layers of complexity that lie beneath the surface of any child's circumstances are worth keeping in the social care worker's frame of reference.

Deeply scored patterns of very disturbing and destructive behaviours and family secrets, defensiveness and a palpable atmosphere of fear within the family home hinted at themes of menace, cruelty and vindictiveness in this very young boy's family environment. Deeply rooted cultural influences as he was growing up and the very powerful enduring legacy that remained following his father's death provided the scaffolding that framed his life and his future and all were to challenge those in whose care he was. It also indicated to anyone with a thinking head on their shoulders how necessary it is to expand your perspective from the initial points of contact if you are to have any truthful and realistic understanding of a child's life circumstances. The good enough worker is never satisfied that they know everything; we can easily miss vital clues along the way if we are not alert to the signals that often come our way. Sometimes those signals are clear but we still miss them.

There have been many recent positive and progressive developments in the legislative and policy areas relating to the safeguarding and protection of children, which it is not necessary to outline here. However, if we are to avoid the pitfalls of the past we will need to be constantly attentive to the parameters of our practice.

A number of important questions arise for me and, I believe, for the good enough worker in the aftermath of significant enquiries, perceived failures and a public perception of grossly inadequate and dysfunctional safeguarding. Has the pendulum now swung so far in the opposite direction that we are now adopting an extreme sense of our own professionalism and in real danger of being hyper-defensive in our practice? Is the system becoming so heavily weighted in favour of safety that we are at risk of throwing the baby out with the bathwater and stifling the very process of care?

Is the system in danger of becoming so over-regulated that our professional working lives are more and more governed by bureaucracy and time-consuming red tape, dominated by ever-intrusive box ticking? Is there a sense that it's increasingly imperative to 'cover your back', keep looking over your shoulder, ever mindful of heightened scrutiny and surveillance?

At the much bleaker end of this scale I would be very fearful of any further trend or thrust towards what I would term the *standardised machine*, whereby there is an expectation that we as professionals just fit, never questioning, into a working model where uniformity is the great common denominator. We need to determinedly resist the level of bureaucratic intrusion that has a corrosive impact on the work, that drains away scarce and invaluable energies, that restricts precious time and attention for essential and often critical interpersonal individual work.

There is also the need to be watchful that associated rules and regulations are not invasive in the young people's lives, that personal initiative is not impeded and that there is appropriate space for creative and innovative thinking and action. We need to be using our peripheral professional vision to ensure that our own practice does not become perverted by the very structures that are intended to enhance it. At times we can, unwittingly and despite our best intentions, drift towards and become a perfect fit for the standardised machine.

Competent, professional caring in a structured, planned, safe environment, with an emphasis on nurturing experiences and providing opportunities for healing and renewal is the task that the good enough worker has to aim for to be of benefit to those for whom they care. The nuts and bolts, day-to-day, complex, demanding, challenging task in working effectively with vulnerable people might be further outlined as follows in terms of what the good enough worker consciously aims for.

- To help those we work with to cultivate an atmosphere of care and respect for themselves and others around them.
- To help them to begin to understand themselves and their emotions.
- To enable them to explore their past life experiences and future potential.
- To help them understand the nature of groups and to be sensitive towards the needs of the individual within the group.
- To give them a sense of moral and social values, particularly in critical areas such as respect, responsibility, honesty, truth and justice.

- To work towards giving them a clear sense of their own self-worth and a strong sense of their own identity.
- To guide them along their own path of self-discovery and self-determination.
- To liberate them in their own individuality.

In the context of direct individual work, Carl Rogers continues to be a significant influence for me, with his emphasis on the integrity of the relationship, unconditional positive regard for individuals, the capacity for empathy at the forefront and bringing your genuine self to the process.

Jack Phelan has written a really interesting piece on the stages of child and youth care worker development (Phelan 2009). He explores the process of professional development, describing the levels of professional progression, from the evolving capable care giver to the treatment planner and change agent to the free-thinking creative professional. He outlines the tasks, internal processes and supervisory strategies for each of these stages of development in a really clear and concise way that I find very beneficial, understanding and insightful.

TEAMWORK AND INTERDISCIPLINARY WORK: COLLABORATION, COLLUSION AND CONFUSION

Effective teamwork is a pivotal and central force in holding things together. One of the maxims that immediately springs to my mind is that 'each individual has a responsibility for the actions of the team as a whole and the team has a responsibility for the actions of each individual.' I have always been impressed with how congruous this concept of teamwork is. It feels rounded and holistic. I like the idea of individual and collective responsibility looping around itself and completing a circle. Ownership by each and everyone is a clear expectation, and nobody is left off the hook. The openness of the decision-making process is implicit. For me it has always carried within it a naturally outward-looking agenda; the transactional nature of the internal thinking and talking is intended for external deployment. The teamwork is only ever a means to an end and never an end in itself.

There is an implied onus on individuals to be single-minded enough to stand on their own two feet, to honestly and courageously express their views and thoughts. This is the strength of character that the young people need if real advocacy is to be experienced.

Also inherent in the process is that each individual's opinions will be valued. Anyone with a contribution to make will be encouraged to do so and their views must be heard and considered. I am reminded of an incident when I was responding to an eleven-year-old boy following a verbally rebellious outburst. I felt I was doing quite well with my guidance and direction until the point when he hawked up an unmerciful spit that landed at my feet. Now, apart from a spit like that being worth any number of words, the next thing that shot out of his mouth was the question, 'How would you like to live in a house where people work?'

I remember fumbling around in a feeble attempt to respond to both the symbolism of the spit and the content of his comment as I struggled internally with my own professional embarrassment. On bringing this back to the team, we had a lively discussion which centred on the collective realisation of how the young people have to learn to live within our working lives too and how they have to reconcile and come to terms with this.

There is, of course, always the point that sometimes they have as much trouble with us as we might have with them. There is also the inescapable artificiality of the care environment and the obvious sensitivities required in making it a more bearable and productive environment.

I have had the privilege of attending and contributing to many team meetings where very strong, divergent and opposing views were expressed, and vigorously contested and defended, and yet a mutual sense of professional respect remained intact afterwards. Effective teamwork, at its optimum, allows for individuals with very different personalities, widely differing approaches, outlooks and attitudes to learn how to function effectively together. A primary acknowledgement of that very diversity and an understanding of its vibrancy and dynamism is a major asset. In my view, young people in care benefit hugely from having access to different personalities; at times the outgoing extrovert, at others the quieter, more sedate individual. They all have a significant role to play and there is not one personality type to fit all – God forbid! The good enough worker can live and work in such an environment, which may be threatening and overpowering at times.

Conflict is never far from the surface in group dynamics and is a normal and expected experience. Conflicting views and opinions should be embraced rather than ending up with people embroiled in negativity. Conflict has a constructive role to play and should not be feared or avoided as this may stagnate and stifle the team's capacity to grow and develop. There should always be the space and freedom for the more pessimistic views to be stated – this also takes courage and provides a healthy balance in any discussion. There needs to be a strong foundation on which professional respect and trust can be built. Tolerance is an essential attribute; tolerance of each others' idiosyncrasies, perceived inadequacies and imperfections. This may well mean placing some thoughtful restrictions on our own reactions and responses.

On the flip side, in every group situation there is the potential for undesirable elements to emerge, often with serious consequences. These more destructive drives and forces come in all shapes and sizes: power struggles, factional alliances, subversive and counter-subgroups. At a more base and unacceptable level there can be ridicule, bigotry, discrimination, favouritism and bullying. Courage and determination feature prominently in addressing each and every one of these darker forces; otherwise, these underlying elements can remain hidden, nameless but nonetheless a toxic dread that can poison, paralyse or disable the team. Together with appropriate management – watchful, vigilant and considerate – participation from everyone is necessary if the team is to have the capacity to grow and develop and to thrive. If not addressed in a team/management context the results can be devastating for individual workers, whose confidence, idealism and commitment can be fractured and at times destroyed.

The good enough worker aspires to develop a professional atmosphere that is essentially enabling, a working environment, underpinned by a sound ethos and a philosophy, where individuals can feel secure in the knowledge that the more noble concepts of justice, equality and truth can thrive and that any destructive drives that emerge will be courageously challenged.

An extension to effective teamwork is the crucial importance of interdisciplinary and inter-agency work. This is where the effective worker is able to demonstrate real professionalism in a way that does credit to and enhances social care as a profession. A central finding emerging from every single enquiry related to child protection and welfare tragedies held in both the UK and Ireland is the abysmal failure of the different professional groups and agencies to successfully work together. The needs of vulnerable people overlap and go beyond the boundaries of responsibility and loyalties of the different professional groups. Safeguarding and protection is not confined to any one agency. How responsibility is distributed requires a co-ordinated approach in a collaborative sharing of knowledge and skills in order to determine wisely what constitutes any vulnerable person's best interest.

This whole area is obviously not without its challenges and risks. There are many tensions and possible flashpoints. Power differentials, perceived ownership of 'expertise', assumptions and stereotypical perceptions around roles and functions, defensive practice, competitiveness and false loyalties are some of the pointers to the professional minefield that needs to be navigated at different times (Blyth & Milner 1990).

I once did an exercise with a family we were working with from which emerged an array of all the professionals that were involved with them in one way or another: social workers, social care workers, teachers, public health nurse, doctor, community workers, community welfare officer, counsellor, psychologist, Gardaí, drug treatment key worker, St Vincent de Paul support worker. This vast army of 'experts' all operated in isolation with little or no communication or co-ordination. There was the unavoidable sinking feeling that all that was being achieved by this extensive array of resources was increasingly needy and incompetent individuals. In that particular instance, reasonably successful efforts were made to bring most of these professionals together, which produced a more cohesive way of providing support for the family.

One really good protocol for inter-disciplinary and agency work has been developed in the north inner city of Dublin by YPAR (Young People at Risk). The family is centrally involved and participates fully from the outset. The model is proving to be very beneficial for all involved and ultimately provides more cohesive support with better outcomes for families.

I have yet to meet a child, no matter how serious the adversity they had been exposed to, who didn't retain a deep sense of loyalty and attachment to their own family. Their sense of belonging and of their very identity as a person are absolutely and profoundly linked to family. Professional commitment to maintaining links to a child's family of origin is paramount. The sad reality is that many young people who find themselves homeless have significant residential care histories. In my view, in many of these cases there is a very simple and practical underlying reason – their family connection had been seriously disrupted, jeopardised or severed because insufficient attention had been given to keeping it intact and supporting it (Whelan 1984).

CONCLUSION

Separation and loss are recurring major themes for young people in care. One of the primary resources they need in response to this scenario is the kind of safe environment where appropriate time and space are available, where they can mourn and grieve their losses, where feelings can find a place to take root, where healing can be facilitated, where they can reconcile their dark and damaging thoughts and memories. The strategies and techniques required to facilitate and enhance any or all of the above need to be grounded in real and meaningful relationships that assist vulnerable people at a basic level to be sufficiently freed up within themselves to experience the joy, laughter and happiness of a more enriching life.

An eight-year-old boy in our care used to come down from upstairs cloaked and veiled from head to foot in white sheets and shawls. Like a ghostly apparition, he would float silently around the room and although he caught each person's attention he remained detached and aloof. He would make absolutely no communication, other than a wry smile, as initially his peers and staff struggled to relate to him. He would remain in character in a trance-like state over extended periods of time; and these episodes were repeated on many occasions. The staff team became increasingly concerned with this perceived 'altered state of mind' and the decision eventually came that we needed to have him appropriately assessed.

The psychiatrist found nothing wrong with him, no psychosis of any kind, and was of the opinion that the child was using this technique quite effectively as a self-protective coping mechanism. Naturally, this was reassuring for us all and considerably reduced the tension. What he was effectively doing was generating a force field around himself that insulated and shielded him from his psychological pain. He eventually moved on from these episodes as he settled and began to feel more secure. I have always been intrigued by the way children can use their imagination to push back against the pressure of reality.

Relationship-building should be approached with warmth, vitality and responsiveness: it should be non-possessive; an enabling experience that allows individuals to drop the façades that we all use and hide behind. As social care workers we should not be fearful of letting our feelings show. It is so much more enriching and rewarding when you can authentically be yourself. There is nothing more insulting for vulnerable people than having to experience the condescending and patronising offence that is characterised by superficial, shallow or pretentious responses.

Be aware that you may make mistakes and sometimes might make the wrong decision. The work is complex and tricky at the best of times and, with the best will in the world, we sometimes get it wrong. However, always have an expectation of yourself that you will learn from your mistakes.

You should not be afraid to acknowledge mistakes. Trying to cover up and being evasive will only compound any difficulties that arise. You should also apologise when appropriate – taking responsibility for your own actions is really good role modelling. It is only human nature to get it wrong occasionally and as long as we can honestly feel we are doing our best, this is an area around which we should try to become more insightful. I have made many mistakes during my own working life and expect that I will make some more.

Having an openness to learning is a prerequisite because the learning associated with this work is so expansive and never-ending. The good enough worker never really reaches the point where they can say that they've arrived.

Some situations are so complex, dense and subterranean that they are virtually unresolvable. This is a tough concept to accept – particularly for one who believes that 'hope springs eternal' and in the 'rule of optimism'. The reality is that there are sometimes limits to what we can hope to achieve and actually achieve. This should never diminish our efforts towards helping individuals feel more buoyed up in their lives.

I was at a conference at which John Diamond, the then Director of the Cotswold Community, spoke about how important he felt it was to work in a non-moralistic, non-blaming way and without vindictiveness, and that one of the abiding challenges in the work is to survive without vindictiveness.

I also believe that you have to develop a capacity for forgiveness. Vulnerable people in need of care can carry huge burdens of loss, considerable baggage and hidden agendas, which can be manifested in very destructive reactions. Social care workers, being on the front line, can be the prime recipients for verbally abrasive and physically aggressive outbursts. When the dust settles and understanding dawns, the ability to forgive can be a powerful ally and hugely therapeutic for all.

And finally ...

Here are some things to be mindful of:

- Old school uncommon sense.
- Develop and retain both an ability and a desire to reflect on your own practice, always moving towards being more honest with yourself.
- Be alert to any situations or issues that might contaminate your own ability to move forward emotionally.
- Check your own impulses and become more skilful around self-regulation and containing your own biases and prejudices.
- Be very suspicious of anything that diminishes, undermines or degrades the veracity of meaningful relationship-building.
- Best practice is not a fixed concept – it is open to a variety of influences at any given time. Keep in touch with contemporary thinking and evidence-based examples of sound practice (Buckley *et al.* 2006).
- Develop a vision for the work that's underscored with credible and relevant values and principles and that encourages an active ownership in the process.

- Balance your responses between being over-restrictive and too permissive.
- Be considerate and sensitive towards your colleagues: acknowledge their accomplishments; make space for supporting them; and be pro-active in seeking support for yourself when you need it.
- Don't take yourself too seriously. Lighten up a little and never stop honing your sense of humour.
- Know when to listen and – more important – hear what is being said.
- Cultivate a positive mindset around supervision, use it intelligently and expect a high standard of participation both from the process and from yourself.
- You do not have to allow any damaging external management from the margins go unaddressed; find an appropriate way to respond.
- In the context of caring for children and supporting families, deepen your awareness and appreciation for life's little mercies.
- Never underestimate the value of common decency – remember your manners when dealing with children and their families and maintain the basic professional courtesies towards your colleagues.

Chapter 25
The Good Manager: Moral Discernment and Courage

John Molloy

At no stage in my career have I ever felt comfortable in management. In fact, those who know me will tell you that I still have that awful habit of straying on to 'the floor' whenever I get the chance. I should know better. It is not that I am good on the floor. It is more the case that I am trying to avoid what I should be doing – the boring routine of managing!

Years ago, one of my former bosses told me that as a manager I was like Winston Churchill: 'You are brilliant in times of war, but a total disaster in times of peace!' He went on to tell me that I fed off crisis situations. When there were none, I was nearly compelled to create one, just to feed the addiction!

Next year I will arrive at the end of my current contract of employment. By coincidence, this will happen at the same time as my thirty-third year as a manager. It is with this in mind that I felt it might be appropriate for me to reflect on the 'wherefores and whys' of management, almost as an exercise to help me make sense of what it is that keeps me going, what it is that has compelled me to turn up for work day after day for more than thirty years.

Please do not think I am claiming to be a 'good manager'. I am not. I am very much a believer in the 'Peter Principle', which states that we continue to be promoted in our career until we find our level of incompetence. In fact, if I was truly honest, I would have to say that I have spent the last thirty-plus years waiting to be found out!

A DUTY TO CARE

One of the great privileges I experience as a manager happens in the course of interviewing applicants for the role of social care worker. In the midst of this chore, which can sometimes go on for two or three days, every now and then some young new graduate with very limited employment experience walks into the room and performs in a way that enlightens, inspires and chastises old hands like me for forgetting how precious our work is. I sit in awe as they speak with no inhibitions about their belief in the goodness of humankind, their aspirations to help and to care, and indeed to change the world, one young person at a time.

The good manager nurtures and nourishes these young workers, empowering and enabling them, helping them to work within frameworks that protect them, not only from the politics and the cynicism and frustrations of our work, but also from themselves. Above all, the good manager will do nothing that inhibits, blocks, withers or crushes that core of beliefs and aspirations that these young workers own.

The reality is that no matter how hard we try as managers, the work of social care seems very difficult at times. The attritional effects of stress, compromise and what we see as litanies of failures to meet the high expectations we set ourselves as individuals and organisations, can lead young workers into a world of burnout and disillusionment.

In supervision, when I as a manager sit opposite a worn-out or burned-out worker who is full of self-doubt, anger or carelessness about their work, I try to play back an imaginary recording in my head of that first interview. I try to hold that picture in my head of the believer and crusader who sat opposite me just a few short years before, inspiring me and giving me hope for the future. Instead of dismissing their hurt, or blaming their ineptness, or defending myself against their unspoken accusations, I find it easy – by mentally replaying that interview tape – to want to return the inspiration, to offer support, to care for and mind these workers.

The unspoken accusation may not come from them; it might well be from within. Have I as a manager done this to them? Should I have seen it coming? Did I expect too much? Did I take them for granted?

It is from this reflection that I move forward. How do I stop this happening again? What must I do to be better at this job? Even after more than thirty years, it is still not too late for me to ask what I should do to improve. What must I do to be a good manager?

EVIDENCE-BASED PRACTICE: STANDARDS AND INSPECTIONS

There is a school of thought, or rather a school of management, operating today that has developed on the back of regulation and prescription. Managers who espouse this school of thought run services that are geared towards passing inspections and being accountable. They stress the need to sign off on forms, list outcomes and police practice.

Child care legislation has copper-fastened the drive towards evidence-based practice. Inspection after inspection has pushed us further down this road. It would seem that eventually we will arrive at a stage where managers will be automated form-fillers who are so tied into their systems that they will not need to leave their office. Instead they will be too busy developing pie charts and bar charts evidencing patterns of behaviour, delineating peaks and troughs, reflecting the ups and downs of each child's placement, with different colour codes to clearly show the effectiveness of each new intervention.

The school of management that I refer to – those who develop a proficiency for doing well in the inspection process because of their technical know-how in evidencing control, efficiency and accountability – can operate without regard for risk-taking or creativity, or even moral judgement, in what Joseph Dunne would call a 'practitioner-proof mode of practice', a system 'minimally dependent on the discretion or judgement of individual practitioners' (Dunne 2011:17).

The evidence-based approach draws managers and organisations into a world where registration depends on proving that standards are met. Rather than recognising that the standards are only the baseline framework, for a service that is struggling they can become the only framework. This approach does not recognise the very difficult, stressful, human – or should I say flawed – nature of our work. But more of that later.

It would be wrong of me to dismiss inspections, to dismiss managers who operate on these system-based approaches. It is important for us to remember how we arrived at this situation. Years of abuse scandals, years of dismissing young people's opinions, years of secrecy and closeting young people away in the care system demand that we operate in a way that is transparent, purposeful and effective, not to mention caring. We have no right to look down our noses at a system that has brought so much improvement to our services.

Sometimes social care workers complain of the negativity they experience in the inspection process. A few years ago a small group of social care workers in one of my organisation's homes complained about the process. As a result of what happened I undertook to do much more preparatory work with my social care teams before the next round of inspections. I undertook to perform occasional root and branch audits of all aspects of the casework of each child in our service. I looked for changes and omissions that happened 'accidentally' or just through the passing of time, and not the passing of decisions. It took me three full days to trawl through each case, and a further half day to write up a full report. It was difficult to find the time, but after doing the first one, I soon found it important to make the time for more.

Of course I found shoddy work. I found poor practice. This was named in my reports. However, I also found many, many examples of good work, most of which was under-reported or merely hinted at.

When I drew up my reports on these cases, naming the areas that were poor, but complaining that staff under-reported or minimised their good work; that they did not evidence their good care practices appropriately, I made sure everyone had the chance to read through these reports. Not only that, I also went around individual team members letting them know of individual pieces of work I had come across which really impressed or surprised me. I let them know that I had caught them doing good work. I could see their heads lift and, even more important, everyone's work improved dramatically.

The function of the inspection process is not to baby or mind social care staff. It is there to ensure that our young people are minded and cared for appropriately with commitment and love, as much as accountability and transparency; but wouldn't it be really something if there was as much of an emphasis on the positive in its evidence-based approach as there is on the negative?

To back this up, the Ofsted report *Outstanding Children's Homes* (2011) was a really refreshing and inspiring read, and really helpful to any manager struggling to ensure that their service is operating well. In that document Ofsted pulled together the traits of twelve well-managed centres as examples of best practice.

I often think that, human nature being what it is, if we dwell on the negative, and we constantly work for consistency, then the only consistency we can arrive at will be mediocrity.

It is the role of the good manager to rise above this negativity and to ensure that our policing of practice demands that we catch our staff doing good work; that we let them know they are caught, and that their work is regarded as important.

My experience has shown that this approach has led to improved standards of care for the young people. It has also shown that I have to name poor practice far less often.

MANAGEMENT TRAINING

Social care is not as unique as some would have you believe. It has obvious difficulties that can be very stressful. On the one hand, it does not run like a factory conveyor belt tinning tomatoes, but neither does it have the stress levels of nursing in an A&E department. We fall somewhere in between. Our centres can be lovely, warm, welcoming places, full of love and laughter, but the very nature of the hurt and hardship our young people endure can bring with it raw anger, rejection and our own serious questioning of what we are trying to do. It is at times like this when our training seems deeply inadequate.

How do you train new managers to accept that with the best will in the world they cannot cure everything; that not everything is fixable; that it is not just a question of working harder and the result will follow; that it is not simply planning and organisation that is needed?

Social care managers are seldom involved in what you might call a 'solutions-based focus' or 'problem solving'. Beyond following the regulations for social care centres, we are required, in the words of Elizabeth Campbell, to 'anticipate and understand how moral and ethical values such as justice and fairness, honesty and integrity, kindness and compassion, empathy and respect for others can be upheld or violated by seemingly normative practices' (2011:82).

While this might sound like a very basic requirement of our role as managers, it is only when we move into the realm of weighing up decisions that we must make – where impartial judgement over conflicting requirements comes into play – that the role of the manager becomes much clearer.

Joseph Dunne wrote that social care is often more about predicaments than problems:

> *A predicament is a point of intersection of several lines of consideration and priority that, though pulling in different directions, are interwoven tightly in a complex web. Attempts to unravel any of these strands singly may only introduce greater tangles in others.*
>
> (Dunne 2011:22)

While this might sound complicated, it goes some way to explain the predicament I sometimes find myself in. How do you make decisions when the best you can use as a guideline is the goal of doing the least amount of damage, or causing the least amount of hurt? There is little that management training can do to help in situations like that.

Of course, it is true that leadership, core skill knowledge, mentoring, coaching, legal knowledge and accountability are important factors in training. Policing practice, knowledge of group dynamics, ability to manage change – all of these things are important and should be at the heart of all training. Much more than this, though, it should be remembered that the bread and butter of management is decision-making. A manager must decide. They must make decisions.

The one thing that is not tolerated by social care staff is having a manager who has to over-think every decision, who has to meet with his or her supervisor, who prevaricates and delays. You can see the thought process at work: 'What happens if I do this? What happens if I do that?' What happens in the end is that nothing happens; nothing other than the fact that every single team member, every single young person in the organisation is looking on, judging and dismissing. It is on the basis of decision-making that we are judged. It is from this one aspect of our role that leadership, credibility and authority emerge.

All the fine words written about partnership, about consultation, coaching, mentoring and minding might read well in a book, but they mean absolutely nothing if the manager is not trusted and is not a credible person. The confidence that emanates from the manager is what secures and holds a team together. The other side of this is even clearer to see. When the team lose confidence in the decision-making of a manager a kind of paralysis can set in, where social care workers have to second guess what happens next before they can commit themselves to any course of action. Confidence is based primarily on the quality of the decision-making process.

We all know that when a small child falls and hurts themselves, the first adult to pick them up and rescue them becomes trusted in a very real way. Management is like that too. When a manager takes a team through a crisis or trauma they will be judged in a way that lasts.

- How do you hold a team through unplanned discharges?
- How do you hold a team through a serious assault on a staff member?
- How do you hold young people and staff through a death, through the suicide of a young person?
- How do you hold a centre through the abuse of a child?
- How do you sack staff?
- How do you make people redundant?

And even, how do you recognise and deal with the back-biters and rumour-mongers who subvert the positive forces in the team? Not the ones who disagree on the basis of principle – they are valuable members of the team. I'm talking of the ones who never come out into the open – the subversives. It may have been these Susie Orbach was describing when she wrote of 'the Jungian concept of the "shadow", which posits that there are always forces at work that seek to undo or do the opposite of our conscious intent and overt intentions of the organisations in which we work' (Orbach 2011:7).

Victor Frankl (1989) questioned the difference between a prisoner breaking rocks in a prison yard and a sculptor breaking rocks in a studio. One is being punished, the other is working towards a goal. It is not a long journey from one to the other.

MORAL DISCERNMENT

Everyone in the organisation, and even some outside it, looks to the manager for direction, for confidence, for some form of truth, for some kind of affirmation of hope and clarity of vision – the mark of a real leader. This is when the manager has to fall back on experience, intuition, knowledge and even personality. Everything comes into play, even things that the manager may not be expecting from themselves, running a fine line between recklessness and timidity, sometimes coming up with what George Sheehan (1983) described as 'new versions of trust, subtlety and intimacy – a well-developed professional wisdom'. It is hard to define what is meant by this. The one area that cannot be taught on any course is wisdom.

That said, we have to find some way of imparting this wisdom from older managers to new managers, and even to the leaders within the team. There must be some way of sharing this wisdom; of helping others become wise. To go back to George Sheehan, we need 'managers who have the right instinct for people, who are expert in those things that cannot be taught and know just what to do and say when facing another human being' (Sheehan 1983:117). This wisdom, framed against the backdrop of the organisation's ethos, the personal and professional values of the manager, and accountability to the professional goals or visions of the social care team, could well be what Vokey and Kerr call 'moral discernment', which they describe as 'the ability to arrive intuitively at a sound moral judgement in the face of complexity in a way that can incorporate, without being limited to, analytical or deliberative forms of human cognition' (Vokey & Kerr 2011:66).

What distinguishes the good social care manager from their peers in this and other fields is this 'moral discernment', this ability to be professionally wise. It is not something that is preachy, sanctimonious or lecturing. It is the culmination of all you have experienced, learned, valued and even dreamt. 'You learn to use everything that happened in your life in creating the character you are working on' Marlon Brando said about acting; 'You learn to dip into your unconscious and make use of every experience you ever had' (Sheehan 1983:117). The same could be said of being a manager.

This is a long way from the mentality of the 'evidence-based practice' mantra. It encourages wisdom as a 'capacity for engaged understanding and discerning judgement' (Dunne 2011:13).

In contrast, the manager who makes decisions in a fickle way based on expediency, the short-term view or failing to recognise what is important may get results, but they will be achieved at the cost of their credibility, trust and authority – all criteria that are needed in a good manager or leader.

Long ago, in the last century, my boss came to me to consult on the performance of a novice assistant house parent. I expressed the strong opinion that this young worker was both inept and unsuited to the work; and this confirmed his view. The outcome of this consultation was that she was dismissed. On the following day, at the end of her shift, my boss offered to drive her to the bus stop when she was going home. On that three-minute trip, he sacked her, leaving her to deal with this news alone on her one-hour trip home. Three weeks later he described to the board of management the long, supportive discussion he had had with her, going through the long process of getting her to gradually come to a realisation that although 'her heart was in the right place', this work would 'take too heavy a toll on her emotionally'. He actually told the board that this girl had resigned. I was dumb-struck to hear him lie so blatantly. To this day I have never understood why he did this, or why he did not take the time to dismiss this worker in a way that showed even a little humanity. I never trusted him again; not only that, but from that day forward, even when his motives were appropriate, I could never give him credit for anything good he did. His motives were always questionable in my mind.

SUBVERTING PROFESSIONALISM

There may be some who would claim that the care regulations we implement are founded on moral discernment, are born out of professional wisdom. No doubt those involved in the drafting of these standards created and penned each one in a way that reflected a moral yearning to advocate for young people and ensure their rights. But no sooner had the ink dried on some of these documents than the subjective, so-called realist interpretations came into play.

The impact of abuse scandal reports introduced 'staff protection' practices. Phrases like 'not leaving yourself open to allegations' and 'no over-emotional involvement' became components in this new professional practice. Instead of being impartial, there is almost a new goal to be impersonal; not just impersonal or without emotion, but self-righteously subverting the wisdom out of which the written standards were formed.

Sometimes it is helpful to remind ourselves of the origin of words and to look back at previous meanings. The word 'professional' in the past did not represent the embodiment of impersonal, efficient dealings with clients. Its older use was in the sphere of healing, religious life and education. It comes from the word to profess: to state that 'This is how I want to live my life; this is what I believe in!'

There are times, though, when life without that judgement would seem much simpler.

Again, going back to the concept of evidence-based practice, or looking at performance management systems, there is no permission to act unless the evidence is there. There is no licence for responses based on intuition or gut feelings. I have met managers who will not deal with conflicts of contradicting claims or judgements unless there are written statements for them to act upon ... just in case there are legal repercussions! You all know what I am talking about – 'Have you got that in writing?'

Of course, these are the exceptions. In his book *How to Manage* (2011), Jo Owen divides the criteria involved in management into three sections: IQ (intelligence quotient); EQ (emotional quotient) and PQ (political quotient, or political intelligence). PQ is the ability to get things done. It is a term used in the business world, and while it might be confused with wisdom or moral discernment, it is often based on a sense of street-smartness, a sense of good timing and cleverness. A manager with high PQ may be driven as much by self-serving motivation as by adhering to some kind of organisational ethos. And while it might sound Machiavellian, managers with high PQ have an enviable gift for identifying issues towards which it might be better to turn a blind eye. They are the masters of expediency. The reason why I used the word 'enviable' is that there are clear boundaries around the areas they manage. Areas of risk are only invaded when taking short cuts.

COURAGE TO ACT

For many people, coming into management is simple. If you believe that your way is a good way of caring for young people, and that others could learn from your vision of care, then in some ways, you are duty-bound to come into management. Using your vision and your beliefs, and assuming that you can communicate and lead, you can achieve the role of facilitating a group of people, whom you hope will be like-minded, to work with you to achieve this vision.

When obstacles arise in the team you work around them. You bring your wisdom into play. You know deep down that if you can fix this problem or that problem or the next problem, you will see things change. Sometimes it is as straightforward as that.

At other times, you end up dealing with that 'Jungian shadow', as Susie Orbach (2011) described it; the corrupting, subversive element in an organisation that cannot easily be identified. How do you deal with that? There is no road map for this kind of problem. There is just an innate wisdom that tells you that you must take this problem on. You park your own prejudices. You leave your own comfort zone. You consult to verify your intuition and you observe. If you can take this on, your team grows and becomes stronger. The outcome for the young people improves. Job satisfaction improves. Stability and continuity improve. The team, the young people and the organisation thrive.

When the opportunity comes, you must take it. That is what being a manager is about. If you fail to take it, the world will not fall flat. Often no one will notice. You will fall flat because you have shirked your duty.

Moral discernment demands bravery.

CONCLUSION

It takes courage to make a manager realise that his or her job description is not just to police practice and to manage staff. It is to facilitate and remove all obstacles and all negativity that prevent the team from offering the very best care to the young people that their collective potential allows.

That negativity may well come from above. In order to fulfil your job description you must have the courage to manage and to educate your own line managers and administrators, no matter how daunting the task. It may be that the only way that the team of workers in your centre will be respected is by you as a manager insisting on that respect. That takes courage.

Moral discernment is that quality that good managers have that drives this courage, so that it is not just the isolated act, or the act in isolation within the staff team. It is the way in which the manager approaches everything; every opportunity, every opening that allows not just for the advancement of social care workers within his or her team, but of all social care workers.

If we believe that what we do is important and meaningful, and that the care we offer to our young people makes a real difference in their lives, then we, as managers, must have the bravery to use every opportunity to profess the courage to act. 'Courage', according to Paul Tillich, is 'the universal and essential self-affirmation of one's being' (Tillich 1952); it is how you live always, not just on occasion.

To become a good manager, you must have clarity of vision. There may well be times when you set yourself unreasonable goals, or adopt a short-term view, or fail to recognise what is important. Wisdom is the gift of being able to recognise these shortcomings and to rectify them. Our role as managers is judged on how we make decisions, particularly at times of crisis and conflict. The good manager makes these decisions with moral discernment and courage. From this all the other positive criteria for management emanate.

It is from such decision-making that staff are encouraged to move beyond the baseline of evidence-based practice to standards where consistency is not found in mediocrity – where consistency is the stepping stone to standards of excellence.

No Womb at the Inn

Bless me father for I have sinned
Now my belly's all agrown
There's a child inside this child
Sinner's seeds are fully shown

Now they say, there is no room here.
No wains allowed, I'll have to go
They're sorry but the rules are written
Move to Galway; this beoir says no.

Sixteen years of different faces
Kind eyes, knife cold, none your own
Caravans, shelters, locked up places
Packed and moved from home to home

God, I swear, this one they won't get
Tugging on the cord, they are
Shifting eyes and whispering walls
I'll break out, and run afar

Not for mine, the care of strangers
Not for mine, another mam
They won't take what's mine, I own her
Blood is blood, God cess, be damned.

Squirming, kicking life inside me
Holy God, I'll raise her right
This here wain is not for taking
Mary, give me strength to fight.

When she comes, I don't want nothing,
Father, can you hear me prayers
Just for me to mind me own one
But I don't think there's one who cares.

Caroline Coyle

Bibliography

Abramovitz, R. and Bloom, S. (2003) 'Creating sanctuary in residential treatment for youth: from the "well-ordered asylum" to a "living-learning environment"', *Psychiatric Quarterly* 74(2), 119–35.

Aggleton, P., Hurry, J. and Wilson, J. (2001) *Young People and Mental Health.* Chichester: John Wiley & Sons.

Alzheimer's Society (website) 'Types of Dementia' <http://www.alzheimers.org.uk/site/scripts/documents.php?categoryID=200362> accessed 28 July 2013.

— 'Learning Disabilities and Dementia' <http://www.alzheimers.org.uk/site/scripts/documents_info.php?documentID=103> accessed 28 July 2013.

— Fact Sheet 401: 'What is Alzheimer's Disease?' <http://www.alzheimers.org.uk/site/scripts/documents_info.php?documentID=100> accessed 28 July 2013.

Anghel, R. (2011) 'Transition within transition: How young people learn to leave behind institutional care whilst their carers are stuck in neutral', *Children and Youth Services Review* 33, 2526–31.

Anglin, J. (2002) *Pain, Normality and the Struggle for Congruence.* New York: Haworth Press.

— (2003) 'Pain, normality, and the struggle for congruence: reinterpreting residential care for children and youth', *Child and Youth Services* 24, 1–2.

Anglin, J. and Knorth, E. (eds) (2004) *International Perspectives on Rethinking Residential Care.* New York: Kluwer Academic/Human Sciences.

Arnold, L. (1995) *Women and Self-Injury: A Survey of 76 Women.* Bristol: Bristol Crisis Service for Women.

AWCC (Association of Workers with Children in Care) (1978) *The Athlone Papers.* Dublin: AWCC.

Babiker, G. and Arnold, L. (1997) *The Language of Injury: Comprehending Self Mutilation.* Leicester: BPS Publications.

Bailey, B.A., Hare, D.J., Hatton, C. and Limb, K. (2006) 'The response to challenging behaviour by care staff: emotional responses, attributions of cause and observations of practice', *Journal of Intellectual Disability Research* 50(3),199–211.

Barton, S., Gonzales, R. and Tomlinson, P. (2011) *Therapeutic Residential Care for Children and Young People: An Attachment and Trauma-Informed Model for Practice.* London: Jessica Kingsley.

Bartunek, J., Trullen, J., Bonet, E. and Sauquet, A. (2003) 'Sharing and expanding academic and practitioner knowledge in health care', *Journal of Health Services Research and Policy* 8(2), 62–8.

Bates, B., English, D. and Kouidou, G. (1997) 'Residential treatment and its alternatives: a review of the literature', *Child and Youth Care Forum* 26(1), 7–51.

Bellefeuille, G. and Ricks, F. (2010) 'Relational inquiry: a child and youth care approach to research', *Children and Youth Services Review* 32, 1235–41.

Berridge, D. and Brodie, I. (1996) 'Residential Child Care in England and Wales' in M. Hill and J. Aldgate (eds), *Child Welfare Services: Developments in Law, Policy, Practice and Research*. London: Jessica Kingsley.

Bettelheim, B. (1976) *The Uses of Enchantment: The Meaning and Importance of Fairy Tales*. New York: Vintage.

Biestek, Felix (1961) *The Casework Relationship*. London: Unwin Hyman.

Blanchard, Kenneth (1990) *The One Minute Manager*. Harper Collins.

Blyth, E. and Milner, J. (1990) *The Process of Inter-Agency Work in Taking Child Abuse Seriously by the Violence Against Children Study Group*. London: Unwin Hyman.

Bowlby, J. (1965) *Child Care and the Growth of Love*. UK: Penguin.

— (1973) *Separation: Anxiety and Anger*. USA: Basic Books.

Brendtro, L. and du Toit, L. (2005) *Response Ability Pathways*. Cape Town: Pretext.

Brendtro, L. and Larson, S. (2006) The Resilience Revolution. Bloomington, IN: National Education Service.

Brendtro, L. and Shahbazian, M. (2003) *Troubled Children and Youth: Turning Problems into Opportunities*. Illinois: Research Press.

Brendtro, L., Van Bockern, S. and Clementson, J. (1995) 'Adult-wary and angry: restoring social bonds', *Holistic Education Review* 8, 35–43.

Bridges, W. (2004) *Transitions: Making Sense of Life's Changes*. Cambridge: Da Capo Press.

Bronfenbrenner, Urie (1979) *The Ecology of Human Development: Experiments by Nature and Design*. Cambridge, MA: Harvard University Press.

— (1996) *The State of Americans: This Generation and the Next*. New York: Free Press.

Bryant, D. and Wasik, B. (2001) *Home Visiting: Procedures for Helping Families*. USA: Sage.

Bryant, D., Wasik, B. and Lyons, C. (1990) *Home Visiting: Procedures for Helping Families*. USA: Sage.

Buckley, H., Howarth, J. and Whelan, S. (2006) *Framework for the Assessment of Vulnerable Children and their Families: Assessment Tool and Practice Guide*. Dublin: Trinity College Research Centre and University of Sheffield.

Byrne, L. (2000) 'Practice Placement in Social Care Education', unpublished MA dissertation, Cork IT.

Byrne-Lancaster, L. (2012) 'Proposal for Research: Learning on Social Care Practice Placement', unpublished PhD research proposal, IT Sligo.

— (2013a) 'Social Care Threshold Concepts: Indicators Derived from Agreed Social Care Definitions', Social Care Ireland Annual Conference: Changes, Challenges, Opportunities. Limerick: SCI.

— (2013b) 'Social Care Practice Placement: A Stage Approach to Occupational Learning', 16th Irish Academy of Management Conference: Scholarship of Integration: Engaging Communities of Practice and Learning. Waterford: Irish Management Academy.

Campbell, Elizabeth (2011) 'Teacher Education as a Missed Opportunity in the Professional Preparation of Ethical Practitioners' in Liz Bondi, David Carr, Chris Clarke and Cecilia Clegg (eds), *Towards Professional Wisdom*. Surrey: Ashgate.

Canham, Hamish (1998) 'Growing up in residential care', *Journal of Social Work Practice* 12(1), 63–75.

Care (1972) *The Care Memorandum on Deprived Children and Children's Services in Ireland*. Dublin: Care.

Care Inquiry (2013) *Making not Breaking: Building Relationships for our Most Vulnerable Children*. London: HMSO <http://www.nuffieldfoundation.org/sites/default/files/files/Care%20Inquiry%20-%20Full%20Report%20April%202013.pdf>.

Carr, A. (2006) *Family Therapy: Concepts, Process and Practice* (2nd edn). Chichester: John Wiley & Sons.

Carrigan Report (*Report of the Committee on the Criminal Law Amendment Acts (1880–5) and Juvenile Prostitution*) (1931). Dublin: Department of the Taoiseach.

Carroll, M. and Holloway, E. (1999) *Training Counselling Supervisors: Strategies, Methods and Techniques*. London: Sage.

Centre for Independent Living Limerick (2011) 'History of Independent Living' <http://www.limerickcil.com/history.html>.

Children's Rights Alliance (2010) 'Joint Press Statement (IFCA, IAYPIC and Children's Rights Alliance)' <http://www.childrensrights.ie/resources/joint-press-statement-ifca-iaypic-and-children%E2%80%99s-rights-alliance> accessed 3 December 2013.

Clutterbuck, D. (2002) *Learning Alliances: Tapping Into Talent*. London: CIPD.

Colley, H. (2003) *Mentoring for Social Inclusion: A Critical Approach to Nurturing Mentor Relationships*. London: Routledge Falmer.

Conners, R. (1996) *Self Injury in Trauma Survivors*. USA: American Orthpsychiatric Association.

Cooper, J. and Vetere, A. (2005) *Domestic Violence and Family Safety: A Systemic Approach to Working with Violence in Families*. London: Whurr.

CORU (Health and Social Care Professions Council) (2012a) *Criteria and Standards of Proficiency for Education and Training Programmes*, Version 1. Dublin: CORU.

— (2012b) *Social Care Workers* <http://www.coru.ie/regulated-professionals/professions-to-be-regulated/social-care-worker/> accessed 18 Feburary 2012.

— (2013) *Framework for a Code of Professional Conduct and Ethics*. Dublin: CORU.

Courtney, Damien (2003) 'Social Care Education and Training: Towards a National Standard', Welcome Address, 3rd annual IASCE Conference, Cork, 16–17 October.

— (2012) 'Taking Stock: The Development of Social Care Education and Training in Ireland', Keynote Speech, Social Care Ireland Conference, Kilkenny.

Crimmens, D. (1998) 'Training for residential childcare workers in Europe: comparing approaches in the Netherlands, Ireland and the United Kingdom', *Social Work Education* 17(3), 309–20.

Croyle, K.L. and Waltz. J. (2007) 'Subclinical self harm: range of behaviours, extent and associated characteristics', *American Journal of Orthopsychiatry* 77(2), 332–42.

CSO (Central Statistics Office) (2012) *This is Ireland: Highlights from Census 2011*, Part 2 <http://www.cso.ie/en/census/census2011reports/>.

Cussen Report (1936) *Report of the Commission of Inquiry into the Reformatory and Industrial Schools System*. Dublin: Stationery Office.

CYC-Net (International Child and Youth Care Network) (website) <http://www.cyc-net.org> accessed 3 December 2013.

D'Arcy, K. (2003) *Working Backwards: Tertiary Sector Views on the Resources Available for Care of Young People with Severe Emotional and Behavioural Difficulties in Ireland*, Irish Paediatric Association.

Davys, A. and Beddoe, L. (2010) *Best Practice in Professional Supervision: A Guide for the Helping Professions*. London: Jessica Kingsley.

DECLG (Department of the Environment, Community and Local Government) (2011) *National Housing Strategy for People with a Disability* 2011–2016 <http://www.environ.ie/en/DevelopmentHousing/Housing/PublicationsDocuments/FileDownLoad,28016,en.pdf>.

de Róiste, Á. and Dinneen, J. (2005) *Young People's Views about Opportunities, Barriers and Supports to Recreation and Leisure*. Dublin: National Children's Office.

De Shazer, Steve (1984) 'The imaginary pill technique', *Journal of Strategic and Systemic Therapies* 3(1), 30–4.

Devlin, S., Healy, O., Leader, G. and Hughes, B.M. (2011) 'Comparison of behavioral intervention and sensory-integration therapy in the treatment of challenging behavior', *Journal of Autism and Developmental Disorders* 41:1303–20.

DoH (Department of Health) (1970) *Reformatory and Industrial Schools Report*, chaired by District Justice Eileen Kennedy (Kennedy Report). Dublin: Stationery Office.

— (1996a) *Report on the Inquiry into the Operation of Madonna House*. Dublin: DoH.

— (1996b) *Standards in Residential Centres and Guide to Good Practice*. Dublin: DoH.

— (2001) *National Standards for Residential Centres*. Dublin: DoH.

— (2012) *Value for Money and Policy Review of Disability Services in Ireland*. Dublin: DoH.

DoHC (Department of Health and Children) (2000) *Statutory Registration for Health and Social Professionals: Proposals for the Way Forward*. Dublin: DoHC.

Digney, J. (2010) 'Advice to Child and Youth Care Staff', CYC Online <http://cyc-net. org/cyc-online/cyconline-oct2010-digney.html> accessed 16 November 2013.

Digney, J. and Gaffney, P. (2006) 'What do you take in your tea?', *Relational Child and Youth Care Practice* 19(4), 46–9.

Dima, G. and Skehill, C. (2011) 'Making sense of leaving care: the contribution of Bridges model of transition to understanding the psycho-social process', *Children and Youth Services Review* 33, 2532–9.

Do Something Different (website) <http://www.dsd.me> accessed 3 December 2013.

Doel, M., Sawdon, C. and Morrison, D. (2002) *Learning, Practice and Assessment*. London: Jessica Kingsley.

Dolan, P., Canavan, J. and Pinkerton, J. (2006) *Family Support as Reflective Practice*. London: Jessica Kingsley.

Dooley, B. and Fitzgerald, A. (2012) *My World Survey: National Study of Mental Health in Ireland*. Dublin : Headstrong/UCD School of Psychology.

Doyle, J. and Lalor, K. (2009) 'The Social Care Practice Placement: A College Perspective' in P. Share and K. Lalor (eds), *Applied Social Care: An Introduction for Students in Ireland* (2nd edn). Dublin: Gill & Macmillan, pp. 165–82.

— (2013) 'The Social Care Practice Placement: A College Perspective' in K. Lalor and P. Share (eds), *Applied Social Care: An Introduction for Students in Ireland* (3rd edn). Dublin: Gill & Macmillan, pp. 151–66.

Doyle, Paddy (1989) *The God Squad*. London: Corgi.

Dunne, Joseph (2011) 'Professional Wisdom in Practice' in Liz Bondi, David Carr, Chris Clarke and Cecilia Clegg (eds), *Towards Professional Wisdom*. Surrey: Ashgate.

EC (European Commission) (n.d.) *How to Write Clearly* <http://ec.europa.eu/ translation/writing/clear_writing/how_to_write_clearly_en.pdf>.

Emerson, E. (1995) *Challenging Behaviour: Analysis and Intervention in People with Learning Disabilities*. Cambridge: Cambridge University Press.

— (2001) *Challenging Behaviour: Analysis and Intervention in People with Severe Intellectual Disabilities* (2nd edn). Cambridge: Cambridge University Press.

Emerson, E. and Einfeld, S.L. (2011) *Challenging Behaviour* (3rd edn). Cambridge: Cambridge University Press.

EPIC (Empowering People in Care) (2011) 'HIQA Follow-up Report on Foster Care Still Damning' <http://www.epiconline.ie/hiqa-follow-up-report-on-foster-care-still-damning.html> accessed 3 December 2013.

— (2012) *My Voice Has to be Heard: Research on Outcomes for Young People Leaving Care in North Dublin*. Dublin: EPIC.

Eraut, M. (1997) 'Perspectives on defining "the learning society"', *Journal of Educational Policy* 12(6), 551–8.

— (2000) 'Non-formal learning and tacit knowledge in professional work', *British Journal of Educational Psychology* 70, 113–36.

Erskine, R. G. (1998) 'Attunement and involvement: therapeutic responses to relational needs', *International Journal of Psychotherapy* 3(3).

Farrell, G.A., Shafiei, T. and Salmon, P. (2010) 'Facing up to "challenging behaviour": a model for training in staff–client interaction', *Journal of Advanced Nursing* 66(7), 1644–55.

Farrelly, T. (2013) 'Evidence-based Practice in Social Care' in K. Lalor and P. Share (eds), *Applied Social Care: An Introduction for Students in Ireland* (3rd edn). Dublin: Gill & Macmillan, pp. 122–34.

Favazza, A. and Rosenthal, R. (1993) 'Diagnostic issues in self mutilation', *Hospital and Community Psychiatry* 44(2), 134–40.

Ferguson, H. (2011) *Child Protection Practice*. UK: Palgrave Macmillan.

Fewster, G. (2013) *Relational Child and Youth Care: Principles and Practices*. Cape Town: Pretext.

Fitzmaurice, E. (2013) 'Managing Challenging Behaviour' in K. Lalor and P. Share (eds), *Applied Social Care: An Introduction for Students in Ireland* (3rd edn). Dublin: Gill & Macmillan.

Fitzpatrick, C. (2012) *A Short Introduction to Understanding and Supporting Children and Young People who Self-Harm*. London: Jessica Kingsley.

Frankl, Victor (1989) *Man's Search for Meaning*. London: Hodder & Stoughton.

Garfat, T. (2011) 'Discovering Camphill: a personal narrative', *Scottish Journal of Residential Child Care*, Autumn. Available at <http://www.celcis.org/resources/scottish_journal_of_residential_child_care_oct_nov_2011>.

Garfat, T. and Fulcher, L. (eds) (2012) *Child and Youth Care in Practice*. Cape Town: Pretext.

Garfat, T., Fulcher, L. and Digney, J. (2013). *The Therapeutic Use of Daily Life Events* (training manual). Cape Town: Pretext.

Gendlin, Eugene T. (2007) *Focusing*. Bantam Press.

Gilligan, R. (2009) 'Residential Care in Ireland', in M.E. Courtney and D. Iwaniec (eds), *Residential Care of Children: Comparative Perspectives*. New York: Oxford University Press, pp. 3–19.

Gilmore, M. (2012) 'Placement in Social Care', Social Care Ireland Anual Conference: Changes, Challenges, Opportunities, Limerick.

Ginott, Haim (1972) *Between Teacher and Child*. New York: Macmillan.

Goleman, Daniel (2002) *The New Leaders: Transforming the Art of Leadership into the Science of Results*. New York: Little, Brown.

Government of Ireland (1989) *Children Act*. Dublin: Stationery Office.

— (1991) *Child Care Act*. Dublin: Stationery Office.

— (2001) *Children Act*. Dublin: Stationery Office.

— (2004) *National Disability Strategy 2004*. Dublin: Stationery Office.

— (2005) *Health and Social Care Professionals Act*. Dublin: Stationery Office. Available at <http://www.irishstatutebook.ie/2005/en/act/pub/0027/index.html>.

— (2006) *Institutes of Technology Act.* Dublin: Stationery Office.

— (2007) *Health Act.* Dublin: Stationery Office.

— (2012) *National Vetting Bureau (Children and Vulnerable Persons) Act.* Dublin: Stationery Office.

Griffin, E., Arensman, E., Wall, A., Corcoran, P. and Perry, I.J. (2013) *National Registry of Deliberate Self Harm Annual Report 2012.* Cork: National Suicide Research Foundation.

Grunwald, K. and Thiersch, H. (2009) 'The concept of the "lifeworld orientation" for social work and social care', *Journal of Social Work Practice* 23(2), 131–46.

Hanlon, N., McWilliams, A. and Quinlan-Cooke, S. (2006) 'Practice Teaching and Learning in Social Care: Reflections on a Course Development' in T.A. O'Connor, *Social Care in Ireland: Theory, Policy and Practice.* Cork: CIT Press, pp. 327–43.

Hanrahan, Ginny (2009) 'Lead the Way, Follow, or Stand Aside', Joint IASCE/IASCW Conference, *Social Care Education and Practice: Learning Lessons Together,* Sligo.

Hawkins, Peter and Shohet, Robin (2012) *Supervision in the Helping Professions* (4th edn). Maidenhead: Open University Press.

Hawton, K. and Rodham, K. (2006) *By Their Own Young Hand: Deliberate Self-harm and Suicidal Ideas in Adolescents.* London: Jessica Kingsley.

Heard, Dorothy and Lake, Brian (1997) *The Challenge of Attachment for Caregiving.* London and New York: Routledge.

Heslop, P. and MacCauley, F. (2009) *Hidden Pain: Self-injury and People with Learning Disabilities.* Bristol: Bristol Crisis Services for Women.

HETAC (Higher Education and Training Awards Council) (2010). *Awards Standards – Social Care Work.* Dublin: HETAC.

HIQA (Health Information and Quality Authority) (2012) *Health Information and Quality Authority Inspection Reports* <http://www.hiqa.ie/social-care/find-a-centre/childrens-centre/ballydowd>.

— (2013) *National Standards for Residential Services for Children and Adults with Disabilities* <http://www.hiqa.ie/publications>.

Holden, M.J. (2009) *Therapeutic Crisis Intervention Student Workbook* (6th edn). Ithaca, NY: Cornell University Residential Child Care Project.

Holt, S. and Kirwan, G. (2012). 'The "Key" to successful transitions for young people leaving residential child care: the role of the keyworker', *Child Care in Practice* 18, 371–92.

Howard, Noel (2012) 'The Ryan Report (2009): a practitioner's perspective on implications for residential child care', *Irish Journal of Applied Social Studies* 12(1), 4 <http://arrow.dit.ie/ijass/vol12/iss1/4>.

Howarth, J. (ed.) (2002) *The Childs' World: Assessing Children in Need.* London: Jessica Kingsley.

HSCPC(Health and Social Care Professionals Council) (2011) *Criteria and Standards of Proficiency for Education and Training Programmes: Guidelines for Education Providers*. Dublin: CORU.

HSE (Health Service Executive) (2009) *The Education and Development of Health and Social Care Professionals in the Health Services 2009–2014*. Dublin: HSE.

— (2010) *Roscommon Child Care Case: Report of the Inquiry Team to the Health Service Executive*. Dublin: HSE.

— (2011) *Time to Move on from Congregated Settings: A Strategy for Community Inclusion* (Congregated Settings Report). Dublin: HSE.

— (2012) *New Directions: Review of HSE Day Services and Implementation Plan 2012–2016*, Working Group Report. Dublin: HSE.

— (2013a) *Performance Report* <http://www.hse.ie/eng/service/publications/corporate/performance reports/2013pr.html>.

— (2013b) *National Office for Suicide Prevention Annual Report 2012* <http://www.nosp.ie> accessed 1 October 2013.

— (2013c) *Self-Harm* <http://www.hse.ie/eng/health/az/S/Self-harm/Diagnosing-self-harm.html> accessed 2 October 2013.

Hughes, D. (2004) 'An attachment-based treatment of maltreated children and young people', *Attachment and Human Development* 6, 263–78.

— (2006) *Building the Bonds of Attachment: Awakening Love in Deeply Troubled Children*. New York: Aronson.

— (2009) *Attachment-Focused Parenting: Effective Strategies to Care for Children*. New York: Norton & Co.

Hughes, L. and Pengelly, P. (1997) *Staff Supervision in a Turbulent Environment: Managing Task and Process in Front-line Services*. London: Jessica Kingsley.

IASCE (Irish Association of Social Care Educators) (2000) *Working Models: A Manual for Placement Supervision*. Carlow: St Patrick's College

— (2004) Minutes of IASCE Meeting, January <http://staffweb.itsligo.ie/staff/pshare/iasce/> accessed 18 February 2012.

— (2006) *Supervision Course* <http://staffweb.itsligo.ie/staff/pshare/IASCE/supervision_course.htm> accessed 5 June 2007.

— (2012) *Practice Placement Policy* <http://staffweb.itsligo.ie/staff/pshare/IASCE/praciceplacement_policy.htm> accessed 18 January 2013.

— (2013) *Practice Placement Manual*. Sligo: Big Fish Press.

IASCW (Irish Association of Social Care Workers) (1988a) *Code for Care Workers*. Dublin: IASCW.

— (1988b) *The Ennismore Papers*. Dublin: IASCW.

IFCA (Irish Foster Care Association) (2012) 'Lack of Assessment Significant Cause of Concern', press release, 17 July <http://www.ifca.ie/news2/press-release/17th-july-2012-lack-of-assessment-significant-source-of-concern/> accessed 3 December 2013.

ILO, ICN, WHO and PSI (International Labour Organisation, International Council of Nurses, World Health Organisation and Public Services International) (2002) *Framework for Addressing Workplace Violence in the Health Sector*. Geneva: ILO.

Inckle, K. (2007). *Writing on the Body? Thinking through Gendered Embodiment and Marked Flesh*. Newcastle: Cambridge Scholars Publishing.

Inclusion Ireland (2013) *Information Pack: A Guide to Disability Law and Policy in Ireland* <http://www.inclusionireland.ie/sites/default/files/documents/information_pack-final.pdf>.

INTO (Irish National Teachers' Organisation) (2004) *Managing Challenging Behaviour: Guidelines for Teachers*. INTO.

Irish Times (1972) 'National Council for Educational Awards', 28 March.

Iwaniec, D. (2006) 'Introduction: An Overview of Children in Public Care' in D. Iwaniec (ed.), *The Child's Journey Through Care: Placement Stability, Care-Planning, and Achieving Permanency*. Chichester: John Wiley & Sons.

James, I.A. (2011) *Understanding Behaviour in Dementia that Challenges: A Guide to Assessment and Treatment*. London: Jessica Kingsley.

JCSCP (Joint Committee on Social Care Professionals) (2002) *Final Report*. Dublin: HSE, for Department of Social and Family Affairs.

Johns, Christopher (2013) *Becoming a Reflective Practitioner*, 3rd edn. West Sussex: Wiley-Blackwell.

Jones, A. (1998) *104 Activities That Build: Self-esteem, Teamwork, Communication, Anger Management, Self-discovery, Coping Skills*. Lusby, MD: Rec Room.

Jones, L. and Landsverk, J. (2006) 'Residential education: examining a new approach for improving outcomes for foster youth', *Children and Youth Services Review* 28, 1152–68.

Kadushin, A. (1976) *Supervision in Social Work*. New York: Columbia University Press.

Kadushin, A. and Harkness, D. (2002) *Supervision in Social Work* (3rd edn). New York: Columbia University Press.

Kahan, B. (1984) 'The State of the Art' in T. Philpot (ed.), *Group Care Practice: The Challenge of the Next Decade*. Surrey: Business Press International, pp. 5–9.

Kahan, B. and Banner, G. (1969) *Residential Task in Child Care* (Castle Priory Report). Banstead: Residential Care Association.

Kelleher, P., Kelleher, C. and Corbett, M. (2000) *Left Out on Their Own: Young People Leaving Care in Ireland*. Dublin: Oak Tree Press.

Killeen, Aoife (2013) 'Our Right to Independent Living: Your Choice or Mine?', paper presented at the Social Care Ireland Conference, Limerick, 21 March.

— (2014) 'The Divide at 65: Implications for Domiciliary Care Delivery for Older People with Physical Disabilities in Ireland', unpublished PhD thesis, Cork IT.

Kilner, Simon (2013) 'Helping Children with Focusing: Guidelines for Companions' <http://www.focusing.org/children>.

Kirschenbaum, H. and Henderson, V. (eds) (1989) *The Carl Rogers Reader*. New York: Houghton Mifflin.

Knorth, E., Harder, A., Zandberg, T. and Kendrick, A. (2008) 'Under one roof: a review and selective meta-analysis on the outcomes of residential child and youth care', *Children and Youth Services Review* 30, 123–40.

Krishnamoorthy, A. and Anderson, D. (2011) 'Managing challenging behaviour in older adults with dementia', *Progress in Neurology and Psychiatry* 15(3), 20–6.

Lalor, K. and Share, P. (eds) (2013). *Applied Social Care: An Introduction for Students in Ireland* (3rd edn). Dublin: Gill & Macmillan.

Lalor, K. and Share, P. (2013) 'Understanding Social Care' in K. Lalor and P. Share, *Applied Social Care: An Introduction for Students In Ireland* (3rd edn). Dublin: Gill & Macmillan, pp. 3–18.

Landy, S. and Menna, R. (2006) *Early Intervention with Multi-Risk Families: An Integrative Approach*. USA: Brookes.

Lentin, Louis (1996) *Dear Daughter*. Dublin: RTÉ.

Levenkron, S. (1999) *Cutting: Understanding and Overcoming Self-Mutilation*. New York: Norton.

Levy, Terry M. and Orlans, Michael (1998) *Attachment, Trauma, and Healing*. Washington DC: CWLA Press.

Linehan, M.M. (1993) *Cognitive-behavioural Treatment of Borderline Personality Disorder*. New York: Guilford Press.

Long, N. (2007) 'The therapeutic power of kindness', *Reclaiming Children and Youth* 5(4), 242–6.

Lyons, D. (2013) 'Learn About Your Self Before You Work with Others' in K. Lalor and P. Share (eds), *Applied Social Care: An Introduction for Students in Ireland* (3rd edn). Dublin: Gill & Macmillan, pp. 98–108.

McCafferty, Nell (1981) *In the Eyes of the Law*. Dublin: Ward River Press.

McCann James, C., de Róiste, A. and McHugh, J. (2009) *Social Care Practice in Ireland: An Integrated Perspective*. Dublin: Gill & Macmillan.

McColgan Report (West of Ireland Farmer Case) (1998). North Western Health Board.

McGuinness, C. (1993) *Report of the Kilkenny Incest Investigation*. Dublin: Stationery Office.

McHugh, P. and Byrne, M. (2011) *Survey of the Research Activity, Skills and Training Needs of Health and Social Care Professionals in Ireland*. Dublin: HSE.

McMahon, L. and Ward, A. (eds) (1998) *Intuition is Not Enough: Matching Learning with Practice in Therapeutic Child Care*. London: Routledge.

McSherry, D., Larkin, E., Fargas, M., Kelly, G., Robinson, C., MacDonald, G., Schubotz, D. and Kilpatrick, R. (2008) *From Care to Where? A Care Pathways and Outcomes Report for Practitioners*. Belfast: Institute of Child Care Research, Queen's University Belfast.

McSweeney, F. (2012) 'Student, practitioner or both? Separation and integration of identities in professional social care education', *Social Work Education* 31(3), 364–82.

Melton, G., Lyons, P. and Spalding, W. (1998) *No Place to Go: The Civil Commitment of Minors*. Lincoln, NE: University of Nebraska Press.

Minuchin, P., Colapinto, J. and Minuchin, S. (1998) *Working with Families of the Poor*. New York: Guilford.

Moran, P., Coffey, C., Romaniuk, H., Olsson, C., Borschmann, R., Carlin, J.B. and Patton, G.C. (2011) 'The natural history of self-harm during adolescence and young adulthood: population-based cohort study', *The Lancet* 379(9812), 236–43. DOI:10.1016/S0140-6736(11)61141-0.

Morgan, M., Brosi, W.A. and Brosi, M.W. (2011) 'Restorying older adults' narratives about self and substance abuse', *American Journal of Family Therapy* 39(5), 444–55.

Morrison, T., Hathaway, J. and Fairley, G. (2005) *Staff Supervision in Social Care: Making a Real Difference for Staff and Service Users*. London: Pavilion.

Murgatroyd, Steve (1996) *Counselling and Helping*. London: British Psychological Society/Methuen.

Myers, D. (2006) *Exploring Psychology* (8th edn, in modules). UK: Worth.

NALA (National Adult Literacy Agency) (website) <http://www.nala.ie> accessed 5 October 2013.

NCEA (National Council for Educational Awards) (1992) *Report of Working Group on Caring and Social Studies*. Dublin : NCEA.

NDA (National Disability Authority) (2002) *Towards Best Practice in Provision of Health Services for People with Disabilities in Ireland*. Dublin: NDA.

— (2009) *From Sheltered to Open Employment for People with Disabilities in Ireland*. Dublin: NDA.

Newburn, T. and Shiner, M. (2005) *Dealing with Disaffection: Young People, Mentoring and Social Inclusion*. Cullompton, Devon: Willan.

NSRF (National Suicide Research Foundation) (2010) *National Registry of Deliberate Self Harm in Ireland Annual Report 2010*. Cork: NSRF.

Nussbaum, Martha (2003) 'Dr True Self: review of *Winnicott: Life and Work* by F. Robert Rodman', *New Republic*, 27 October.

— (2012) *Philosophical Interventions: Reviews 1986–2011*. USA: Oxford University Press.

O'Connor, T. (2009) 'Social Care and Social Change: Future Direction or Lost Opportunity?' in P. Share and K. Lalor (eds), *Applied Social Care: An Introduction for Students in Ireland* (2nd edn). Dublin: Gill & Macmillan, pp. 99–109.

— (ed.) (2013) *Integrated Care for Ireland in an International Context: Challenges for Policy, Institutions and Specific Service User Needs*. Cork: Oak Tree Press.

O'Connor, T. and Murphy, M. (eds) (2006) *Social Care in Ireland: Theory, Policy and Practice*. Cork: Cork IT.

Ofsted (Office for Standards in Education, Children's Services and Skills), UK (2011) *Outstanding Children's Homes*. UK: Ofsted.

Oireachtas Committee (1996) *Kelly Fitzgerald, A Child is Dead*. Western Health Board.

OMCYA (Office of the Minister for Children and Youth Affairs) (2009a) *Report of the Commission to Inquire into Child Abuse* (Ryan Report). Dublin: OMCYA.

— (2009b) *Report of the Commission to Inquire into Child Abuse (Ryan Report) – Implementation Plan*. Dublin: OMCYA.

O'Neill, E. (2004) *Professional Supervision: Myths, Culture and Structure*. Ireland: RMA Publications.

Orbach, Susie (2011) 'Work is Where We Live: Emotional Literacy and the Psychological Dimensions of the Various Relationships There' in Liz Bondi, David Carr, Chris Clarke and Cecilia Clegg (eds), *Towards Professional Wisdom*. Surrey: Ashgate.

Osmond, J. (2005) 'The knowledge sprectrum: a framework for teaching knowledge and its use in social work practice', *British Journal of Social Work* 35, 881–900.

Osterling, K. and Hines, M. (2006) 'Mentoring adolescent foster youth: promoting resilience during developmental transitions', *Child and Family Social Work* 11, 242–53.

Osuch, E.A. and Payne, G.W. (2009) 'Neurobiological Perspectives on Self-injury' in M.K. Nixon and N.L. Heath (eds), *Self-injury in Youth: The Essential Guide to Assessment and Intervention*. New York: Routledge.

O'Sullivan, Eoin (2009) *Residential Child Welfare in Ireland, 1965–2008: An Outline of Policy, Legislation and Practice*. Paper prepared for the Commission to Inquire into Child Abuse. Dublin: Stationery Office.

Owen, Jo (2011) *How to Manage*. New Jersey: Prentice Hall.

Pawson, R., Boaz, A., Grayson, L., Long, A. and Barnes, C. (2003) *Types and Quality of Social Care Knowledge Stage Two: Towards the Quality Assessment of Social Care Knowledge*. London: Centre for Evidence-Based Policy and Practice, ESRC UK.

Payne, M. (2013) *Modern Social Work Theory* (4th edn). UK: Palgrave.

Phares, E. (1976) *Locus of Control and Personality*. New Jersey: Gilver Burdett.

Phelan, J. (2009) 'The Wounded Healer as Helper and Helped: A CYC Model' <http://www.cyc-net.org/cyc-online/cyconline-mar2009-phelan.html> accessed 16 November 2013.

— (n.d.) *Stages of Child and Youth Care Worker Development*, CYC-net <http://www.cyc-net.org/phelanstages.html> accessed 12 October 2013.

Piggott, J., Williams, C., McLeod, S. and Barton, J. (2004) 'A qualitative study of supports for young people who self harm in residential care in Glasgow', *Scottish Journal of Residential Child Care* 3(2), 45–54.

Pinkerton, J. (2012) 'Understanding young people's transitions from state care: the need for connections', *Diskurs Kindheits- und Jugendforschung* 3, 309–19.

Pinkerton, J. and Coyle, D. (2012) 'Leaving care: the need to make connections', *Child Care in Practice* 18(4), 297–308.

Proctor, Brigid (1986) 'Supervision: A Co-operative Exercise in Accountability' in A. Marken and M. Payne (eds), *Enabling and Ensuring: Supervision in Practice*. Leicester: National Youth Bureau/Council for Education and Training in Youth and Community Work.

QQI (Quality and Qualifications Ireland) (website) 'National Framework of Qualifications' <http://www.qqi.ie/Pages/National%20Framework%20of%20Qualifications.aspx>.

Reilly, M. (2008) *Report on an Inspection of Loughan House Open Centre by the Inspector of Prisons*. Dublin: Inspector of Prisons.

Rix, Juliet (2013) 'Why are love and care no longer part of child social work?', *The Guardian*, 6 November <http://www.theguardian.com/society/2013/nov/06/social-work-looked-after-children-love-care> accessed 16 November 2013.

Rogers, Carl (1951) *Client-centered Therapy: Its Current Practice, Implications and Theory*. London: Constable.

— (1980) *A Way of Being. Boston*, MA: Houghton Mifflin.

RTÉ News (2013) 'HIQA Inspectors not Assured Children were Safe' <http://www.rte.ie/news/2013/0221/368944-hiqa-inspectors-not-assured-children-were-safe/> accessed 3 December 2013.

Ruch, G. (2005) 'Relationship-based practice and reflective practice: holistic approaches to contemporary child care social work', *Child and Family Social Work* 10, 111–23.

St Catherine's Association (2013) *Policies*. Ireland: St Catherine's Association.

Sanderson, H. and Lewis, J. (2012) *A Practical Guide to Delivering Personalisation: Person-centred Practice in Health and Social Care*. London: Jessica Kingsley.

Schön, D. (1983) *The Reflective Practitioner: How Professionals Think in Action*. New York: Basic Books.

Selekman, M.D. (2006) *Working with Self-Harming Adolescents: A Collaborative, Strengths- Based Therapy Approach*. New York: Norton.

Seligman, M. (2002) *Authentic Happiness: Using the New Positive Psychology to Realize your Potential for Lasting Fulfilment*. New York: Free Press.

Shannon, Geoffrey and Gibbons, Norah (2012) *Report of the Independent Child Death Review Group*. Dublin: DCYA.

Shardlow, S. and Doel, M. (2009) 'Health and Social Care: A Complex Context for Professional Education' in S.A. Shardlow, *Educating Professionals: Practice Learning in Health and Social Care*. UK: Ashgate, pp. 3–14.

Share, P. (2009) 'Social Care and the Professional Development Project' in P. Share and K. Lalor, *Applied Social Care: An Introduction for Students in Ireland* (2nd edn). Dublin: Gill & Macmillan, pp. 58–73.

— (2013) 'Social Care Practice, Professionalism and Post-professionalism', in K. Lalor and P. Share, *Applied Social Care: An Introduction for Students in Ireland* (3rd edn). Dublin: Gill & Macmillan, pp. 42–57.

Share, P. and Lalor, K. (2009) *Applied Social Care: An Introduction for Students in Ireland* (2nd edn). Dublin: Gill & Macmillan.

Sharry, J., Madden, B. and Darmody, M. (2001) *Becoming a Solution Detective: A Strengths-based Guide to Brief Therapy*. London: BT Press.

Sheehan, George (1983) *How to Feel Great 24 Hours a Day*. Simon & Schuster.

Sheppard, M., Newstead, S., Di Caccavo, A. and Ryan, K. (2000) 'Reflexivity and the development of process knowledge in social work: a classification and empirical study', *British Journal of Social Work* 30, 465–88.

Sher, L. and Stanley, B.H. (2009) 'Biological Models of Nonsuicidal Self-injury' in M.K. Nock (ed.), *Understanding Nonsuicidal Self-injury: Origins, Assessment and Treatment*. Washington, DC: American Psychological Association.

Shohet, R. (1999) 'Whose Feelings am I Feeling? Using the Concept of Projective Identification' in Andrew Hardwick and Judith Woodhead, *Loving, Hating and Survival: A Handbook for All who Work with Troubled Children and Young People*. Aldershot: Ashgate.

Simply Put (website) 'Plain English Around the World' <http://www.simplyput.ie/about_us_around_the_world> accessed 5 October 2013.

SLMRU (Skills and Labour Market Research Unit) (2009) *National Skills Bulletin 2009*. Dublin: FÁS.

Smail, David (1987) *Taking Care: An Alternative to Therapy*. London: J.M. Dent & Sons.

Smart, Maxwell (2006) 'The Carberry Project', CYC-Online (87) <http://www.cyc-net.org/cyc-online/cycol-0406-carberry.html> accessed 16 November 2013.

Smith, M. (2005) 'Working in the life space', *In Residence: Scottish Institute for Residential Child Care* 2.

Smith, Mike (1998) *Working with Self Harm: Victim to Victor*. Gloucester: Handsell Publishing.

Smith, Roger (2010) 'Social work, risk, power', *Sociological Research Online* 15(1), DOI:10.5153/sro.2101.

Smullens, S. (2013) 'What I wish I had known: burnout and self-care in our social work profession', *New Social Workers Online* <http://www.socialworker.com/home/Feature_Articles/Field_Placement/What_I_Wish_I_Had_Known%3A_Burnout_and_Self-Care_in_Our_Social_Work_Profession/> accessed 28 August 2013.

South Eastern Health Board (2004) *Meeting the Challenge of Challenging Behaviour: the Policy and Vision for the Development and Delivery of Services for People with Intellectual Disabilities and Challenging Behaviour*. Ireland: South Eastern Health Board.

Stapert, Marta and Verliefde, Erik (2012) *Focusing with Children: The Art of Communicating with Children at School and at Home*. PCCC Books.

Stein, M. (1999) 'Leaving Care: Reflections and Challenges' in O. Stevenson (ed.), *Child Welfare in the UK*. Oxford: Blackwell.

— (2006) 'Young people aging out of care: the poverty of theory', *Children and Youth Services Review* 28, 422–34.

— (2012) *Young People Leaving Care: Supporting Pathways to Adulthood*. London: Jessica Kingsley.

Stein, M. and Clayden, J. (2005) *Mentoring for Young People Leaving Care: Someone for Me*. London: Joseph Rowntree Foundation <http://www.jrf.org.uk/system/files/1859354025.pdf> accessed 3 December 2013.

Stepney, P. and Callwood, I. (2006) *Collaborative Working in Health and Social Care: A Review of the Literature*. University of Wolverhampton Learning and Teaching Projects 2005/2006 <www.wlv.openrepository.com>.

Stevens, I. and Furnivall, J. (2007) 'Therapeutic Approaches in Residential Care' in A. Kendrick (2007) *Residential Childcare: Prospects and Challenges – Research Highlights*. London: Jessica Kingsley.

Sunbeam House Services (2013) *Policies*. Bray, Co. Wicklow: Sunbeam House Services.

Sutton, J. (2005) *Healing the Hurt Within: Understand Self-injury and Self-harm, and Heal the Emotional Wounds*. Oxford: How to Books.

Tantum, D. and Huband, D. (2009) *Understanding Repeated Self-injury: A Multidisciplinary Approach*. Basingstoke: Palgrave Macmillan.

Task Force on Child Care Services (1980) *Final Report to the Minister of Health*. Dublin: Stationery Office.

Thomlison, B. (2008) 'Family-Centred Practice' in B. White (ed.), *Comprehensive Handbook of Social Work and Social Welfare*. New Jersey: John Wiley & Sons.

— (2010) *Family Assessment Handbook: An Introduction and Practical Guide to Family Assessment* (3rd edn). USA: Brooks/Cole, Cengage Learning.

Thompson, N. (2008) *The Social Work Companion*. UK: Open University Press.

Thumbadoo, Z. (2011) 'Isibindi: love in caring with a child and youth care approach', *Relational Child and Youth Care Practice* 24(1–2), 210–16.

Tillich, Paul (1952) *The Courage to Be*. New Haven, CT: Yale University Press.

Trevithick, P. (2008) 'Revisiting the knowledge base of social work: a framework for practice', *British Journal of Social Work* 38, 1212–37.

Tuairim (1966) *Some of Our Children: A Report on the Residential Care of Deprived Children*. London: Tuairim.

Twardosz, S. and Lutzker, J. (2010) 'Child maltreatment and the developing brain: a review of neuroscience perspectives', *Aggression and Violent Behavior* 15, 59–68.

UN (United Nations) (2006) *Convention on the Rights of Persons with Disabilities*. UN.

UN Enable (2013) *Development and Human Rights for All* <http://www.un.org/disabilities/index.asp>.

van der Kolk, B. (2003) 'The neurobiology of childhood trauma and abuse', *Child and Adolescent Psychiatric Clinics of North America* 12, 293–317.

Viney, Michael (1966) 'The Young Offenders' articles, *Irish Times* April–May.

Vokey, Daniel and Kerr, Jeannie (2011) 'Intuition and Professional Wisdom: Can We Teach Moral Discernment?' in Liz Bondi, David Carr, Chris Clarke and Cecilia Clegg (eds), *Towards Professional Wisdom*. Surrey: Ashgate.

Walker, S. (2012) *Responding to Self-Harm in Children and Adolescents: A Professional's Guide to Identification, Intervention and Support*. London: Jessica Kingsley.

Walsh, B.W. (2012) *Treating Self-Injury: A Practical Guide* (2nd edn). New York: Guilford.

Ward, A., Kasinski, K., Pooley, J. and Worthington, A. (eds) (2003) *Therapeutic Communities for Children and Young People*: Volume 10 of *Therapeutic Communities*. London: Jessica Kingsley.

Wasdell, D.W. (1979) 'The Holding Environment'. Meridian Programme, Meridian House <http://www.meridian.org.uk/_PDFs/Holding%20Environment.pdf>.

Watchman, K., Kerr, D. and Wilkinson, H. (2010) *Supporting Derek: A Practice Development Guide to Support Staff working with People who have a Learning Difficulty and Dementia*. York: Joseph Rowntree Foundation.

Waterman, A. (2013) 'Pre-placement Preparation', Association of Higher Education Careers Services, UCD, May <http://www.ahecs.ie/task-groups/work-placement-task-group/> accessed 14 September 2013.

Whelan, M. (1984) *Community-Based Child Care in Inner City Dublin*. Dublin: Community-Based Child Care.

White, M. (2007) *Maps of Narrative Practice*. New York: W.W. Norton & Co.

Whitfield, C.L. (1987) *Healing the Child Within: Discovery and Recovery for Adult Children of Dysfunctional Families* (Recovery Classics edn). Arlington, VA: Health Communications Inc.

Whittaker, J. (2004) 'The re-invention of residential treatment: an agenda for research and practice', *Child and Adolescent Psychiatric Clinics of North America* 13(2), 267–79.

Williams, D. (2008) 'Self-injury and Young People in Residential Care: The Experiences of a Sample of Social Care Workers', unpublished MA thesis, School of Social Work and Social Policy, Trinity College Dublin.

— (2011) 'Understanding and supporting young people who self-injure in social care settings', *CURAM*, September.

Williams, D. and Gilligan, R. (2011) 'Self injury and the challenges of responding to young people in residential care: the experiences of a sample of social care workers', *Irish Journal of Applied Social Studies* 11(1), 14–27.

Williams, D. and Lalor, K. (2001) 'Obstacles to the professionalisation of residential child care work', *Irish Journal of Applied Social Studies* 2(3), 6 <http://arrow.dit.ie/ijass/vol2/iss3/6>.

Wilson, K. (2000) 'Therapeutic Intervention' in M. Davies (ed.), *Encyclopedia of Social Work*. Oxford: Oxford University Press.

Winnicott, D. (1965) *The Maturational Process and the Facilitating Environment*. London and New York: Karnac.

— (1969) 'The use of an object and relating through identification', *International Journal of Psychoanalysis*, 50, 711–16.

— (1988) *Babies and their Mothers*. London: Free Association Books.

Woodside, M. and McClam, T. (2011) *An Introduction to Human Services* (7th edn). USA: Brooks/Cole.

Worthington, A. (2003) 'Relationships and the Therapeutic Setting' in A. Ward, K. Kasinski, J. Pooley and A. Worthington (eds), *Therapeutic Communities for Children and Young People*: Volume 10 of *Therapeutic Communities*. London: Jessica Kingsley.

YPAR (Young People at Risk), North Inner City (n.d.) *Co-ordinating Services for 0–18 Year Olds*. Dublin: YPAR.

Zeus, Perry and Skeffington, Suzanne (2008) *Coaching at Work*. McGraw-Hill.

Index

Page numbers in **bold italic** indicate figures, tables, etc.

Please note that the Association of Workers with Children in Care (AWCC) changed its name to the Irish Association of Care Workers (IACW), and this was subsequently changed to the Irish Association of Social Care Workers (IASCW).